Thousand-Miler

Thousand-Miler

Adventures Hiking the Ice Age Trail

Melanie Radzicki McManus

WISCONSIN HISTORICAL SOCIETY PRESS

Published by the Wisconsin Historical Society Press
Publishers since 1855

The Wisconsin Historical Society helps people connect to the past
by collecting, preserving, and sharing stories. Founded in 1846,
the Society is one of the nation's finest historical institutions.

Order books by phone toll free: (888) 999-1669
Order books online: shop.wisconsinhistory.org
Join the Wisconsin Historical Society: wisconsinhistory.org/membership

Printed in the United States of America
Designed by Percolator Graphic Design
21 20 19 18 17   1 2 3 4 5

Library of Congress Cataloging-in-Publication Data

Names: McManus, Melanie Radzicki, 1961– author.
Title: Thousand-miler : adventures hiking the Ice Age Trail / Melanie Radzicki
    McManus.
Description: [Madison, Wisconsin] : Wisconsin Historical Society Press, [2017]
Identifiers: LCCN 2016043299 (print) | LCCN 2016043924 (ebook) |
    ISBN 9780870207907 (paperback : alkaline paper) | ISBN 9780870207914
    (ebook) | ISBN 9780870207914 (Ebook)
Subjects: LCSH: Ice Age National Scenic Trail (Wis.)—History. | Ice Age
    National Scenic Trail (Wis—Description and travel. | McManus, Melanie
    Radzicki, 1961– —Travel—Wisconsin—Ice Age National Scenic Trail. |
    Hiking—Wisconsin—Ice Age National Scenic Trail. | Geology—Wisconsin—
    Ice Age National Scenic Trail. | Natural history—Wisconsin—Ice Age National
    Scenic Trail. | Hikers—Wisconsin—Ice Age National Scenic Trail—Biography.
Classification: LCC QE697 .M454 2017 (print) | LCC QE697 (ebook) |
    DDC 796.5109775–dc23
LC record available at https://lccn.loc.gov/2016043299

To my S.B., of course.

Contents

Ice Age Trail Route

Courtesy of the Ice Age Trail Alliance

My Journey Begins

A journey of a thousand miles must begin with a single step.
—Lao Tzu, Chinese philosopher and poet

A kaleidoscope of colors and shapes whirls outside the car window. If I could focus, even a little, I'd see rolling, green hills. Sparkling sapphire lakes. Golden prairie grasses just starting to burnish to a russet sheen. Stands of pine so thick they're almost ebony in hue. But even the neatly rolled hay bales I love to admire while driving through the bucolic Wisconsin countryside are nearly invisible to my eyes today, appearing merely as smudged amber dots on the horizon. I'm unable to take in the scenic landscape because my thoughts are caught up in a frantic loop, continually reminding me that no matter how many miles we put behind us, more will simply unspool ahead. Something pings my chest. Fear? Anticipation?

Ed and I have already been barreling down the highway at sixty-five miles per hour for more than two hours, and we've still got several more hours to go before reaching our destination: St. Croix Falls, a sleepy town of 2,100 perched on the rocky bluffs towering over the St. Croix River in northwestern Wisconsin.

We'll have zipped along more than 250 miles of highway to get there from our home just outside of Madison, the capital, which squats down low in the center of the state not too far from the Illinois border. A 250-mile car trip is pretty long. My butt is already angrily cramping in protest at sitting so long, and my legs continually twitch around trying to find some new, more comfortable position. But 250 miles pales in comparison to 1,100, especially when covered on foot. Alone. And in remote, unfamiliar territory filled with Lyme-disease-bearing ticks, poisonous plants, bears, wolves, and I'm not even sure what else. Yet that's what's in store for me starting tomorrow, and for every day after that for the next month or so. You see, I'm going to hike the Ice Age Trail.

The Ice Age Trail is an eleven-hundred-mile footpath that gently traces the edges of the last glaciation in Wisconsin. One of just eleven National Scenic Trails, it's in the same vaunted company as the Appalachian Trail, which runs some 2,181 miles from Georgia to Maine, and the Pacific Crest Trail, which winds 2,650 miles from Mexico to Canada, passing through California, Oregon, and Washington along the way. It's also one of just three National Scenic Trails to be coiled entirely inside one state, the other two trails being in Florida and Arizona. Although the Ice Age Trail is a state and national treasure—it's no easy feat to become designated a National Scenic Trail—many people are unaware of its existence, even Wisconsinites. And more than 3.4 million of us live within an hour's drive of some portion of the trail.

Why has the trail never grown in our collective consciousness? Perhaps because it isn't yet complete; about 650 miles of footpaths have been carved into the land so far, stitched together by 450 miles of road, dubbed "connecting routes." Maybe it's because Wisconsin isn't home to an avid hiking culture, like those found in mountainous regions such as Colorado or New England. Or perhaps it's because we midwesterners, long derided by East and West Coast folks as living in "flyover country," have bought into that notion, believing our corner of the United States couldn't possibly be home to anything truly special.

About a year before I began planning my hike, I was one of the clueless who had no idea what the Ice Age Trail was, despite having hiked, skied, and run along numerous segments of the trail for years. Sure, I'd seen the name before, along with the trail's signature yellow blazes. But I never stopped to ponder that I'd used something called the Ice Age Trail in the Kettle Moraine State Forest in the eastern half of the state, and at Indian Lake County Park near my home, and over at Lapham Peak in Delafield, west of Milwaukee, and up at Devil's Lake, Wisconsin's most popular state park. But once I learned what the Ice Age Trail was, I became entranced with the notion of following a one-thousand-plus-mile path all around the state—through hardwood forests and pine plantations, across waving grasslands and lumpy farm fields, over rivers, along a Great Lake, through trail towns big and small. I could get to know my beloved state on an intimate basis, step by step, in a way few other people ever would, unearthing its hidden secrets, inhaling its heady scents, listening as it spoke to me through the sighing wind, the rustling prairie grasses and the creaking forestland. I could become part of the landscape, and the very earth could become part of me. As someone who has always felt a primal connection to my home state, the thought was intoxicating. Seductive. The trail was singing a siren song, and I couldn't resist.

So here I am.

⌒

Ed exits Interstate 94 when we reach Eau Claire, pointing the car north along State Highway 53. The sudden change in speed and direction abruptly halts my obsessive thoughts about the length of my pending hike.

"I need a trail name," I blurt out.

"A what?"

"A trail name. Most people who hike a long-distance trail either pick one out or someone they meet along the way gives them one. If I don't pick a name now, someone will probably give me some dumb name like Fruit Loop or Blondie."

While poking around the website of the Ice Age Trail Alliance, the nonprofit organization in charge of developing, maintaining, and promoting the Ice Age Trail, I'd come across a list of "Thousand-Milers," those who had thru-hiked the entire trail and connecting road routes, as I would be doing, or who had section-hiked all of the trail segments. Both their real names and their trail names were listed. There were Salty, Pins, and Lint. Biscuit and Gravy (they hiked together). Buzz and Ya Comi. And my two favorites: Gray Ghost and Nimblewill Nomad. I loved the way those last two names sounded when spoken aloud, how they looked on paper. I needed a moniker like that. I began poring over lists of trail names on various hiking websites: Dancing Dove, Gypsy, Odyssa. Fire Belly, Rags, Happy Pants. Jackass, Bamboo Bob, Big Daddy D. No name came close to embodying who I was or captured why I was hiking the trail.

"Come on, Ed, help me," I plead. "I can't just be 'Melanie' out there. Right now there's a Mother Goose, a Hiking Dude, and a Papa Bear out on the Ice Age Trail. I need a really cool name like 'Papa Bear.'"

"Mama Bear?"

I roll my eyes. "That's so lame."

"Buttercup?" An ever-so-tiny grin plays at the edges of his mouth; that's one of his silly nicknames for me.

"Be serious."

"Hot Mama? Trail Bait?"

I glare at him.

"Pooky Bear?"

"Stop! You're not helping things."

And then it comes to me. "Valderi!" I shriek. Ed looks puz-zled. "You know, from that camp song 'The Happy Wanderer.'" I begin to sing in an enthusiastic, if off-pitch, voice, "I love to go a-wandering, Along the mountain track, And as I go, I love to sing, My knapsack on my back. Val-deri, Val-dera, Val-deri, Val-dera-ha-ha-ha-ha-ha, Val-deri, Val-dera. My knapsack on my back!" I flash Ed a triumphant grin.

In 1970, our family moved from Chicago to Sheboygan, a quiet city snugged against the shores of Lake Michigan about sixty miles north of Milwaukee. One of the first things my mother did was pack the five of us kids into our family's turquoise Chevy sedan and head for a hiking trail in the Kettle Moraine State Forest. As we grumbled about the heat and mosquitoes and whatever else big-city kids complain about when first faced with the great outdoors, my mother began marching through the woods singing "The Happy Wanderer" in an effort to make the hike fun. The little ditty has quite a catchy tune, and soon the six of us were skipping along the trail, filling the air with Val-deris, Val-deras, and plenty of hearty ha-ha-ha-ha-ha-has. The path we hiked—not just that day, but many times afterward—was the Parnell Tower Loop Trail, a portion of which was also part of the nascent Ice Age Trail. I didn't know it at the time, of course, and even if I had, it would have meant nothing to me.

But now the connection strikes me as perfect, and I explain all this to Ed. Pleased that I've finally found a suitable name, I once again turn to the window and watch the miles fly past.

~

We reach St. Croix Falls late in the afternoon and check into our hotel before heading to Interstate State Park. Founded in 1900, it's Wisconsin's oldest state park and the site of the Ice Age Trail's western terminus. I want to make sure I know exactly where the starting point is so there are no missteps in the morning. I find the western terminus marker, a plaque affixed to a boulder sitting placidly on the park's Pothole Trail. The trail overlooks the St. Croix River and its steeply pitched gorge, dubbed the Dalles of the St. Croix. The air is still and hot right now, with insects noisily whining about the late-afternoon heat. Looking around, I spy a few of the potholes from which the trail got its name.

Potholes are glacial pockmarks, if you will. Fast-moving, sediment-filled streams often flow between a glacier and the rocky terrain beneath it. At times an eddy will form within a stream, picking up debris in the process. As the eddy fiercely swirls the debris around and around, the bits of rock and grit sometimes neatly drill a hole into the bedrock. Large stones can drop into these potholes, too—stones too sizable for the current to hoist back out. These stones swirl around and around in the compact pothole, slowly, gently being smoothed and rounded, until they end up looking a bit like bowling balls. These rocks are called grindstones. I stick my head into one of the potholes, hoping to see a grindstone. It's deep and dark and cool down there, but unfortunately no grindstone lies at the bottom.

Before leaving the park, we duck into the Ice Age Interpretive Center and head for the information desk.

"I'll be thru-hiking the Ice Age Trail starting tomorrow morning," I tell the park employee with a tinge of pride. "Can I sign the hiking register?"

"Hiking register?"

"You know, the one that thru-hikers sign when they're starting out or finishing the trail."

"Oh, we don't have anything like that."

I blink. "There's no register?"

"No. I suppose we should have one, though. That's a good idea." She smiles brightly.

I'm crestfallen. I've read all about the trail registers placed at regular intervals along the famous Appalachian and Pacific Crest

Trails. You sign in at the beginning and end of your hike, plus at various points along the way. Hikers use the logs to communicate with others they've met on the trail—*Hey, Bones, I beat you here, you loser!*—or to jot down their victories, frustrations, or random thoughts. *No blisters so far! Or This sucks! Or I smell really bad!* I figured the Ice Age Trail probably didn't have many registers along the way—it's a long-distance path in progress, after all—but I assumed each terminus would have one.

As I turn away, the ranger waves, cheerily wishing me good luck.

Back in the car, Ed and I now follow the blazes from the park through town. The Ice Age Trail guidebook says it's tricky navigating this first 7.4-mile segment here in St. Croix Falls, especially when the trail leaves the park and begins winding through the city streets. Ed and I have no problem following the blazes, until we get to the spot where the trail exits Riegel Park near the Polk County fairgrounds. At this point, the trail simply vanishes. Ed and I trot up and down the street, trying to figure out where the path continues. The map indicates all you do is cross the street and the trail resumes, but there's no blaze across the street and no trail. I'm glad we decided to undertake this little reconnaissance mission today. I'd hate to be immediately stumped my first day on the trail.

"Hey!" I call out to a man who appears alongside the road. "Do you know where the Ice Age Trail is? It's supposed to be somewhere right around here. I'm hiking it tomorrow morning, and I don't want to get lost right away."

"Nope, sorry," he says, adding, "Will you be hiking it all the way from Interstate State Park?" I nod my head. His eyebrows immediately shoot up and disappear under the fringe of hair covering his forehead. "I hope you know that's about ten miles," he says, locking his eyes onto mine as if to impress upon me the severity of the undertaking. "*Ten miles.*"

I want to say my itinerary calls for hiking 32 miles tomorrow, and then another 1,050 or so after that. Instead I smile, thank him, and turn back to the grassy field in front of us.

"Here it is!" Ed shouts.

"Where?"

"Right here."

"I don't see a thing."

"It's really faint."

I'm standing not more than a foot to the left of Ed, who is pointing at the grassy field we've been walking past for the last fifteen minutes. I see absolutely nothing.

"Stand right behind me." I move behind him and there, almost indiscernible, is a path of sorts. It's really just a foot's width of grass tamped down ever so lightly.

"How do you know this is the Ice Age Trail?" I demand. He points again, this time far across the field, where a speck of yellow winks in the distance. An Ice Age Trail signpost. Why there's one way out in the field and not here at the roadside is a mystery. I should have taken it as an early warning sign.

It's a quarter past six in the morning and the air is already so thick I feel like I'm breathing through a wet washcloth. The forecast for today, August 31, 2013, is a blistering ninety degrees. This will not be pretty. The sky is a gauzy gray, the sun's rays still feeble. I lightly touch the western terminus boulder while Ed snaps the obligatory "start" photo, then trot off down the trail just as a car pulls up and three young men tumble out. I wonder if they're starting a thru-hike, too, but don't pause to inquire.

I weave through the park, head into town, and follow the blazes up and down a tiny esker, which is a serpentine mound of debris that once lay at the bottom of a river coursing under the glacier. I'm led through Riegel Park and now easily find where the trail resumes near the fairgrounds. Soon I pop out into a neighborhood, where Ed is waiting in our car, which is loaded with an assortment of food and water.

"Hey, did you see those three guys in the park?" he says. "I talked with them a little after you left. They're doing the first sixty miles of the Ice Age Trail this weekend. You'd better hurry so they don't overtake you."

"Don't say that!" I say anxiously. "I can't get into a competitive mind-set with people who are hiking sixty miles when I'm doing eleven hundred. Besides, they're guys, and they're a lot younger than me." The trio looked to be in their twenties; I'll be turning fifty-two in a week.

I grab a bite of a peanut butter and jelly sandwich that Ed proffers, refill the bladder in my hydration pack, then hastily begin jogging down the street. Because, darn it, I now feel like I have to stay ahead of those guys.

Ed drops the car at a nearby park and joins me on the trail, now unrolling northbound along the shores of the St. Croix. We skip across a few streams, hop along some rocks, then pop out onto a blacktop road. My first trail segment is finished! Only 115 more to go.

I spy the Ice Age Trail's signature yellow blaze nailed to a post directly across the road in front of us. But as it's set on the post facing us, not nailed on the post's right or left side, what does it mean? Which way do we turn, right or left? I grab the map from my pack. We need to turn right onto a River Road to start along the connecting road route to the Gandy Dancer segment, so my guess is we turn right here. But the spot where we are on the map is tiny and overlaid by both the black dashes indicating the trail and the circles marking the connecting routes. It's possible we need to head left, then take a quick right onto River Road. I scowl at the blaze, sitting calmly in its neutral position, like Switzerland.

"We need to head left," says Ed.

"How do you know?"

"Because of the blaze."

"But it's on the front of the post, not on the right or left. It could mean either."

"We need to turn left. I can tell."

"That doesn't make any sense!"

But Ed is positive we need to head left, so I follow him, stuffing the map back into my pack. Why I'm listening to Ed, I'm not sure. He has a terrible sense of direction; I'm always the designated map reader and navigator. Sure enough, twenty minutes later, seeing no more Ice Age Trail signage and no sign of a River Road, we retrace our steps. Just as we reach the roadside blaze, the three young guys I saw pull up to the western terminus this morning emerge from the woods. They call out hello, give a jaunty wave, then head off without a backward glance. Thanks to Ed's earlier words, I'm annoyed they've passed me. My only consolation is that they're moving awfully quickly given the day's heat and humidity and the number of miles they're hoping to knock off. Unless all three are talented ultra-distance runners, such a pace could spell disaster later on.

"Oh, now I get it," says Ed, interrupting my thoughts.

"Get what?"

"I bet that blaze is for westbound hikers and indicates the St. Croix River segment starts here. Otherwise how would anyone know where to turn into the woods? There's no trailhead sign."

He must be right, because I suddenly recall reading in the guidebook that the connecting routes aren't blazed. Well, I guess it's a good lesson learned.

It's around noon, the temperature well past the ninety-degree mark, when I again run into the three young men, now dejectedly walking along the Gandy Dancer rail trail segment, sizzling in the heat. One has removed his shirt and strapped his backpack to his bare skin. The mother in me wants to tell him that's not a smart idea in this heat and humidity; he'll get sunburned and chafed. But he doesn't appear to be in the mood to listen to advice from some random older woman, so instead I take a turn smiling and waving as I pass the group.

At day's end I've successfully logged my planned thirty-two miles. More impressively, my feet sport only one small blister apiece. My only regret is that I didn't pause to chat with those three young men—because I never got to tell anyone that Valderi is now on the trail.

CHAPTER TWO

Birth of a Trail

We spend millions to go fast. Let's spend a little to go slow.
—RAYMOND T. ZILLMER, ICE AGE TRAIL CREATOR

When the United States was in its infancy, the land was laced with trails. American Indians had tamped innumerable footpaths into the earth long before the Europeans arrived, of course. And once our melting pot full of immigrants established a foothold in the fledgling country, a network of more sophisticated trails began spreading from sea to shining sea to enhance exploration, commerce, and migration. Like arteries efficiently ferrying blood around the body, the trailways pulsed with people, animals, vehicles, and goods, as America's new residents raced around building homes, industries, and new lives. Create trails strictly for recreation? Pshaw! There was no time for that. Nor did most of the immigrants or their descendants worry about preserving and protecting the vast American environment, with its seemingly limitless resources. But that sentiment began to change in the late nineteenth and early twentieth centuries.

As more and more Americans squeezed into ever-swelling cities—cities filled with whirring and clattering machinery

and streets that reverberated with shouts, whistles, and bells—
escaping from such grimy, stressful urban jungles quickly became desirable. Necessary even. And as people began dipping
their toes into the serene, clean, great outdoors, they began to
notice, and voice alarm about, the heedless use of our resources,
which seemed quite limited after all. Congress quickly set to
work establishing national parks to protect our most spectacular
natural tracts: Yosemite, Sequoia, Crater Lake. Grand Canyon,
Grand Teton, Glacier. Acadia, Shenandoah, Rocky Mountain.
But these stunningly beautiful new parks were more romantic
ideas than usable recreational space, as most were tucked away in
isolated pockets in the West, virtually inaccessible to the average
American.

Then, in 1921, a man named Benton MacKaye put forth an
alluring idea: build a smattering of camps atop the spiny Appalachian ridge, where harried city dwellers could escape to unwind.
In the beauty and serenity of the mountains, away from noise and
machinery and crowds, they could work, study, maybe even do a
little farming. A trail would connect the camps, but hiking would
not be the focus. MacKaye proposed the camps stretch from New
Hampshire's Mount Washington in the north to North Caroli-
na's Mount Mitchell in the south. People were greatly intrigued.
But before the camps could become a reality, MacKaye's wife
committed suicide. Devastated, MacKaye stepped back from his
creative proposal, and eventually a man named Myron H. Avery
took over, changing the project's focus from mountaintop camps
to hiking. Aided by a hardworking group of trail enthusiasts, the
activists went to work blazing trails, creating local hiking clubs
along the route for support, drawing maps, and writing guide-
books. In 1937, America's first interstate recreational path was
born: the Appalachian Trail.

Fast-forward a decade or so to the 1950s, when even more
Americans found themselves stuffed into bloated cities and

pining for outdoor recreational escapes. Over in Milwaukee, Raymond T. Zillmer had been doing a lot of thinking. A lawyer by profession, the bespectacled Zillmer was also an avid hiker and mountaineer. On four separate occasions he mountaineered in remote patches of Canada's Cariboo Range in eastern British Columbia. The fourth time, in 1947, he became the first person (along with his son, John) to cross its range east of the Rausch River and the North Thompson. In tribute, the Canucks dubbed a Cariboo peak "Mount Zillmer." Zillmer had also done a lot of trekking in Europe and developed a fondness for the way so many of the trails wandered around the countryside, yet regularly dipped into towns, making it easy to grab a bite to eat or find a place to stay come nightfall. During the 1930s and 1940s, Zillmer closely followed the development of the Appalachian Trail while helping to create and expand the northern and southern units of the Kettle Moraine State Forest here in Wisconsin. Then, in the 1950s, inspiration struck.

Zillmer envisioned a ribbon of parkland winding across, down, and up the state, with Kettle Moraine as its nucleus. This unique, linear park would be a magical place, one where squirrels could leap from tree to tree for more than one thousand miles without ever touching the ground. The map he sketched of his park was long and narrow, first squiggling across the state's northern tier, then scooping a huge "U" into its eastern half before petering out in Kewaunee County. This was no random design, however, but rather a carefully calculated one. For Zillmer's planned parkway was much more than a comely recreational tract. It traced the edges of North America's last glacial advance into Wisconsin, an inventive route that would allow visitors not only to recreate in the scenic outdoors but also to easily see some of the world's most outstanding glacial features.

~

Ray Zillmer's
1958 map

Courtesy of the Ice Age Trail Alliance

The average Wisconsinite might know the state's hilly, lake-bejeweled land was once a glacial playground, but few realize America's Dairyland could easily have been nicknamed the Glacier State or Ice Age Wonderland. To understand how we ended up with prime glacial remains, we need a quick Ice Age primer. For more than one million years, much of Canada and the northern United States was covered in a coat of ice more than one mile thick. In some spots, the ice sheet rose an incomprehensible two miles skyward. During those one million years, the massive ice sheet would grow and recede, grow and recede, over and over and over again. But four of those growth spurts were particularly significant, so geologists named each one after its farthest southern advance. There was the inaugural Nebraskan stage, then the Kansan push, the Illinoian stage, and, finally, the Wisconsinan advance. This final push by the ice sheet ended with a fingerlike poke deep into Wisconsin's belly.

Then, about seventy thousand years ago, the ice began to ever-so-slowly recede for the final time. It took some sixty thousand years before the ice was gone for good, or about ten thousand years before the present day. As a reminder of its long and significant presence, the glacier strewed debris across the continent. But nowhere was that glacial detritus as recognizable, as well preserved, as beautiful, as right here in its namesake locale, Wisconsin. It was this geologic largesse that Zillmer wanted to showcase with his proposed parkway, Ice Age National Park.

Zillmer's idea was cutting-edge. His envisioned parkland, which had a trail in its center, was exceptionally long and narrow, for one thing, decidedly unlike the wide, expansive wilderness tracts that characterized places such as Yosemite and Yellowstone. And while Zillmer wanted the park's route largely to be determined by the glacier's final resting spot, or terminal moraine, he also wanted to ensure it regularly passed through cities and towns so that it would be easily accessible to citizens. This notion was directly opposite to that behind the creation of the Appalachian Trail and the subsequent Pacific Crest Trail, which were designed to pull people as far away from civilization as possible. But Zillmer had that fondness for European hiking trails and promoted the idea of a not-too-remote park that would help connect people with the outdoors. Why drive two or three days to the West to commune with nature? That was a waste of time and money, and most Americans didn't have all that much of either. Far better, it seemed, to play outdoors somewhere close to home.

With this vision in mind, Zillmer in 1958 founded the Ice Age

Park & Trail Foundation, now known as the Ice Age Trail Alliance, or IATA. That year and the next, a bill was introduced into Congress to create the national park, but both times Congress opted not to consider it. In 1960, Raymond T. Zillmer died at age seventy-three. The following year, the National Park Service (NPS) determined Zillmer's park proposal was a no-go because it didn't fit their model; the National Park Service did not yet have in its care any linear parks stretching for hundreds of miles. Plus, a park that sprawling would be a nightmare to administer. The outlook appeared bleak for Zillmer's Ice Age Park. And then, a ray of hope.

Wisconsin officials, trail and park supporters, and the NPS collectively came up with a new idea: the Ice Age National Scientific Reserve. The Scientific Reserve would be an affiliate of the NPS and would comprise nine units scattered around Wisconsin, ostensibly in areas with prime glacial remains to be protected, studied, and showcased. Hiking trails could be built in each reserve, if they weren't already in existence in these parcels of land. And someday, perhaps, these nine units could be linked via a long-distance trail. In 1964, Congress approved the Ice Age Reserve legislation, thanks in large part to the efforts of Democratic Congressman Henry S. Reuss of Milwaukee, a major trail promoter. It wasn't an ideal alternative, namely because several of the Scientific Reserve sites would not be located along the glacier's terminal moraine per Zillmer's vision. But it was a start.

The following year, President Lyndon B. Johnson delivered a special message to Congress on conservation and the restoration of natural beauty, inspired in part by a 1960 Outdoor Recreation Resources Review Commission survey that showed 90 percent of Americans participated in some type of outdoor recreation, with walking being the second most popular activity. During his speech, President Johnson called on the nation "to copy the great Appalachian Trail in all parts of America, and to make full use of rights of way and other public paths." Three years later, in 1968, Congress passed the National Trails System Act, which authorized a national trail system divided into four categories: National Historic Trails, National Recreation Trails, National Scenic Trails, and connecting or side trails. It also proclaimed the Appalachian and Pacific Crest Trails as the United States' first two National Scenic Trails.

National Scenic Trails, according to the new law, could only be authorized and designated by Congress. They had to be designed around areas possessing significant scenic, historic, natural, or cultural qualities and must provide recreational opportunities for users. In general, motor vehicles would not be allowed on these trails. Zillmer's idea, still kicking around amongst his supporters despite the establishment of the Ice Age National Scientific Reserve, soon morphed from that of a national park into a footpath called the Ice Age Trail. Ice Age Trail backers dared to hope that one day their project would become a prestigious National Scenic Trail, one just as heralded as the legendary Appalachian Trail.

Buoyed by the federal government's new program, they got to work building their footpath. Using the Northern Kettle Moraine State Forest's existing Glacial Trail as its foundation, just as Zillmer planned, they constructed mile after mile of new trail. By 1980, about two hundred miles of trail were in place. Their hard work was rewarded that year when President Jimmy Carter signed a law creating the Ice Age National Scenic Trail, the nation's eighth such path. In 1987, Wisconsin named the Ice Age Trail the state's sole State Scenic Trail as well.

Even though it was started in the 1970s, the Ice Age Trail today is only half completed, with many miles of country roads connecting actual trail sectors. Why has it taken so long? After all, the twice-as-long Appalachian Trail was finished in less than twenty years, and that was back in the old days, before modern tools and technology. Ditto with the Pacific Crest. These inaugural National Scenic Trails proved to be exceptions. It typically takes decades to build a long-distance trail. First, trail advocates have to identify trail corridors. Then they must purchase the land or protect it in perpetuity through arrangements such as permanent easements. Sometimes, with a little luck, someone will donate a parcel of land, sell it at a bargain price, or donate "trade lands"—parcels of land outside the proposed trail corridor that can be used to help purchase desired plots, whether by actually trading the donated parcels for others in the trail corridor or, more commonly, selling the donated lands and using the proceeds to purchase desirable plots. The final step is the easiest: physically building the trail.

Initially, the Ice Age Trail footpaths, similar to those of the Appalachian Trail, rolled along a patchwork of purchased land—expensive, but permanent—and private property. In the latter scenario, generous landowners often okayed the creation of a stretch of trail on their property, but sealed the deal through a handshake agreement rather than signing over permanent rights. The problem is, handshake agreements are easily dissolvable. Landowners who become disgruntled with hikers tramping across their property can shut down trail segments without warning. Even those who enjoy hosting the trail may eventually sell their land to someone who doesn't share their sentiments.

Ray Zillmer knew about these dangers and was a proponent of obtaining permanent rights for every inch of the trail. But Henry Reuss disagreed. Congressman Reuss was instrumental in helping the Ice Age Trail obtain National Scenic Trail status, twisting enough congressional arms until the necessary votes were secured. He had faith the trail could be pieced together through the goodwill of private landowners, and felt it would be an unnecessary waste of time and money to secure permanent easements. The snowmobile community relied upon handshake agreements with property owners all the time to secure access to trails, he argued. They didn't have problems with dissolving paths. Neither would the Ice Age Trail.

During the early to mid-1980s, the issue of permanent rights versus handshake agreements was a contentious one to some degree. While trail backers bickered over which method was best, the majority of new trail footage quietly became reality via handshake agreements. The bottom line: it was faster and cheaper. But the folly of these informal accords soon became evident as the trail continually inched forward, then receded, inched forward, then receded, glacierlike, as these arrangements were constantly being struck and dissolved, just as Zillmer feared. The net result was almost zero growth.

Many are surprised to learn that since the Appalachian Trail was completed in 1937, about 99 percent of the trail has been relocated or rebuilt and transferred from private to public ownership. Additionally, a one-thousand-foot-wide corridor surrounding the footpath is now protected so urbanization can't creep too close to the trail. Still, officials say the Appalachian Trail will never really be finished; its path will always shift slightly if land along a more scenic path, or with access to a waterway, becomes available.

The Ice Age Trail is going through a similar rebirth. Today the IATA is trying to purchase the land or secure permanent easements on all current trail segments, plus build new ones to extend the length of the trail. It's no easy feat. Besides needing landowners willing to sell or sign permanent easements, money is needed to purchase more land. The two main governmental entities forking over the funds to help build the Ice Age Trail these days are the state of Wisconsin through its Knowles-Nelson Stewardship Program, and the NPS via the Land and Water Conservation Fund, which it administers jointly with Wisconsin's Department of Natural Resources.

Unfortunately, both are woefully short on resources. The Knowles-Nelson Stewardship Program was included in Wisconsin's 2015–2017 biennial budget, but funded at a much-reduced rate and with a large number of grant stipulations. The program is authorized only until 2020, too, so its existence will undoubtedly be debated in the future. The federal Land and Water Conservation Fund receives all of its money from a small portion of the proceeds derived from offshore oil drilling. In September 2015, Congress allowed the fifty-year-old program to expire. President Barack Obama did reinsert the program into his Fiscal Year 2017 budget recommendations, but its future existence and funding level are questionable. In addition, competition for Land and Water Conservation Fund grants is much more fierce than in the past.

What all of this means is that it's largely up to the IATA to raise the visibility of the trail to secure more private support.

And it's up to trail users to chip in—financially, so more land can be purchased, and physically, by volunteering to help build and maintain the trail.

CHAPTER THREE

Running Like a Girl

*Success isn't how far you got, but the distance you traveled
from where you started.*
—STEVE PREFONTAINE, RUNNING LEGEND

A wide carpet of thick, green weeds unrolls before me, cascading
down a steep ski hill. One step down the hill, and my right knee
twinges. Two steps, and a warning flare of pain shoots up my leg.
Three, and it nearly buckles beneath me. Shifting all my weight
to my left leg, I stop and ponder my situation. Just three days into
my journey, and I'm in trouble. Big trouble.

It all began late yesterday, when I was partway through the
McKenzie Creek segment. Rounding a corner, I ran into a massive patch of overgrown wild raspberries. Nearly shoulder-high,
the thick brambles clawed at my arms and legs, scratching angry,
red tic-tac-toe marks into my flesh. I fought my way through the
patch, hacking at the bushes with my trekking poles as if they were
machetes. But I overlooked a final, devious tendril snaking across
the path like a tripwire. It snared the base of my shin, just above
my foot, and I stumbled. My right knee smashed into a rock em-
bedded in the earth, causing searing pain and a string of expletives.

I walked the pain off over the next few miles and got a good night's sleep. Everything seemed fine the first few miles I hiked today. Until now. Here in the southeastern corner of Burnett County, the Ice Age Trail runs through Timberland Hills, a Nordic ski site featuring twenty-four kilometers of trail carved into a 2,400-acre swath of forestland. The Outer Loop I'm on is described as having "screaming hills." Screaming is right. Clearly, my knee hasn't recovered. Clearly, walking downhill is not an option. So how do I get down this midwestern mountain, and all the others sure to follow in this skiing wonderland?

I seriously consider rolling down the hill. But I've got a pack strapped to my back and trekking poles in my hands. Even if I could throw my pack and poles cleanly down to the bottom of the hill, I'd get pretty dizzy rolling all the way down. Plus, whenever I've rolled down hills in the past—admittedly, it's been a while—I tended to end up rolling sideways. Here, that would land me in the scrubby trailside brush. I ponder scootching down the hill on my butt, a technique I once used on a trail in Wales when I was suffering from a similar ailment. But the weeds are slick with dew and punctuated by muddy ruts. I'll end up sopping wet and filthy, and the day's hike has just begun. That leaves two options: walk sideways or backward down the hill.

Gingerly, I take one step sideways with my right foot. My knee grumbles, then is quiet. Slide, step. Slide, step. Slide, step. After a few minutes pass, I glance up and see I've made it a whopping two yards. This will not do. I turn and face the top of the hill and try walking backward. My knee remains pacified, but I can't see where I'm going and start to become disoriented and dizzy. I turn back to my side. Slide, step. Slide, step. Slide, step. Eventually I manage to get down the hill, face forward, and march on. Minutes later, another hill rises before me. A loud sigh hisses from my lips like a teakettle's whistle as my frustration level approaches the boiling point. I climb to the top, then repeat my step-and-slide trek down its back side. I continue inching along the trail in this fashion for the next five miles, burning through an enormous amount of time. And I don't have time to spare. I'm actually in a race of sorts.

～

Thru-hiking a long-distance trail is challenging. Very few people in America will ever attempt such a thing. Through 2014, about 16,500 people had hiked the entire Appalachian Trail in one attempt since its completion in 1937. That's an average of 214 people a year, although these days—a time when long-distance hiking is enjoying a surge in popularity—some 2,000 to 3,000 annually set out to hike this storied trail. Still, of those 2,000 to 3,000 potential thru-hikers, only about 25 percent, or 500 to 750, will actually complete the trail. A minute slice of those 2,000 to 3,000 who set out each year, maybe one or two a year, or perhaps only one or two every few years, will attempt to set an "FKT" while thru-hiking. *FKT* stands for "fastest known time." If you bag an FKT on a long-distance trail, that means you've covered its mileage faster than anyone else.

Conventional wisdom says that if you're going to attempt to set an FKT on a long-distance trail, you need to cover thirty to fifty miles per day. Ultrarunners—those skilled at running distances farther than marathon length, which is 26.2 miles—try to do this by running as much of the trail as possible, typically spending eleven to thirteen hours on the trail each day. Others prefer to hike the entire time, but spend more hours daily on the trail to cover the same distance. In 2011, Jennifer Pharr Davis set an FKT on the Appalachian Trail of forty-six days, eleven hours, and twenty minutes by hiking sixteen hours per day, sometimes sleeping on the trail to eliminate commuting times. Her FKT was bested in 2015 by ultrarunning phenom Scott Jurek, whose record was then broken in 2016 by ultrarunner Karl Meltzer. So both methods work.

No one had ever tried to set an FKT on the Ice Age Trail until 2007. That year, Verona High School alum and former Wildcat cross-country runner Jason Dorgan set out to cover all one-thousand-plus miles in three weeks, his entire vacation allotment. Jason's reasons were twofold. One, he was an avid ultrarunner and reveled in the challenge. And two, he had long been an active Ice Age Trail backer and volunteer. Jason knew any time someone attempted to set an FKT, it brought attention to the trail. And that was just what the Ice Age Trail needed. The more attention the trail got, the more potential for funding, land donations, and volunteers. So off he went. Twenty-two days and six hours later, he'd set the thru-hike record. The Ice Age Trail now had its first FKT.

I love running, too, and I met Jason through a social running group sometime in the 1990s. I was vaguely aware of his thru-run while it was occurring in April 2007, but I was busy preparing for my oldest child's high school graduation and transition to college. I never paused to ponder what the Ice Age Trail was, where it went, or exactly what Jason was doing out there for three weeks. Then one day in the fall of 2012, I found myself next to Jason during a group run, taking two steps for each one of his long-legged strides. He began reminiscing about his FKT adventure, and this time I listened closely, becoming more and more intrigued.

For the past three years, I'd actually been engaged in a somewhat similar venture. As a travel writer, I had alternated hiking and running along Spain's six-hundred-plus-mile Vía de la Plata several times while writing a guidebook about this famous pilgrimage trail. That birthed a growing fondness for hiking and running along trails—and for undertaking long-distance challenges. The realization that a similar path existed just minutes from my home, and not an ocean away, was exhilarating.

That night, a white film of dried sweat from the run still encrusted on my body, I logged onto the Ice Age Trail Alliance website to do a little research. I learned that to date, only twenty-two people had thru-hiked the trail. I learned that just three of those twenty-two were women. The fastest woman, Sharon Dziengel, completed it in fifty days, which translates to hiking twenty-two miles per day. A thrill shot through me. If I ran the trail the way Jason had, I could easily set the women's FKT. At fifty-one, I was pretty old to set an FKT, but I would be going up against only three women—three women who weren't trying to set a record when they hiked the trail. If I could cover a relatively modest thirty miles per day, I would crush Sharon's time. How fun would that be, especially at my age?

I spent the next nine months planning my attempt, fueled by endless cups of coffee and many hours in front of my computer, trail maps spread all over my desk. I decided to start in St. Croix Falls, heading west to east, and drew up a schedule of where approximately thirty miles per day would take me. Inspecting every connecting route and measuring various alternatives, I tried to pinpoint where I could shave off mileage, even if just a tenth of a mile. While you have to hike every trail segment, plus the roads in between, to officially complete a thru-hike, you don't have to hike the connecting road routes suggested by the Ice Age Trail Alliance in its atlas maps and guidebook. You can take any route you'd like. The IATA's suggested connecting routes are generally the shortest way to get from point A to point B, but they sometimes diverge to take you past glacial features or areas where they hope to build future trail. One particular connecting route scorned by many thru-hikers is the one in between the Chippewa River and Lake Eleven segments, near Cornell. The IATA recommends a circuitous route to keep hikers off of busy State Highway 64, a detour that adds a whopping fourteen miles to the trek. Sure I could handle a little traffic, I swiped the fat tip of my yellow highlighter along Highway 64, instantly saving myself three to four hours of running.

Moving my finger along the trail route, I came to an odd bubble around the Wisconsin Dells area. It was the bifurcation, an anomaly found only on the Florida and Ice Age National Scenic Trails. The bifurcation begins at the end of the Chaffee Creek segment just south of Coloma. At this spot, actually a wayside off of Interstate 39, the trail splits for seventy-five to eighty-five miles (depending which way you go), making sweeping arcs to the right and left before rejoining at Devil's Lake in Baraboo. The eastern half of the bifurcation passes Aldo Leopold's shack and John Muir's boyhood home, providing opportunities to learn about these important environmentalists. The western half showcases the remnants of Glacial Lake Wisconsin, a significant geologic feature. This former massive lake was created when the glacier's Green Bay Lobe, which covered a large swatch of eastern Wisconsin, moved westward and bumped into the ancient Baraboo Hills, grinding to a halt. The two structures blocked the southbound flowage of the ancient Wisconsin River like a dam, resulting in the formation of Glacial Lake Wisconsin. When the glacier eventually began to melt and recede, a drainage path to the south of the blockage opened one day along the Baraboo Hills' eastern flank. Suddenly freed, the vast lake drained so quickly—geologists say just a few days—that its furiously rushing waters effortlessly chiseled the famous dells formations out of the area's soft sandstone.

The path Ray Zillmer originally sketched did not contain a bifurcation. But as time passed, some trail enthusiasts argued his vision had one flaw. If the path unspooled only along the terminal moraine, it would bypass many impressive glacial landforms. In the central part of the state, these included Glacial Lake Wisconsin, the Baraboo Hills, and Devil's Lake State Park, arguably some of the most significant glacial features in the entire state. A linear path couldn't take in all of the glacial riches studding this area, so two proposed routes evolved, which lay to the east and west of the terminal moraine. After much squabbling over the years about whether the eastern or western trail should be used, the NPS solved the dispute in 1987 by noting loop trails were allowed on National Scenic Trails. Therefore, one route could be considered the "real" trail and the other its side loop. With both the eastern and western trails approved, it made no sense to quibble over which was the real trail and which was the side loop, and the NPS didn't require such a designation. So today hikers have a choice of taking either half of the bifurcation if they wish to officially complete a thru-hike.

For me, the choice was clear. Without pausing, I glided my highlighter over the eastern route, which was shorter and had more trail segments. Trail segments are generally the more scenic paths, plus are easier on the feet than concrete or asphalt.

As painstaking and time-consuming as the process was to determine my connecting routes, that was the easy part of the planning process. Next I tackled lodging. Camping wasn't an option if I was going to be moving so fast. I couldn't run with a tent, sleeping bag, and camping stove lashed to my back. All I planned to tote was a modestly sized hydration pack that could hold water, snacks, maybe dry socks and some bandages, and my phone. So I made arrangements to stay with friends or family who lived near each day's end point. In areas where I didn't know anyone, I booked stays at motels or inns. In some of the trail's most remote northern reaches, I calculated I would need to drive as much as a full hour to get to the closest lodging, and then another hour back again in the morning, a frustrating waste of time. No wonder Jennifer Pharr Davis unrolled her sleeping bag right on the Appalachian Trail many a night.

Next I started stocking up on energy bars and snacks to fuel me during my run-hike, neatly stacking dozens of the rectangular bars into an old shoebox. I bought a jug of some kind of recovery drink mix to down immediately after finishing each day's mileage to help replenish whatever nutrients the trail sucked from my body that day, and a half-dozen pairs of woolen athletic socks, which dry out quickly if they get wet. I bagged up nine pairs of running shoes over the months, some new, some old; I could wear the old, worn-out pairs a day or two each and then pitch, leaving three or four good pairs to rotate daily. This would be critical if some got too wet to wear for a day or two. Plus, rotating shoes daily is always recommended, in part to prevent hot spots and blisters.

Poking around a back shelf of our closet, I found an old canvas bag. About the size of a large satchel and festooned with several wide outer pockets, it seemed perfect for a medical kit. I tricked it out with a wide assortment of bandages, plus mole skin, gauze, scissors, tweezers, antibacterial salves, and muscle rub. I tossed in ibuprofen, needles to pop blisters, antibacterial wipes, petroleum jelly to ward off chafing, and some antacids and antidiarrheal tablets—because you never know. In went mosquito and tick repellent, sunscreen, lip balm, and aloe. Finally, after reading about ultrarunners' frequent use of duct tape on supersized blisters, I added one bright red roll before standing back in admiration. I had just created one kick-ass medical kit.

Although many thru-hikers travel unassisted, that wasn't an option for me if I was going to nab an FKT. So my final task was putting together a crew: people who would help me for a day or two, shadowing me on the trail in their vehicle all day. They would meet me at road crossings or other designated spots, ready to resupply me with fresh water, more snacks, dry socks, different shoes—whatever I might need or want. They would also shuttle me to the trail in the morning and to my lodging at night. My husband agreed to take the first ten days, when I would be farthest away from our home base in Sun Prairie. My younger sister signed on for three days. My parents took three more. Our younger daughter, home for just a few weeks before heading off to a three-month contract job in New York City, agreed to help me during her final five days in Wisconsin. Friends filled in the rest.

By this point I was exhausted from my months-long preparations, humbled by the offers of crewing assistance, and overwhelmed by the details involved in patching together such an adventure. Now all that remained was the easy part: running eleven hundred miles.

◆

I knew injuries were a possibility before I set foot on the trail. One of the most common to beset long-distance hikers or runners is tendinitis, an inflammation of the tendons caused by overuse. The best way to avoid this is to build your mileage slowly, hiking eight or ten miles a day at first, gradually building up to fifteen- or twenty-mile days. If you're trying to set an FKT, however, you have to knock it out of the ballpark on day one. I was well positioned to do this, being a daily runner and overall exercise fanatic. And with my planned precautions, such as changing my shoes every day and alternating periods of running with walking so that I would constantly be using different muscle groups and gaits, I figured I had a good chance of completing the hike injury-free. What I hadn't factored into the equation was the possibility of stumbling on rocky terrain—much less on day two.

Fortunately, the Timberland Hills segment seems to have been my knee's Achilles heel. After that segment, the knee stops protesting too much. No, I still can't run on it. But I can hike as much as I want. And for whatever reason, the subsequent downhills in the following Grassy Lake segment don't bother it. So I motor ahead, hoping the knee will heal itself over the next few days, allowing me to effortlessly fly along the trail.

By midafternoon, the agony of Timberland Hills is a distant memory. I enter the Bear Lake segment and calculate I have just three or four hours of hiking left. There are 4.2 miles to Bear Lake, which ends at the Boy Scouts' L. E. Phillips Scout Reservation, then a final 5.9 on a connecting route. Bear Lake runs through a hummocky mix of woods and marshland, passing several lakes. According to the "Hiker-2-Hiker" notes passed on to me by IATA volunteer Sharon Dziengel—the kindliest person, I've come to discover, in addition to being the woman whose record I'm somewhat guiltily trying to beat—previous thru-hikers say it can be confusing to follow the trail in here, so I make sure I'm concentrating. The first mile is delightful, a barely there trail that twists and winds playfully through thick woods. Just as I'm thinking this might be my favorite trail segment so far, the yellow arrows and blazes abruptly stop.

The last arrow I'd followed, not more than a quarter mile back, had pointed me to the left along a path that curved 180 degrees, directing me straight back the way I'd just come. I had thought that was odd at the time but assumed the path would curve back again. But now that I don't see any blazes or arrows, I figure I must have overlooked the proper path. Or perhaps I have somehow started following the signs for westbound hikers. I turn around and begin walking back to that last arrow for a reanalysis.

But it's gone. Disappeared. Vanished.

In fact, the very trail I'm on—a mere scuff in the dirt, it's true, but the only thing remotely resembling a trail in this dense tangle of trees and undergrowth—ends right where I'm standing. It doesn't arc back into that 180-degree curve I'd followed minutes ago. Just minutes ago! I slowly turn around in a circle, my heart now racing. I don't see a single yellow arrow or blaze anywhere, in any direction. How can I have lost the trail when all I've done is turn around and walk back exactly the way I've just come? This makes no sense whatsoever. There has to be a marker lurking here somewhere. I walk back and forth, back and forth, on the little path. Nothing. Panic begins to claw at my throat. Faint strains from the 1960s TV series *The Twilight Zone* echo in my head. My mind now frozen, my feet begin randomly stumbling through the woods, a few minutes this way, a few minutes that way, in some kind of primal, blind attempt to spot a flash of yellow. To find my way. Regain my bearings. All

I accomplish from my efforts is to slice up my arms and legs by thrashing through the brush.

I force myself to stop flailing about and think. *Think!* Okay, I saw some white and red blazes before. I'd assumed they were Boy Scout trails since the Bear Lake segment ends at a Boy Scout camp. I'll follow one of these paths; surely one will lead me to the camp, where I'll rejoin the Ice Age Trail. Carefully looking all around me, I spot a red blaze alongside a tiny trail. I exhale loudly in relief. Then, shaking my limbs to get rid of the stress, I begin hiking once more. But that red blaze turns out to be the sole one, and the path similarly peters out after a short distance. A wave of nausea passes through me. I start to feel almost dizzy with panic and fear. What the heck is happening out here? I *am* in the twilight zone!

Grabbing my trail map from my pack, I see there's a road about a half mile west of the trail. If I use my compass, I should be able to bushwhack my way to the road, interestingly named 13¾-16th Street, and call Ed to pick me up. It will be disappointing not to complete this segment, but it's not cheating. Sharon Dziengel told me thru-hikers have to complete every segment to the best of their ability. This means if you get lost and end up taking a shortcut, that's fine as long as your intent was to hike the entire segment. Besides, if you get lost, chances are you'll end up hiking more miles rather than fewer. Glancing at my phone, I breathe a sigh of relief to find I have cell service. I place a quick call to Ed.

"I'm lost in Bear Lake!" The words tumble out in a squeaky crush. "There are no blazes anywhere! I'm going to try and bushwhack my way to the road. When I make it, I'll call you so you can pick me up. By any chance is there a Scoutmaster at the camp who can give any information about this trail?"

"The place appears to be deserted," he says. "Abandoned, actually. And by the way, I just got here. I had a heck of a time finding the camp. It's kind of a strange place." *Of course it is. Because this whole area is in some strange vortex!*

I fish out my compass, and a sinking feeling hits me. I first learned how to read a compass a few years back, when Ed and I entered an adventure race that necessitated its use. It wasn't hard to use, but I'd forgotten the steps involved. Think. *Think!* I fiddle with the dial and watch the red arrow spin to the left, then to the right, then to the left again. But it's no use. I can't remember how to use the thing. Shoving it back into my pack, I pull out my cell phone again. I know there's a compass somewhere on here. I locate it, tap it into action, and slowly turn until I'm facing the direction it says is west. Pushing away branches just waiting to spear my eyeballs, I begin picking my way through the woods. I wonder if I'm walking through huge patches of poison ivy; one of my sisters-in-law told me it was bad right now. But I don't know what poison ivy looks like. Yes, I know the saying, "Leaves of three, let them be." But every darn plant in the forest seems to be three-leaved.

Stop fixating on poison ivy! Concentrate. Concentrate!

I've walked only a dozen steps when the compass begins spinning wildly. "Recalibrate," it tells me. I do, but it keeps insisting I need to recalibrate it. The phone compass is a bust, too. I'm so screwed. I give a little hiccup-sob, which embarrasses me even though I'm alone, and stumble in the direction I think is west.

And then, a miracle.

A wide, dirt parking lot with a service road leading out the far end opens up before me in a small clearing. I run into its sandy expanse and reach for my phone yet again.

"Ed, I found a road!" I say, not pausing to catch my breath. "I don't know where it leads, but I don't care. I'm not going into that forest again. I'm taking this road. Just pray it doesn't lead farther into the wilderness." Click.

Five minutes later, the logging road spits me out on 13¾-16th Street, and I whoop for joy. Soon Ed and I are speeding toward the start of the connecting route, the woods surrounding Bear Lake quickly receding in the distance. I don't look back.

CHAPTER FOUR

Fighting with the Trail

If you can find a path with no obstacles, it probably doesn't lead anywhere.

—FRANK A. CLARK

Just four days in, Ed has already developed an efficient crewing routine. He drops me off at the day's starting point, then drives to the next spot where the trail crosses a road. Parking the car, he starts walking on the trail toward me so he can provide me with some company and explore a little of the trail himself. Every five minutes of hiking, he pauses to find some sticks, then carefully sets them in the dirt so they form the appropriate Roman numeral: V means that spot is five minutes from the car, X is ten minutes, and so on. He does this because every time he hikes in and finds me, I immediately bark, *"How far away is the car?"*

I can't help it.

It seems silly, I know. But it's like clockwork. I'll be hiking along in the woods, enjoying the scenery, having a merry old time. My mind will easily gloss over thoughts of my dwindling water supply, which gets warmer and less palatable by the hour, or the fact that I've long ago licked from my lips the crumbs from my last snack. Yet the sight of Ed is some kind of trigger for thoughts of the car, laden with food and water. I'm suddenly desperately hungry and thirsty, and a torrent of tantrum-like questions flows out of my mouth like lava down the side of a volcano.

"How far until the segment is over?"

"Is the water in the car still cold?"

"Did you happen to bring any snacks with you?"

With his Roman numeral stick system in place, he can patiently point out each mark and tell me exactly how much longer I have to hike until I hit the mother lode stuffed in our car. I know why he's doing this, and I'm ashamed at my outbursts. But I can't help it. Really.

The entrance to the Hemlock Creek segment comes at the end of $28^{11}/_{16}$th Street in Birchwood. Its first dozen or so yards run alongside someone's home, and the passage is as smooth and lovely as a manicured golf course. That's why I'm shocked when I reach the bridge over Pigeon Creek, and it's smothered in an overgrown tangle of nastiness. Out come the trekking poles. I hadn't needed them during the morning's Tuscobia segment, which tags along on part of the wide, smooth, seventy-four-mile Tuscobia State Trail. In its rail heyday, one passenger train, one freight train, and eleven logging trains clicked and clacked along this route daily, all part of the Omaha Line. In 1965 the line was abandoned, and local Hulda Hilfiker—clearly a visionary for her time, and with a cool name to boot—led the successful drive to convert it to a recreational trail. That was in 1966, just a year after Wisconsin's Elroy-Sparta Trail became the nation's first rail trail.

In an ideal world, the Ice Age Trail, when completed, would be composed entirely of neatly trimmed singletrack, or trail not much wider than your two feet, to afford hikers the most rustic, scenic experience possible. But creating such a trail today is expensive and time-consuming. So when the desired route inches near a state recreational trail or rail trail already in place, it only makes sense to piggyback. The Ice Age Trail does this eight times, gliding along portions of the Gandy Dancer, Tuscobia, Mountain–Bay, Badger State, Sugar River, Glacial Drumlin, Lake Country, and Ahnapee Trails as it winds its way through the state.

I haven't minded occasionally hiking on recreational paths. The flat, groomed trails are a nice change of pace after rugged singletrack, such as the over-foliated path I'm plunging into here in Hemlock Creek. I slash and hack at the vegetation obscuring my passage across the bridge, muttering angrily as the sun beats down upon me from its lofty perch, causing rivulets of sweat to course down my back.

"This is ridiculous," I cry aloud in frustration. "I can't believe this is classified a National Scenic Trail. It's barely a trail at all! Who would ever want to hike this?"

Stomp, slash, mutter, sputter.

The minute I step off the bridge, I walk straight into a thick, bristly patch of weeds that snags my pack, slashes my arms, and stealthily wraps a belt of burrs around my waist.

"I DID NOT SIGN UP FOR THIS!" My harsh cry momentarily pierces the velvety silence, then is gone, the angry words floating away over the treetops.

If I yell out loud on the Hemlock Creek segment and no one is there to hear it, did I really make a sound?

My anger released, I disentangle myself from the scrub and soldier on with a sigh. This hike is not at all what I thought it was going to be—a pleasant, injury-free skip along well-manicured trails. Clearly, despite my research and preparation, I had set out on my hike a trail ingénue. The Ice Age Trail I'd cut my teeth on closer to home was largely composed of paths that wound through state and county parks: Kettle Moraine, Lapham Peak, Indian

Lake, Devil's Lake. With park personnel to help keep those paths smooth and a steady flow of foot traffic, these trails are generally in pristine condition. Hit one on a bad day and you might end up hiking through grass up to your calves or getting burned by some wild parsnip arcing across the trail. So that's what I presumed the entire Ice Age Trail would be—a happy-go-lucky path, neat and tidy, rolling around the state without a stain on its stockings.

Yes, I'd noticed signs stating the trail was maintained by volunteers. But I hadn't stopped to ponder what that meant before setting out. So when I call some trail volunteers a few days later, seeking intel on some of the upcoming segments, they fill me in. The Ice Age Trail is organized into twenty-one volunteer chapters, each tasked with trail outreach and promotional activities within their communities. But the chapters' main activity is to maintain the trail miles in their area. That involves clearing brush and downed trees, replacing missing or worn blazes and markers, and a host of other tasks. In trail-dense regions, such as here in the Northwoods, it's a Herculean task. If a tree is downed over the trail five miles into a segment, someone has to hike in there hauling the often-heavy tools to remove it from the trail, then hike back out—easily a day's work or more. In summer, after spring's rush of new growth, miles of trail are likely to be overgrown and in need of a good trim, a project that can take a crew of people days—a big commitment for volunteer workers who have other obligations. Then there's Mother Nature. In 2011, a twister unleashed its fury on a one-mile stretch of the upcoming Parrish Hills segment in Langlade County, downing trees and scattering blazes, effectively erasing any traces of the footpath. As of 2016, a temporary reroute around the devastated patch of land was still in place. Someday soon, volunteers hope, the original trail will be re-created using a GPS device that still contains a map of the old route.

While the tornado that ripped through Parrish Hills was incredibly destructive, an ensuing salvage-logging operation didn't help matters any. Salvage logging occurs when a natural disaster hits a forest, such as a wildfire, flood, insect infestation, or, in this case, tornado. Logging companies move into the devastated area afterward to harvest whatever useful, marketable timber is left, rather than leave it to decompose. After the 2011 tornado, Langlade County, owner of this patch of land, authorized a salvage logging operation. Between the twister and salvage work, a pretty stretch of trail was reduced to little more than a sad, bald patch of earth.

Here's another thing I didn't realize: Wisconsin is still being actively logged, especially here in the Northwoods. I had naïvely thought the practice had been felled a century ago, when Wisconsin's mighty forests had been logged into near-obliteration. Logging companies often can't, or simply don't, avoid the Ice Age Trail. When some loggers down blazed trees, they kindly try their best to leave trail markers in the vicinity to help hikers. But others don't, heedlessly buzzing through the forest. Logging companies don't always notify the IATA when they're in the area, either, whether it's because they don't realize they should, don't have the time, or don't care. That leaves things, once again, mainly up to the volunteers, who try to regularly hike the segments to uncover any such surprises.

So volunteers shoulder an awful lot of the work involved with the trail. And some chapters simply don't have enough help. They don't have an army of boots on the ground. Or if they do, those boots might belong to the gray-haired set who are less able to slash thickets of wild raspberries with ease. Younger members often work full-time and have families, which equates to limited hours available for volunteer work. In land-rich chapters, too, members might live an hour's drive from the trail; if you've got four hours to give, your round-trip commute leaves you with just two for actual trail work.

When I later tell colleague Karen Berger about my assumption of groomed trails heading into my thru-hike, she emits a deep chuckle. Berger is a hiker extraordinaire. She's nabbed the Triple Crown of Hiking, having thru-hiked the Appalachian, Pacific Crest, and Continental Divide Trails, among scores of others. She's also a widely published author of hiking tomes, most recently having penned *America's Great Hiking Trails* (Rizzoli, 2014), which was a *New York Times* bestseller in the Travel category. "When I hiked the Continental Divide many years ago," she says, "the vast majority of the trail was not marked." Even today, she says, the trail has some spots where you have to bushwhack, guided by a map, compass, and GPS.

As I battle through the Hemlock Creek segment, I realize that as much as I've been crabbing to myself these past four days about the annoyance of swimming through bristly thickets, tripping on tangled vegetation, and searching for errant blazes, there's something very rewarding about making it through such a stretch. I'm going mano a mano every hour with the same gnarly terrain Wisconsin's first settlers faced. If they could explore the territory and carve out a living here, with nothing to guide them except Native American footpaths and animal trails, I can certainly pick my way along a manmade trail, no matter how rough around the edges. And every time I do, I become a little more confident.

∼

Something is wrong. I've been hiking along a wide, regularly blazed logging road for a few miles now, but I haven't seen a blaze for about a quarter mile. I keep turning around to see if I can at least spy one on the opposite sides of the trees, placed there for westbound hikers—a tip I learned at this year's Ice Age Trail Alliance conference during the hiker panel—but nada. So I retrace my steps to make sure I haven't overlooked an arrow along with that last blaze. Nope. So back I go down the logging road.

But after a half mile this time, I still haven't seen a blaze on either side of the road, in either direction. I know in my gut that this is not the way. What am I missing? Once again I return to the last blaze, sitting on a post on the left side of the path. This is an official blaze. It's not worn or tilted; nothing about it is unusual. No, going straight has to be the right way. For the third time I head down the path, this time hiking about three-quarters of a mile before clenching my teeth and turning around. Now I'm standing at the post again. I've got to be missing something right here. What is it? I carefully scan both sides of the road.

And there it is.

A small brown sign with a yellow arrow is nailed to a tree on the right. It's pointing me off the logging road and onto a nearly invisible trail. The small brown sign blends in with the bark on the tree, plus is partially covered by some dense herbage sprouting up from the base of the tree. Between a ghost of a trail and a tiny, hidden arrow, it's no wonder I missed this turn. But I've wasted forty-five minutes jogging up and down the logging road, the equivalent of nearly three miles of hiking, so I'm annoyed. Stomping onto the tiny path, I almost immediately run into Ed.

"Where have you been?" he demands, irked. "I thought I'd run into you forty-five minutes ago. I wasn't prepared to hike this long."

"Tell me about it. I was lost for the last forty-five minutes."

I explain the hidden blaze and path, then realize the situation could have been much, much worse. If Ed had popped onto the logging road while I was hiking ahead, searching for a blaze, he would have continued westward on the trail, heading back toward the trailhead. Then, when I finally got onto the correct path, we'd be hiking in opposite directions. It dawns on me that we need some kind of contingency plan, especially with the spotty phone service up here. Jason had told me that during his record-setting thru-run he would draw an X in the dirt if he crossed a road and his crew wasn't waiting as expected. That's what we'll have to do.

I click along the trail with my trekking poles, hiking faster and faster, mad about the hidden marker and the forty-five minutes I've wasted. About the stupid mosquitoes that are so much thicker in this dense foliage. About the heat and humidity. I emerge from the woods at last and march up to the car, yanking on the handle. I need water. Now! But the car is locked. And in my haste to get here, I apparently got ahead of Ed, who has the key. I kick the tire in frustration, then a second time for good measure. Why didn't I think to carry my own car key?

Ed arrives a few minutes later and opens the car, and I refuel, my irritation instantly evaporating like a drop of sweat in the hot sun. And that's when it hits me. I need to be drinking more. That's why I keep getting so easily annoyed near the end of every segment. I'll learn the following year, while on a guided hike into the Grand Canyon, that the classic signs of dehydration are being disoriented, irritable, and combative—fittingly remembered with the acronym DIC. "When you start acting like a DIC," the guide will tell our group, "you need to drink more water."

"The good news is, you don't appear to have torn your meniscus," the chiropractor says as she pushes my right knee this way and that.

I'm cheered by the news, although I hadn't considered the possibility that I might have torn it.

"Do you think your cold laser can help?"

"Yes, I do," she says, as she places a small wand on various painful spots on and around my knee. The wand is connected to a machine that pulses light at a specific, low-level wavelength; the treatment is supposed to fight inflammation and reduce scar tissue and pain, among other things.

We're staying with Ed's mother in Eau Claire, about an hour from the trail. Since it's a larger city with easy access to medical care, I take a chance and see if a chiropractor can help with my knee. I need to start running again. Before I leave, she hands me a slip of paper with the name of another chiropractor, Dr. Curt Draeger, who practices in Antigo.

"Dr. Draeger has a much more powerful laser than mine," she says. "And he works with a lot of athletes. If your knee is still giving you problems when you reach Antigo, give him a call."

～

Chippewa Moraine, one of the nine units in the Ice Age National Scientific Reserve, is one of the prettiest segments on the entire Ice Age Trail. More than twenty kettle lakes polka-dot the landscape, which also consists of dense forestland. During spring migration, this is a popular pass-through for red-headed and hairy woodpeckers, scarlet tanagers, and yellow-throated vireos, among other species. I stop in at the Obey Ice Age Interpretive Center that sits just off the trail to top off my water, and I briefly peruse the exhibits. The ranger behind the desk tells me I might run into Stanley, a black Lab owned by a neighbor.

"He's real friendly, so don't be worried," he says. "But he might hike with you a long time. He loves to be out in the woods."

As if on cue, a thick-set black Lab comes loping up to me the minute I return to the trail.

"Hey, Stanley!" I call out. "Do you want to go for a hike today?"

Stanley apparently does, because he stays with me for nearly all of the remaining 5.8 miles of trail. He methodically bounds ahead of me, sniffing the vegetation, dirt, rocks, whatever catches the fancy of his 220 million olfactory receptors, then turns to look at me as if to say, "You're still coming, right?"

At one point, with Stanley well down the path ahead of me, I pause a few minutes to snap some photos. Suddenly I sense a presence right next to me. Looking down, I see good old Stanley. He's gazing at me with a very concerned look in his big, brown eyes, as if to say, "You're okay, right?"

Near the end of the segment, Ed jogs up; he has parked the car in the lot at the trailhead a little way ahead.

"This is Stanley. He is just the sweetest dog! He's been with me ever since the interpretive center, and he's been pretty attentive, always making sure I'm nearby and okay."

The words are barely out of my mouth when the trail leads us across a small road and Stanley takes off like a bullet—a dog on a mission. Stanley is racing toward a farm off to our left. A paddock sits behind the farmhouse, corralling some horses, while a small pen on the side holds a caramel-colored calf. Ed and I both gasp as we see Stanley—kind, gentle Stanley—fly into the pen holding the calf and begin chasing it in circles. I can see the terror in the calf's eyes even from here. It begins bellowing in fright, frantically racing around the tiny pen, Stanley nipping at its heels. Twice the calf crashes into one of the metal railings, which bristle with barbed wire. Now a cat flies up out of the pen, as if on a springboard, then scampers away, wanting no part of this lunacy. The horses gather in a tight clutch near the fence and begin whinnying nervously, stamping their hooves and tossing their manes. We've got to do something. One of these animals will get hurt. I reflexively step toward the farm, but Ed reaches out a hand and stops me.

"Keep moving," he says curtly. "It's not our dog."

He's right, I realize reluctantly. We head back into the forest, my heart hammering as I try to block out the sounds coming from the farm. Seconds later a gunshot rings out, and my heart sinks. Although Stanley is clearly in the wrong, he shouldn't be shot. Is this what happens up in the Northwoods? Does Wisconsin have its own patch of *Deliverance* country?

With a terrific rustling, Stanley bursts out of the brush and sits at our feet, panting. I'm relieved he hasn't been shot, but I'm not happy about the trauma he just caused.

"You were very naughty, Stanley!" I scold, shaking my finger in his face. "Bad dog!" He looks up at me with those big, brown eyes, then scampers off down the trail. I wonder if the ranger at the interpretive center knows about this side of Stanley?

CHAPTER FIVE

Into the Wild

Wilderness is not a luxury but a necessity of the human spirit, and as vital to our lives as water and good bread.
—EDWARD ABBEY, AUTHOR, *DESERT SOLITAIRE*

"Open this now," says Ed, pressing a brightly wrapped present into my hands.

"I don't want any birthday presents now," I protest, puzzled and peeved. My birthday is still two days away. Ed knows how much I love my birthday. How much I love to celebrate my birthday *on my birthday* and not on any other day. I don't want to open even one present early. But he persists.

"You *have* to open this now." A car whizzes by, then another. I hardly feel like opening birthday presents while I'm standing on the gravel shoulder of a state highway, trekking poles in hand. But Ed rarely insists on anything, so it must be important to him. I open the soft, lumpy package and find carefully tucked inside two blaze-orange technical shirts. They're so bright, I almost have to shield my eyes.

"It's dangerous walking on the side of a highway," he says protectively. "Put one of these on now." Great. Now, in addition to opening one birthday present early, I have to strip on the side of the highway. But Ed is so concerned, I quickly slip off the shirt I have on and don one of the orange ones as he nods approvingly. Then, promising to meet me two or three miles up the highway, he hops in our car and disappears down the road.

As of this day in September 2013, an Ice Age Trail thru-hike entails covering some 450 miles of connecting road routes in addition to the 650-some miles of trail. But the Northwoods where I started is thick with trail; thus far, I've encountered only around forty miles of blacktop or gravel connecting routes, most of them parceled out in two- or three-mile increments, with one fifteen-miler tossed in for fun. But today will be different. Today's schedule calls mainly for hiking from the end of the Chippewa River segment, just west of Cornell, to the Lake Eleven segment, tucked into a swath of the state's mighty Chequamegon-Nicolet National Forest. The Ice Age Trail Alliance's suggested connecting route is nearly forty miles long, because it eschews the most direct route—along busy State Highway 64—in exchange for safer passage on a series of small country roads. Since I'm trying to set a thru-hike record, I elect to walk along State Highway 64's shoulder for about twelve miles, hence Ed's concern. But doing so will mean a twenty-five-mile connecting route versus a forty-miler. For me, the choice is easy.

My first few hours along the road are surprisingly pleasant. I'd heard many hikers complain about the tediousness of the trail's connecting routes, how they're boring and ugly and miles and miles long. But after stumbling, hacking, and slashing my way through some pretty rugged terrain for the past week, I enjoy clicking my way along the highway with my poles. The pavement is smooth. The air is free of pesky mosquitoes. Nothing is scratching my arms or legs.

About twelve miles in I hang a right on County Highway H, then take a left on Polley Lane. I'm now paralleling Highway 64 on a smaller road, which I can stay on for seven miles before I have to jump back onto 64. What I hadn't realized—what I couldn't have realized—when I plotted this route on paper was that Polley Lane's first few miles are gravel. After a mere mile on the rocks my feet begin to ache. I try to do some running, thinking that changing my gait may help, but my sore knee is still not ready for that. To make matters worse, once again a plump, golden sun hangs high overhead, shooting down blistering, laser-like rays. I shade my eyes and look as far down Polley Lane as I can, but no trees were thoughtfully planted along her sides for thru-hikers. There's nowhere for me to hide. It's going to be just me and the sun for the next few hours.

Oh, Mr. Sun, Sun, Mr. Golden Sun, Please shine down on me!

That's another thing I'm learning about thru-hiking a long-distance trail. Songs that mock and bedevil you can get stuck in your head.

"Hey!" Ed calls out. He's leaning against the car, waiting for me. "Do you need any water or snacks? Boy, are you lucky—what a great day for walking!"

I scowl as I hand him my empty water bottle to refill.

"It's not a great day! It's too hot. There's no shade. And this gravel hurts my feet."

"Oh, I didn't think of it that way," he says, handing me back a full bottle. "I guess it's just great weather if you're the person crewing. Well, I'll see you in another few miles." And off he goes in a spray of gravel.

The sun's biting rays have mellowed into a warm hug when I finally reach Lake Eleven and slip into the cool embrace of the Chequamegon-Nicolet National Forest.

◦～◦

The Chequamegon-Nicolet National Forest is one of Wisconsin's treasures, blanketing more than 1.5 million acres of northern

Wisconsin, albeit in scattered chunks of land. At some 858,400 acres, the Chequamegon half of the forest dots portions of Ashland, Bayfield, Price, Sawyer, Taylor, and Vilas Counties. The Nicolet side, at 661,400 acres, resides in Florence, Forest, Langlade, Oconto, Oneida, and Vilas Counties. The Ice Age Trail runs through a boxy chunk of the southernmost stretch of the Chequamegon portion, specifically the Medford District. And it's a miracle that it does so.

America's nineteenth-century logging boom decimated northern Wisconsin's forests, including the Chequamegon, leaving little more than brush fields, stumps, and burned acreage in its wake. Pine was the preferred species to harvest in the nineteenth century. Once the pines were wiped out, around the start of the twentieth century, when Wisconsin led the world in lumber production, the loggers turned to the hardwoods, felling mainly yellow birch and hemlock.

Thankfully, an alarm bell eventually sounded somewhere in the skeletal remains of our nation's great forests, and so in the late 1920s and early 1930s, the federal government took ownership of much of the land that would become Wisconsin's national forests. Then, in 1933, President Franklin Delano Roosevelt created the Civilian Conservation Corps (CCC), which led the charge in saving Wisconsin's Northwoods. The CCC was a group of unemployed men, eighteen to twenty-five years old, who worked to whip America's natural resources back into shape. In Wisconsin and elsewhere, corpsmen reforested the land, controlled the too-rampant forest fires, carved out recreation areas, and built roads. Thanks to them, my next two days will be spent in one of the most delightful slices of the Ice Age Trail.

～

The Chequamegon is a dream. I float along winding paths of the softest pine needles, pass royal-blue lakes twinkling from the sun's kisses, and skim over weathered boardwalk groaning with character. Yes, I encounter a few rough sections with overgrown plants and downed trees, but they don't bother me. I'm too enthralled. Because this is the wilderness, pure and simple. Many of us think of the wilderness as those vast tracts of land in Montana and Wyoming and Nevada. Or maybe in New Mexico, or northern Maine. But Wisconsin? We don't have wilderness! We have "up north." Everyone goes up north to recreate. It's a land of cottages and lakes, pontoons and water skis, deer stands and snowmobile trails. It's a little wild and woolly, sure, but you don't find large expanses of land devoid of people, filled only with plants and birds and animals.

Unless, that is, you're hiking the Ice Age Trail.

Here in the remote Chequamegon, I feel like I'm a million miles away from the rest of humanity. The forest stretches skyward in a thick tangle of branches, blocking out all sound from the outside world. But it's not the same as the silence when you're at church or in the library. In those places, people cough or sniffle, air conditioning or heating kicks in, cars pass on the street. The quiet of the Wisconsin wilderness is a strikingly different experience. Here there are no soft thumps or whirs or whines—none of those ever-present background noises you never realize are there until they're not. It's like being wrapped in a thick, velvety robe, or a cushy layer of bubble wrap. The feeling is isolating, yet incredibly peaceful—so peaceful I want to bottle it up so I can pour it around myself when I'm back home and life gets too frenzied. I pause in the middle of the forest and close my eyes, letting the Chequamegon's essence seep into my pores.

⁓

The idea that being outside is good for you is not new. For quite some time now, ever since kids began spending their childhoods glued to televisions, then Game Boys, Xboxes, computers, and now smartphones, various experts have been raising the cry that we need to get our kids back outside. Richard Louv wrote in *Last Child in the Woods* about behavioral problems in children that he believes are linked to spending too much time indoors. Kids need to run around, play, get their hands dirty. Even better, they should be doing these things in the great outdoors, not the inner city. It doesn't have to be Yellowstone or Yosemite or the Grand Canyon; your nearby county forest or even a local park will do.

Children aren't the only ones who can benefit from spending time outdoors. Innumerable studies show that immersing yourself in nature can do everything from boost your creativity to lower stress, depression, and angst. It can even increase your self-esteem. A daily dose of nature may help us avoid becoming sick; one Japanese study showed women who spent six hours in the woods over a two-day period had more illness-fighting white blood cells in their bodies during the following week. Another found that people who were exposed to 46 percent more sunlight after surgery used 22 percent less pain medication per hour.

I've always enjoyed being outside, and I spend a fair amount of time in the fresh air and sunshine. Yet I'm still noticing an enormous difference in both my physical and mental health while out on the trail. Sure, I've got this knee thing going on. And my feet sprout new blisters daily, little mushroom caps that surround my toenails and ring my ankles. But I'm sleeping deeply and feeling stronger by the day. And my back and shoulders, which normally ache from hours of sitting before a computer, feel fantastic—even though they're not used to having a pack strapped onto them for ten hours a day.

Mentally, my stress levels have taken a nosedive, too (not counting the frightening Bear Lake incident). I never realized how draining it is to run a business, a household, a family. Out here on the trail, I don't fret over whether Ed is remembering to pay the bills, rake the lawn, feed the dog, clean the house, lock the doors at night, or mail all of this month's birthday cards—the ones that I so carefully wrote out ahead of time, stamped, and labeled with the days he should set each one out in the mailbox to ensure a timely delivery. I'm not fretting about the upcoming holidays—how many will dine with us on Thanksgiving, what do the kids want for Christmas, when will Maura be flying home—or trying to remember which month I always get the carpets cleaned (is it November or February?). I'm not reading the newspaper every morning, so I'm not disquieted about the war on terrorism, the economy, or the Packers' record. My life is simple: run, walk, eat, sleep, repeat.

~

Eight days into my thru-hike, I reach the western half of the Mondeaux Esker segment. By now I've passed, or hiked upon, innumerable glacial treasures, most of which I haven't been able to recognize or appreciate. But the Mondeaux Esker is different.

Numerous rivers and streams once coursed at the base of the mighty glacier that blanketed the earth, collecting sediment along their bottoms. When the glacier eventually receded and melted, and the rivers and streams underneath flowed away, the piles of sand and gravel in their beds remained, now visible as towering, serpentine ridges called eskers.

Huffing my way up one side of the Mondeaux Esker, I realize it's trying to tell me its story. An overlooked, insignificant mound of dirt in its first incarnation during the Ice Age, it's now one of the glacier's finest, most impressive remains. It's defying me not to recognize this and to pay homage to its splendor. Today, finally, I do. But my newfound insights aren't over.

When I reach the top of the esker, my quads on fire, I'm on a narrow path rolling along the ridgetop, earthen flanks pitching steeply downward on either side. Understanding now what this esker once was—the tiniest, most inconsequential part of the glacier, a pile of rubble at the bottom of a no-name stream buried under thousands of feet of ice and might—I'm finally able to grasp some sense of the long-ago glacier's immensity. Of how incomprehensibly far it must have stretched skyward. And this realization takes my breath away.

Sunday, September 8, is my fifty-second birthday. I resume my trek on the Mondeaux Esker segment, quickly coming upon the Mondeaux Dam Recreation Area. Clustered around the sprawling Mondeaux Flowage, it comprises four campgrounds, a swimming beach, picnic facilities, and the Mondeaux Dam Lodge. The lodge, a historic structure built by the CCC, is now a seasonal grill and concession stand. According to previous hikers, Steve here at the lodge makes an awesome pizza. If I hadn't hurt my knee and the trail wasn't so rough, I would have arrived here yesterday in the afternoon and been able to sample one of his pies. But I'm behind schedule, so now I've arrived early on a Sunday morning when the grill is locked up tight. None of Steve's famous pizza for me.

Instead, I carefully pick my way across the Mondeaux Esker's challenging rocky-rooty-swampy eastern half, cross the short, scruffy Pine Line, then enter the hilly confines of the East Lake segment. The trail winds northeast, leading me to within two miles of the Price County line, where a flood of emotions hits me so intensely I stop in my tracks.

CHAPTER SIX

Rooted to the Trail

*Life can only be understood backwards; but it must be
lived forward.*
—SØREN KIERKEGAARD, DANISH PHILOSOPHER

Joe Gruntman was a blunt, no-nonsense kind of guy who didn't
like to take orders from anyone except himself. Standing a stocky
five feet, eight inches tall, he had a bushy moustache and large,
bulbous nose that cast a shadow over the lower half of his face.
Joe's favored attire was a pair of heavy twill trousers held up by
wide suspenders, a blue, button-down work shirt, and a sturdy
pair of shoes that covered his ankles. Often, he'd pull a newsboy-
style cap over his shock of thick, dark hair.

Family lore says Joe's decision to pack his bags and leave Bo-
hemia for America may have been a hasty one. In 1903, shortly
before he said good riddance to European soil, Joe—who was
my great-grandfather—attended a dance where his sweetheart,
Marie Tourek, was in attendance. Local custom dictated that if a
gentleman paid to dance with a certain lady, or if she was identi-
fied as his girlfriend, no other gent was allowed to trip the light
fantastic with her. So Joe had reason to call foul play when another

man whirled away with Marie. A scuffle ensued, and the other man challenged Joe to a duel. Joe was in love, but he wasn't stupid. The fifty-fifty odds of a duel weren't to his liking, so he left—not only the dance, but the country. Marie, my great-grandmother, joined him.

Although no immigration records for either person can be located, what is known is that they both traveled in steerage, a popular option for impoverished American immigrants in the late nineteenth and early twentieth centuries. It wasn't a pleasant voyage. Steerage passengers were relegated to rows of bunks in the lower deck of a ship—the spot where the crew typically stashed the cargo—while better-heeled passengers enjoyed upper-deck accommodations that were reasonably spacious, clean, and airy. Toilets were often pots or pans; the barely edible food furnished by the ship was ladled out of huge kettles, much like at a soup kitchen. Not surprisingly, the air in steerage was fetid and stale, and illness was rampant. The two must have wept with joy when they finally disembarked in America.

Joe and Marie, who married at some point, initially settled in Chicago, where their first two children, Anna and Joseph, were born. Joe worked as a common laborer, but since he didn't like taking orders from anyone he soon quit and moved the family to a quiet farm on the southeastern edge of Wisconsin's Sawyer County. The nearest city of note, some fifteen miles east, was Phillips, the county seat of neighboring Price County.

This region of Wisconsin's Northwoods was a magnet for the Czech, Slovak, and Moravian immigrants who were flooding the country at that point in time. Although the state's prosperous lumbering era had recently ended, immigrants were lured to the area by promises of cheap land. The land was a bargain, it was true, but that was because it was nothing more than a barren patchwork of stumps and burned-over tracts devastated by forest fires. But the immigrants, including my great-grandparents, didn't care.

They cheerfully grabbed a plot, rolled up their sleeves, and began to farm the once-mighty forest.

Like the farms of many immigrants, theirs was a simple subsistence operation. Joe and Marie grew a smattering of vegetables for themselves: onions, carrots, celery, snap peas, green beans, potatoes, cabbage. They also owned a few milking cows and raised pigs, chickens, and geese. Joe regularly went deer hunting to pad the larder and, being interested and talented in this sort of thing, gathered all manner of medicinal plants, which he carefully hung from the rafters to dry. Daughters Mae and Josephine, my grandmother, soon rounded out their family.

∽

Rooted to the patch of earth where the trail prompted this ancestral reverie, I unconsciously turn my gaze to the north, toward Phillips. As I stare silently ahead, a gentle breeze caressing my face, the stories I've long heard of my great-grandfather's life play before my eyes as if on a movie reel.

∽

In the fall of 1918, the Spanish flu pandemic began storming around the world. People quaked at the thought of this deadly illness, which was especially terrifying because it came on quickly. You could be fine in the morning and dead by nightfall. Ominously, it was healthy adults, those twenty to fifty years old, who were most likely to contract the flu and perish. (To this day, it is still unknown why this was so.) If you didn't actually succumb to the influenza itself, you would often die due to its complications, such as pneumonia. The Spanish flu eventually struck 20 to 40 percent of the earth's population, killing an estimated 50 million people, including nearly 675,000 in the United States.

In Wisconsin, more than 103,000 citizens contracted the flu between September and December 1918, when the outbreak peaked in the state. The Wisconsin State Board of Health convened a special meeting to address the crisis; afterward, all state physicians, including those who had retired, were required to treat people who contracted the flu, while citizens were instructed to wear masks as a prophylactic.

The Spanish flu outbreak was serious business. If someone in your home contracted the flu, or even was suspected of having it, an immediate quarantine was imposed, which included slapping up a scarlet-letter-like placard on your house's entrance that blared, "Warning! Influenza here. This card must not be removed without authority. Milk dealers must not deliver milk in bottles." The quarantine stayed in effect until you could prove everyone in your home had been fever free for a minimum of four days. Then, before anyone other than a medical practitioner could enter, you had to thoroughly air out your home. The Spanish flu raged on in Wisconsin through the following spring, finally petering out later that year, leaving more than eight thousand fresh graves in its wake.

Like most locales, Phillips and the surrounding countryside were hit by the Spanish flu. Maybe it was his gruffness, or maybe it was his stubbornness and sheer force of will, but the deadly influenza did not strike my great-grandfather nor, thankfully, anyone in his family. But many of his friends and neighbors were not so lucky. Laid low by the illness, some fighting death, they now faced another equally dire problem. Most of these people were subsistence farmers like Joe and Marie, with a small plot of land and, usually, a cow and some chickens or pigs. These animals needed to be fed, and the cows milked, or the families would starve. Yet how could they do such physically demanding chores when they could barely lift their heads up off their pillows? Joe Gruntman was the answer. He may have been unrefined, he may have had a temper, he may have been stubborn as an ox, yet he felt a strong loyalty and kinship to honest, hardworking folks.

Joe woke up extra early each morning that fall while his friends and neighbors ailed, quickly pulling on his boots and snapping his suspenders in place. Marie had his breakfast ready—a cup of black coffee and a thick slice of bread slathered with lard, then sprinkled with coarse salt—which he quickly downed before kissing her on the cheek and heading out for the day. The sky was still pearl gray as it transitioned from night to day, and Joe's boots made a gentle crunching sound as he walked up the gravel path to the first barn. His friends at the adjacent home, softly lit by kerosene lamps, heard him coming and were comforted, knowing they wouldn't lose their animals, their food, their livelihoods. Once the cow was milked and the animals fed, Joe marched into each home, quarantine be damned, and made a big pot of soup for the family. As he left for the next farm, his friends weakly waved their thanks to him from the bedroom window.

Joe's neighbors never forgot his sacrifice during the Spanish flu pandemic. Years later, my mother, one of Joe's granddaughters, was initially aghast at some of the rude things she would hear her grandfather say to others—*Why are you wearing that ugly shirt? I can't believe you painted your house such a crappy color!*—until her mother, Josephine, said not to worry. No one minded. They knew it was just Joe being Joe. They knew that behind those blunt and often impolite words was a truly remarkable, kind man.

Snapping back to reality, I resume my trek, pushing northeast through the mixed hardwood forest. Crossing the headwaters of the Black River, I hear the unmistakable sounds of a deer leaping through the woods. Once again my heart catches and I stop.

Sometime around 1930—the exact year was never jotted down in family annals—Joe and a buddy headed out into the woods to go deer hunting. By then all four kids were grown and gone, and it was just Joe and Marie at home. The men split up and a short while later a shot rang out. Then a pause, followed by a deep, throaty, anguished scream. A scream so loud, my grandma Josephine would later say, that the folks back in town two miles away could hear it. Joe's friend, seeing movement in the woods, had raised his rifle, aimed, and fired. But the motion he saw in the distance wasn't a deer.

The friend rushed over to find Joe lying on the ground, a hole blown through his left arm, blood pouring out. Horrified and panic-stricken, he fled, leaving Joe on the ground, bleeding profusely. Somehow, Joe survived. But his arm didn't. It was later amputated some two or three inches above the elbow, and Joe never went hunting again. Over the ensuing years he never discussed the incident, nor ever spoke ill of the friend. When a child would ask what happened to his arm, Joe would solemnly reply that it was shot off when he was in the army.

Joe Gruntman loved children and doted on his six grandchildren, especially after Marie died in the fall of 1940, leaving Joe a widower at the age of fifty-eight. He was particularly close with my mother, Bobbie, the only child of his youngest daughter, Josephine. My grandfather died very young, when my mom was just three years old, forcing my grandma Josephine to work full-time to support the family. To help out, Joe watched my mother every summer for a month at his home in Phillips. He built her a swing and then a little playhouse, which he furnished with a big Victrola that he purchased at an auction, plus some dishes he found at the city dump. He took her with him into the woods to go berry picking, and he let her go with him when he'd walk along the roadside plucking the herbs and medicinal plants he would later hang from the ceiling in the workshop area of his garage. Once they were dried, he'd use them to make teas and healing poultices. Adept with his disability by then—he could split wood, clean fish, row a boat, drive a car, and bake bread one-handed—he would delight my mom by showing her what he called "my patents," the various devices he created to assist him in doing things when one hand just wouldn't suffice.

But while kind to children, he could be mischievous, too. He loved to play "pull my finger" with his grandkids. And once, when Bobbie was about four years old and just learning Bohemian, he taught her a little ditty. The rest of the summer, whenever they went out visiting, Joe asked her to sing it for his friends. She happily complied, proud of her accomplishment, and the men rewarded her efforts by laughing and clapping. Years later, when my mother was fluent in Bohemian, she recalled that little song one day and burst out laughing. Her grandfather and his friends hadn't been applauding her because she sang so well, or because she was a cute little kid. No, they were chortling because her grandfather's song roughly translated to: "There were once three men. Which one took a crap in the hay?"

～

My great-grandfather reluctantly left Phillips for good in 1955, spending the final three years of his life with my mother and grandmother in Chicago. He died in 1958, three years before I was born.

My family doesn't have many photos of my great-grandfather as a young husband and father. But the few I have, now yellowed and curling at the edges, often show him cradling a rifle, a dead deer hanging upside down from the tree behind him, or sitting in his Sawyer County farm field on a horse-drawn wagon. In my favorite photo, which is still surprisingly sharp, he's standing near a stand of birch trees, a dead wolf slung over one shoulder like a sack of grain. His left hand casually holds its back legs, while his right clutches the barrel of his rifle, its stock resting lightly on the ground. He's standing sideways, turning to look at the camera with no expression on his face. I can't tell if his dark, bushy moustache is hiding a slight frown or a little grin, but I like to think the latter.

What a fascinating man my great-grandfather was. He left his family and country when barely out of his teens, never to see them again. During his lifetime he managed to eke out a living both in Chicago and Wisconsin's Northwoods, where he skillfully slayed deer and wolves. Uneducated, he figured out how to treat everything from pimples to ulcers to heart ailments with nature's bounty. Although a bit of a renegade and a rogue, often blunt and graceless, he helped his neighbors during a worldwide pandemic. When a friend left him to die in the woods, bleeding profusely, he survived and let go of his arm, and any anger, with grace.

My great-grandfather is buried in Phillips' Lakeside Cemetery, right next to my great-grandmother. I've visited their graves several times and driven past the spot where their home in Phillips once stood. During those visits, I never felt a whisper of his presence. Yet standing here deep in the woods, so close to his home turf, his spirit suddenly floods through my body so strongly my heart aches. Did he venture this far south when he was deer hunting? Am I passing some of the plants he would have carefully plucked from the earth to prepare his various medicinal concoctions? Would he be annoyed that his great-granddaughter can't identify poison ivy, let alone just about any other plant in these woods? If he was alive, what would he think of my trek? Would he be proud of me, or think I'm crazy?

Thoughts swirl through my head like dry leaves in an autumnal wind. My heartbeat echoes in my ears. I'm feeling an intense connection to this land. To these woods. To this trail. The blood coursing through my veins carries some of the same DNA as the blood that flowed through Joseph Gruntman's veins. That flowed out of his arm that fateful day in the woods. Perhaps, just maybe, here in these very woods where I'm standing. Joseph Gruntman loved Wisconsin and this particular sliver of it. And that love, that passion, somehow was passed on to me. It doesn't matter that I was born in Chicago, or that I grew up on the sandy shores of Lake Michigan in Sheboygan. Every cell in my body is crying out that my roots are right here. That this is my land. That this is where I belong.

And I never would have known this if I hadn't decided to hike the Ice Age Trail.

CHAPTER 7

Wolves and Coyotes and Bears, Oh My!

Black bears rarely attack. But here's the thing. Sometimes they do.
—Bill Bryson, author, *A Walk in the Woods*

Day ten. I'm about eighteen miles behind schedule, or roughly half a day off. That's not too bad, seeing as I've got some 250 miles under my hydration belt. I'm averaging just under twenty-eight miles per day, not the thirty-two I'd hoped. I still can't run much due to my knee, but it really doesn't seem to matter because the trail is simply too tough up here. I know the hills will shrink, and the vegetation will loosen its stranglehold on the earth, once I round the Antigo area and begin the plunge south toward Janesville. And when I clear Kettle Moraine on the climb back north to Sturgeon Bay and the eastern terminus, I'll be greeted by a wealth of fairly flat connecting routes and rail trail, perfect for making up time.

More worrisome than the fact that I'm half a day behind schedule and can't run much is that now my right foot is hurting. Specifically, the padded part just underneath all of my toes. That area has been painful and red the last few days. I think maybe

I've developed a huge blister deep underneath my skin, where I can't see it. And since a lot of the skin in and around my toes has split open with the stress of my ambitious mileage, I'm nervous an infection has set in around this hidden blister.

Shaking these troubling thoughts from my head, I concentrate on the day's schedule. I'm hoping to finish hiking Wood Lake, then tackle Timberland Wilderness, Camp 27, Newwood, and Averill-Kelly. Giving Ed a wave, I plunge into the leafy, green Wood Lake segment, which winds through the scenic Taylor County Forest. The Ice Age Trail guidebook says this segment is quite remote and is home to black bears, wolves, and coyotes. I'm not too worried about wolves and coyotes, but the idea of running into a black bear unnerves me. I know they're not aggressive like the giant grizzlies out west. And everyone I've met who has hiked the Ice Age Trail assures me they're big babies that run away the minute they see, smell, or hear a human. But on August 16, two weeks before I began my hike, I read about Abby Wetherell.

Twelve-year-old Abby Wetherell was running on a dirt road near her home in Michigan's Wexford County, which sits in the northern half of lower Michigan, when a black bear inexplicably raced toward her. Screaming, she began running as fast as her slender, preteen legs could carry her. The bear caught Abby, knocking her to the ground, growling and clawing at her face and legs. She played dead and the beast eventually trotted away, only to come after her again when she got up and ran to a neighbor's home. Thankfully, the neighbor was able to scare the bear off for good. But Abby, whose injuries included severe lacerations to her thigh, puncture wounds, and bruises, had to be airlifted to a hospital, where she underwent surgery.

Normally, bear attacks occur when a mother is protecting her cubs, especially when you're talking about the less-aggressive black bears found in Wisconsin. But there was no evidence that cubs were nearby when Abby was attacked. So what I take from

Abby's tale is this: Some black bears in the Upper Midwest will maul innocent females running through the woods, even if their cubs aren't around.

I think about Abby as I'm winding my way through the Taylor County Forest and I become a little uneasy. What are you supposed to do if faced by a black bear? Is it run away or stand still? Stare it down or look away? Play dead or draw yourself up large? If it charges, are you supposed to punch it in the nose, or is that what you do if a shark is swimming toward you? Why, oh why, didn't I look this up before I got on the trail?

Eerily, not two minutes later I spot a pile of bear poop in the middle of the trail. Or, to be more accurate, bear scat. No, I've never seen any before. But I'm sure this is it. It's a pretty big pile, for one thing. And black bears, which can hit 280 to 350 pounds when fully grown, are the biggest animals pooping out here in the woods. Plus the soft mound is filled with berry seeds, and everyone knows bears like berries. I scurry past, then pick up the pace. That scat looked pretty fresh.

~

I actually had a near-encounter with a black bear on day three, back in Grassy Lake. Ed had parked at the trail's terminus on 30th Avenue and began walking back toward me. It was an exceptionally pleasant afternoon, the air soft and fresh, the mosquitoes taking a respite from their incessant buzzing around my face. Walking around a bend, I spied a smattering of tiny sapphire lakes winking at me from both sides of the trail, so I paused to take some photos. As I was clicking away, I spotted Ed approaching with a purposeful stride. Something was up. Just as he reached me, he abruptly stopped and grabbed a thick stick lying near my feet, then brandished it like a club.

"Now, don't panic," he said, causing my heart to instantly start hammering. "But I just saw a bear. Back there, around that bend."

He was pointing to a spot not more than a dozen yards away. We looked at each other silently.

"What do we do?" I said.

"I don't know. It's probably gone by now. I hope it is, anyway."

"Well, I'm almost at the end of this segment. I'm not going to turn around and rehike everything I just hiked."

"Stay behind me then."

I zipped my camera back into my pack and tucked in behind Ed as he began bravely marching back down the trail.

"ISN'T IT A NICE DAY OUT?" I said to Ed in a loud voice. Vaguely recalling some advice about making a lot of noise to avoid bear encounters, I wanted them to know that we were coming.

"YES, IT IS, MELANIE," he yelled back.

Our voices were strained. Pathetically fearful. This would be comical to watch, I thought, if it was happening to somebody else. In minutes we reached the spot where Ed had spied the furry hulk. A light wind sent the leaves chattering. We both peered into the woods anxiously—Ed looking to the left, me to the right—as we slowly put one foot in front of the other, continuing our loud, inane conversation.

"I JUST LOVE HIKING, ED, DON'T YOU?"

"YES, MELANIE. HIKING IS SO MUCH FUN."

Nothing.

Finally Ed exhaled loudly, signaling we were out of danger. "Since the bear is gone, I'll tell you something else," he said. "It was so close to me, I saw it blink."

⌒

I don't want to see any blinking bears. Luckily, none are hanging around Wood Lake today, and when I hike through Timberland Wilderness the only scary thing I encounter is a dense patch of bramble that etches angry red marks into my bare arms and exposed thighs. Stumbling out of the segment, I head south on gravelly Tower Road, my 1.9-mile connecting route to Camp 27. It's early afternoon and I'm hot and tired, but I know Ed will be waiting with a car full of supplies, so I focus on that. Soon I spot him. He's not alone.

A tall man stands next to Ed, a giant backpack at his feet. The man is trim, with white hair and a closely clipped goatee. Clad in gray hiking pants and a green, short-sleeved T-shirt, he has clearly been affected by the heat—perspiration has soaked a large, emerald *V* into the front of his shirt. He's dabbing at his equally sweaty forehead with a red farmer's handkerchief, and I notice his right hiking boot is untied, its laces lying limp and defeated on the dusty gravel.

"Are you Papa Bear?" I call out excitedly. Ever since learning that one "Papa Bear" is thru-hiking the trail right now, plodding west while I race east, I can't wait to run into him. Surely someone with such a fuzzy, friendly, fun trail name will be an interesting character.

"No," says the hiker, looking at me quizzically. "I'm Pat Enright."

Pat, sixty-one, tells me he's out here because he and a friend always planned to hike the Appalachian Trail. Problem was, they never quite got around to it. "One day, I realized the Appalachian Trail was never going to happen," Pat says. "So I decided to do this." "This" is hike a trail in his home state, where it's easy to get to trail segments and easy to resupply. Pat had elected to section-hike the trail, a popular option.

Thru-hiking, as I'm doing, involves hiking a long-distance trail end to end in one attempt. For partially completed trails like the Ice Age Trail, this means hiking both trail segments and connecting road routes. While most thru-hikers start hiking and don't stop other than to take a rest day here or there, some thru-hikers will leave the trail for a few days or even a week or two if they have other obligations, eventually returning to pick up where they left off. On some trails, such as the Appalachian, thru-hiking rules specify that your hike must be completed in twelve months or less to be officially considered a thru-hike. But the Ice Age Trail is more flexible. Even if you step off the trail for an extended period of time before returning—years, even—once you finish the entire trail, you're considered a thru-hiker.

Section-hikers, as the name implies, hike the trail in sections. For completed trails such as the Appalachian Trail, that might mean hiking all of the trail miles in one state, or hiking from one town to another. Hikers can define *section* however they'd like. When it comes to the Ice Age Trail, *section-hiking* means hiking all the trail segments, but not the connecting road routes. While thru-hikers more often than not hike the trail in order, whether east to west or west to east, section-hikers will often hike the Ice Age Trail's trail segments in random fashion. Maybe they'll hike all of the trail segments close to their home, for example, then hike segments they happen to be passing while on business trips or visiting relatives. To tick off segments they're rarely near, they might plan a weekend or weeklong trip.

Pat Enright's friends told him he would be nuts to hike the Ice Age Trail, whether thru-hiking or section-hiking, and even if the path was in his own backyard. It didn't deter him, nor did the thought of hiking solo. Sure, he'd prefer company, he tells me when we meet up on the trail, "but I couldn't find anyone crazy enough to go with me!"

Pat started his trek April 1, walking from Hartman Creek midtrail to the eastern terminus in Sturgeon Bay. Over the summer, he tackled the stretch from Hartman Creek to Kettlebowl near Antigo. Then, starting August 31—coincidentally, the same day I got on the trail—he began his final stretch: Kettlebowl to the western terminus in St. Croix Falls. In long-distance hiker lingo, he's doing a flip-flop—a hike that begins and/or ends midtrail—although he doesn't realize this. He simply wanted to hike the trail in both spring and fall, watching the seasons unfurl before him, and to skip most of the bug-laden summer. His strategy is to hike campsite to campsite, which typically means covering thirteen or fourteen miles a day.

I quiz Pat about the trail that lies before me. Anything to be wary of? Words of wisdom? Best practices?

"Everything's pretty easy to follow," he says. "There's really nothing to worry about. Well, just the Kettlebowl."

"What's the Kettlebowl?"

"It's a longer segment near Antigo. Part of it is on a ski hill. But the blazing's not very good in that segment. I got all turned around. Fortunately I eventually hit a logging road and had a brief period of cell reception so I could figure out which way to go. But I don't like that feeling of being lost. It's rather unpleasant." An understatement, to be sure.

As Pat talks, I hear a light tinkling. I look for its origin and spy a small silver bell hanging from his belt. It's a bear bell, he says. You wear one and it jingles while you walk, which tells the bears you're coming. That way, you won't startle them; startling them can cause an attack. When Pat was hiking the previous spring he hadn't worn a bear bell, even though spring is the season when cubs are born and bears are likely to be testy. He hadn't even hung up his food at night when camping, common practice in bear territory, as food easily accessible on the ground often attracts the animals. He didn't see the need. Now, though, he has bears on the brain. Because, like me, he'd read about Abby Wetherell.

With some twenty-two thousand bears in the state, most of them clustered in the state's northern tier (i.e., right here), I wish I had known about bear bells before I set out. I would have wrapped them around my body like a string of Christmas tree lights. I suddenly feel almost naked without them. And vulnerable. I need to get out of bear territory quickly. Once I make it through the Antigo area, I should be safe.

I leave Pat leaning against his backpack, resting, and enter Camp 27. Almost immediately an enormous beaver dam comes into view. Stretching more than one hundred feet, it's the passage across a sprawling wetland area. My trekking poles will come in handy here, as beaver dams tend to be lumpy and bumpy, pockmarked with easily overlooked holes waiting to ensnare an unsuspecting foot. I begin carefully picking my way across, pausing to photograph a profusion of comely wildflowers rimming the dam. As I focus the lens, I realize the flowers are humming. Loudly. Hundreds—no, I'm sure it's thousands—of bees are slowly drifting from flower to flower, their heavy droning emanating from the blossoms in undulating waves. It sounds like an angry buzzing to me. Or at the very least a stern, *Don't interrupt us, we're hard at work* chorus. Which is worse, I wonder—being chased by one black bear or by one thousand angry bees? My mind begins playing its own version of a game I remembered from childhood, "I Was Going on a Picnic":

I was going for a nice hike, when I had to walk through a bunch of nasty bramble.

I was going for a nice hike, when I had to walk through a bunch of nasty bramble and walk without a bear bell.

I was going for a nice hike, when I had to walk through a bunch of nasty bramble, walk without a bear bell, and pass one thousand bees.

Quickly putting away my camera, I scuttle across the dam, the bees' somber intonation slowly fading behind me in the thick summer air.

∽

That night in our motel room, I realize Pat Enright is the first hiker I've seen on the trail, and I'm ten days in. Well, that's not quite accurate. There were those three young men the first day, plus a mother and son in the McKenzie Creek segment on the second day. Still, that's just five people in ten days. And none of them were thru-hiking. I boot up my laptop and start to poke around on the Ice Age Trail Alliance website to see what I can discover about this elite group I'm (hopefully) about to join.

As of this day in early September 2013, just twenty-two people have thru-hiked the trail, nineteen men and three women. Okay, I knew that. What else? Fifty-seven people have completed section hikes, thirty-one men and twenty-six women. One person, a Tom Menzel, is on the Thousand-Miler list, but there's a question mark in the column listing whether he thru- or section-hiked. In fact, there are a bunch of question marks by the entries of the trail's first group of hikers. That's because back in the trail's early days, there were so few thru- and section-hikers that it wasn't necessary for the Ice Age Park & Trail Foundation (IAPTF), the IATA's preceding body, to track them. Staffers were easily able to pull the hikers' names out of their mental checklists if and when necessary. Everything was done on the honor system, too. If someone said they'd thru-hiked the trail, the person was believed. No recognition was afforded those who completed this impressive feat, either.

Around 2001, IAPTF employee Drew Hanson realized this situation needed to be remedied. The Ice Age Trail was long— really long—and hiking it was an accomplishment. The other major National Scenic Trails, such as the Appalachian and Pacific Crest Trails, all tracked their hikers. It benefited everyone—the hikers, the IAPTF, the state, even the nation—to do the same. Hanson got to work. Deciding the Appalachian Trail's "2,000-Miler" program was the best model, he created a similar version for the Ice Age Trail, dubbing it the "Thousand-Miler" program. There was a slight kerfuffle over whether the name should instead be "1,200-Miler," the trail's estimated total mileage once completed. But any trail's total mileage continually swells and shrinks due to land issues and other considerations, so some argued that since it was possible the trail would end up being closer to 1,100 miles, or even 1,300, the moniker "1,200-Miler" could wind up inaccurate. Others simply noted "Thousand-Miler" was more poetic, and in the end that name prevailed.

In late 2002 or early 2003, the first Thousand-Miler application was unveiled. Fill one out once you completed a section hike or thru-hike of the Ice Age Trail, and you officially became a "Thousand-Miler." You were also formally recognized at the IAPTF's next annual conference and awarded a certificate of completion. IAPTF staff then began tracking down all of the previous section- and thru-hikers they could find, asking them to please fill out this new form so a complete and accurate database could be created. Most responded, but not everyone, which is why Tom Menzel and a few others have question marks by their names.

Interestingly, the IAPTF received one out-of-state application that was missing some key pieces of information. Not wishing to mistakenly bestow prestigious Thousand-Miler status on someone, Hanson called the hiker to obtain the required-but-missing info. It was a good call, as it turned out the applicant had not hiked the entire Ice Age Trail, or even one tiny segment. In fact, the applicant had never even set foot in Wisconsin. His daughter filed the application on his behalf. He was elderly now, she said. Frail. But he had been an avid hiker in his earlier years and regularly regaled his kids with tales of the trail. She thought it would be fun to give him a hiking award in recognition of these tales, and randomly selected the Ice Age Trail's new Thousand-Miler program as a way to do so. An odd, if tender, story. Hanson politely declined.

Continuing to peruse the list of Thousand-Milers, I spy some notable accomplishments. Allison Vincent was two years old in 1997 when she finished her thru-hike in a blazing forty-nine days, an unbelievable accomplishment for a toddler. Since Allison was accompanied by her parents, Kathy and Mark, she presumably had a little help along the way (or all of the way). Her placement on the Thousand-Miler list caused a bit of a ruckus among those who felt the honor should be reserved for people who hike the trail using their own foot power, not someone else's. But the IATA decided that while Allison was carted along the trail, she did have a Thousand-Miler experience, and thus deserved the recognition. At the other end of the age spectrum is Irene Cline, the oldest person to achieve Thousand-Miler status for her section-hike. Irene embarked upon the challenge in her early seventies and hiked her final segment at age eighty-six.

The most intriguing name on the list of Thousand-Milers, however, is the one at the very top: Jim Staudacher. Jim was twenty when he thru-hiked the infant trail in the summer of 1979. Incredible, considering so few Wisconsinites realize the Ice Age Trail exists today, let alone thirty-some years earlier. How did Jim know about the trail way back then, and what in the world made him decide to thru-hike it? Fascinated by this Ice Age Trail pioneer—who was planning his ambitious, groundbreaking adventure in 1979, while I, about the same age, was merely planning my next evening out at the disco—I make a mental note to track him down someday to find out his story.

CHAPTER EIGHT

Jim Staudacher, Trailblazer

The person who follows the crowd will usually go no further than the crowd. The person who walks alone is likely to find himself in places no one has ever seen before.
—ALBERT EINSTEIN, THEORETICAL PHYSICIST

Jim Staudacher may have grown up in Shorewood, Wisconsin, a tidy, upscale village clinging to the Lake Michigan shoreline just north of Milwaukee, but he was no cream puff city slicker. For five or six summers, starting when he was a teen, he and his dad packed their camping gear—old military surplus packs, a stove, cast-iron pans, all heavy and cumbersome, not remotely high-tech, but cheap and sturdy—and headed to northern Ontario, Canada. Their mission: to explore the province by canoe, retracing old fur-trapper routes, a passion of his history- and travel-loving father. The two spent weeks and even months at a time gliding along rivers, stomping through the woods, and warmly zipping up in sleeping bags at night.

During Jim's senior year in high school, his friend Dan Daily said he was going to thru-hike the 430-mile Bruce Trail, Canada's oldest and longest marked footpath. (The Bruce Trail is in

southern Ontario and, as of 2016, stretches more than 550 miles.)
Dan invited Jim to join him, and Jim eagerly signed on for the
adventure. And so in the summer of 1977, Jim Staudacher added
"backpacker" to his backwoods résumé.

Hiking the Bruce Trail put an exclamation point on Jim's
childhood forays into Ontario. But it also drove a new desire:
the search for a novel challenge. Jim, by then a six-foot, two-inch,
225-pound man, wanted to undertake another epic hike. One
that was rather tough. Unique. He did some research into hiking
the Appalachian Trail, which was beginning to soar in popularity.
During its first twenty-two years in existence, a mere twenty-two
people had thru-hiked it. That figure inched up to thirty-seven
in the 1960s—still just three to four hikers per year—before
skyrocketing to 775 during the 1970s, when Jim checked into it.
That sounded a little too crowded for him, so he also pondered
tackling the lesser-known Pacific Crest Trail; only 179 people
thru-hiked that path during the 1970s. But then someone suggested he check out the Ice Age Trail. Intrigued, Jim found a
copy of *On the Trail of the Ice Age: A Hiker's and Biker's Guide to
Wisconsin's Ice Age National Scientific Reserve and Trail.* Written by
Congressman Henry Reuss, the representative from Wisconsin
who shepherded through Congress the bill proclaiming the Ice
Age Trail a National Scenic Trail, it was the first Ice Age Trail
guidebook.

Jim pored over the book, fascinated. Although he had driven
all over the state with his dad, he had never really studied Wisconsin's history or geography. Now he thrilled reading about how the
massive Laurentide Ice Sheet of yesteryear sculpted, massaged,
pinched, and poked the land into its current form. He totally got
why Ray Zillmer dreamed of creating a walking trail along the
terminal moraine. And he was beside himself with excitement to
learn about the budding Ice Age Trail, a trail no one had yet hiked
in its entirety. A year later, after he had backpacked up and down

the spiny ridges of Isle Royale National Park, whose topography was also heavily influenced by the glacier, a fantastic dream took shape in his mind and burrowed into his heart: He would become the first person to hike the entire Ice Age Trail. And he would do it by himself—his own personal rite of passage.

⌒

It was a cool fall day in 1978, with rain weeping from the skies and tired leaves drifting down onto lawns and sidewalks, when Jim stepped into Congressman Henry Reuss's Milwaukee office. Rep. Reuss was sort of the Ice Age Trail's gatekeeper at that time, and during Jim's initial due diligence it seemed everyone involved in the development of this new path deferred to him. So Jim figured he should ask Rep. Reuss for approval, or some kind of official blessing, for his novel endeavor. If he was honest with himself, he also wanted the congressman to scrutinize his plans and tell Jim he was on board with the hike. It was an ambitious idea, and Jim had faith in himself, absolutely, but there would be something comforting about the Ice Age Trail's godfather heartily agreeing with and supporting him.

Nerves jangling, palms sweating, the nineteen-year-old gave the congressman a not-all-that-articulate pitch about his plan to thru-hike the trail. He shared an outline of his basic itinerary and then offered to help with trail promotion, if the congressman thought that was a good idea.

Rep. Reuss, while kind and gracious, gently challenged him. Why did he want to hike the Ice Age Trail? Why did he think he could succeed at such a physically demanding endeavor? How would his thru-hike attempt promote the trail? Would it really do any good? Jim made his case as best he could. He knew his answers were awkward and even incoherent at times. But his enthusiasm helped calm him enough to press his case. And it worked. A week later—during which time, he later learned, the congressman's staff was vetting him—he was given the congressman's blessing to hike the trail. Departure date: the summer of 1979.

Now a partner in the endeavor, Rep. Reuss discussed Jim's venture with Sarah Sykes, an assistant in his Milwaukee office. Sarah, twenty-seven, was a petite redhead with a sprinkling of freckles across her nose and cheeks and an oversized pair of plastic-frame glasses that dwarfed her face. Vivacious and energetic, compassionate and generous, she was as captivated by the idea of the Ice Age Trail as Rep. Reuss, and just as committed to helping bring it to life. The two quickly realized Jim's proposed hike was like a gift dropped into their laps. With boots on the ground for the first time, they could have Jim report back to them in real time regarding the condition of every single trail segment, plus offer suggestions as to where prime connections might lie, or note routes that might better capture and showcase the glacial features that spawned its birth. And he could measure the darn thing.

Rep. Reuss's guidebook listed the trail's mileage as 830, but that number was a guesstimate. In 1979, the trail was still very young. It had never been measured in full by one person using one method, Jim learned. Instead, a variety of people had been reporting trail mileage to those in charge using different standards. Some of these folks actually set out and walked the segments to measure the distances, while others merely estimated trail length from maps. The work was all being done in a sincere attempt to determine exact trail mileage, but it simply wasn't that accurate.

Rep. Reuss assigned Sarah the task of helping Jim in his trip planning. In exchange for all of Jim's work, the congressman's office pledged to provide him with maps and Rep. Reuss's personal calling card so he could regularly place long-distance phone calls to Sarah—quite pricey in the 1970s—to keep his office in the loop. Sarah, in turn, would contact Jim's parents to keep them updated on their son's whereabouts. The congressman's office would also cover the costs of shipping him his resupply packages to post offices along the route. The rest of his trip expenses were up to him.

No one—not Rep. Reuss, not Sarah Sykes, not Jim Staudacher—had any idea how much work his trip planning would entail.

～

Once or twice a week, from late October to early May, Sarah and Jim gathered to discuss Jim's options in Rep. Reuss's downtown Milwaukee office—or sometimes in Jim's home, or Sarah's home, or the Milwaukee Public Library, or the Marquette Library. Steaming cups of coffee in hand, they pored over topographic maps and photocopied notes and black-and-white trail photos, trying to piece together a coherent hike. The trail at this time was but a whisper: a curve of dirt here, a strip of gravel over there, some broad swaths of open farmland tattooed with patches of woods where the trail coyly slipped in and out. And lots and lots of road miles in between. The two used the 1976 Ice Age Trail guidebook merely as a starting point for their plans, as they quickly learned during a few field trips to nearby trail segments that it contained a number of errors and trail deviations. Topographic maps and landowner plat maps, they found, were much more detailed and reliable. Jim and Sarah wanted to determine what trail actually existed at this point in time, and if, perhaps, they could identify better routes. The two also spoke with IAPTF officials, chapter volunteers, county and local officials, hikers, and others, seeking guidance and information from every source they could.

Even when Jim left Sarah and returned to the classroom at Marquette University, where he was studying English, Sarah remained hard at work on his pending hike, liaising with the above-mentioned groups and the Wisconsin Department of

Natural Resources. She also worked doggedly to publicize the venture, issuing press releases and setting up television, radio, and newspaper interviews, as Rep. Reuss's office increasingly comprehended what Jim's inaugural thru-hike could mean to the fledgling Ice Age Trail. It could bring attention. Monetary gains. Prominence. Growth. Excitement. The two probably also knew that staying closely involved meant they could have some measure of control over how the Ice Age Trail would be portrayed in the media, an important consideration for the pubescent path.

In 1979, the era of technical fabrics and performance wear was in its infancy. So Jim assembled his tried-and-true outdoors clothing and gear: a JanSport tent, Optimus Svea 123 stove, Vasque boots, and Kelty frame pack, with a tiny Canadian flag patch sewn onto a side pouch in homage to his backpacking debut on the Bruce Trail. He would hike in his usual jeans, nylon or cotton shorts, or wool cargo pants. (Today, cotton shorts and jeans are considered strictly verboten for distance hiking. Cotton is one of the worst materials to wear during physical activity, as it quickly absorbs perspiration but releases moisture slowly, causing the wearer to become easily chilled and chafed.) He did spring for a new Gore-Tex parka, which he purchased at Laacke & Joys in downtown Milwaukee, along with a few other necessities. Jim's Kelty pack weighed a hefty fifty-five pounds when fully loaded with food and water, but it was within backpacking's golden rule of never toting more than one-third of your body weight.

Finally the day of his departure arrived: May 14, 1979. The sky was leaden, the mercury struggled to climb past the forty-degree mark, and a cold wind blew steadily, hardly what one would hope for on the first day of such a massive undertaking. Sarah Sykes, along with Jim's parents, Lucas and Rosemarian Staudacher, gathered to see him off at the trail's eastern terminus, which was then located at the northern tip of the newer Ahnapee State Trail in Door County. Jim scrawled his name into the trail register sitting alongside the path, hugged Sarah good-bye, then stepped onto the trail. His parents stood alongside him, planning to hike the first mile with him. The trio headed off down the old railroad bed toward the town of Maplewood. The first mile passed quickly, and in what seemed like only a few minutes, Lucas and Rosemarian stepped off the trail, leaving Jim alone. After giving them each a quick hug good-bye, Jim adjusted the fifty-five-pound pack strapped onto his back and continued softly crunching along the limestone path. He didn't look back.

The first few weeks of a long-distance hike are difficult for anyone, mentally and physically. The Appalachian Conservancy recommends starting out logging a mere eight miles per day, gradually increasing the distance. This way your body can adapt to its new routine: hiking all day carrying a weighty pack. Occasional zero-mileage days are encouraged to let your body rest. Even with all of these precautions, it typically takes several weeks for the average hiker's body to become hardened to the trail—to not scream at the constant mileage, the great caloric expenditures, the lack of adequate rest, the solitude.

Layered on top of this common trail adjustment period, Jim had to deal with less-than-optimal weather. The first several days, maybe longer, remained chilly, wet, and windy. This wasn't a problem while Jim was hiking, but it was rather unpleasant when he stopped to eat or camp, despite his new Gore-Tex parka and wool cargo pants. From Algoma south, he followed the trail along the shores of Lake Michigan, which quickly became problematic; in the early 1970s, the Great Lakes experienced extremely high water levels, and those levels hadn't dropped much by 1979. The deep water often forced Jim to jump up onto higher ground, and even onto roads when the beach became impassible. But Jim wasn't a distance-hiking newbie. He'd prepared to struggle a bit in the beginning and knew this was all a mere bump in the road, or a bump in the trail, to be more precise. On a personal level, he was still stoked about soaking in Wisconsin's glacial history on foot, still so excited to be out there in nature every day, still thrilled to be achieving his dream of becoming the first thru-hiker on the Ice Age Trail.

Early on, Jim settled into a routine that would carry him through the next several months. He rose with the sun, then made a pot of what he and his dad had affectionately dubbed "mud coffee," which was coffee grounds boiled in a pot, then left to settle on the bottom. While sipping on his mud coffee, he whipped up grits or oatmeal if it was cold out, or grabbed a granola bar if it was warm. Then he quickly packed up and headed out. During his first few weeks on-trail, when spring regularly planted a dewy kiss on the earth each sunrise, he lingered in camp. No use soaking his feet first thing in the morning. Instead, he reviewed his route for the day while the dew slowly burned off. He thought he would be planning each day's hike the previous night, but he found once he finished eating supper, he collapsed into his sleeping bag, too exhausted to do any planning. Too exhausted to even think.

Ideally, Jim walked a few hours in the morning and then, around noon, found a place that had access to water to have lunch. In 1979, finding water along the Ice Age Trail wasn't all that easy. Although Jim carried iodine drops and a crude water filter with him, the water needed to be fairly clear to start with for his drops and filter to render it potable. Often he ended up asking landowners for a drink instead, and luckily most happily complied. After downing his lunch, his main meal of the day, Jim rested an hour or two, using the time to jot notes about his morning walk, pore over upcoming maps, and the like. Then he resumed his hike until the sky turned dusky, at which time he would find a discreet spot along the trail to pitch his tent. After a simple dinner, perhaps some mac and cheese or fruit and trail mix, he slipped into his sleeping bag to recharge for the next day.

~

With Sarah Sykes's assistance—and, in turn, help from the IAPTF, local trail coordinators, Jim's dad, and others—Jim had sketched out tentative road routes to get him from trail segment to trail segment. But he changed many of these almost the minute he began hiking, even deviating from some of the actual Ice Age Trail segments. Besides the issue of high water along Lake Michigan's shore, he quickly found that trail segments crossing private land were often nearly impossible to discern due to broken or missing blazes and stiles, downed trees, and thick scrub. Other trail segments that piggybacked on snowmobile routes would likely be glorious in winter, but now, in the spring and summer, had devolved into swampy passages not conducive to long-distance hiking. Jim dutifully noted the conditions of the various trail segments along with suggested improvements.

Despite challenges with the weather, water sources, and some of the trail, Jim's first two weeks passed uneventfully. And then, adventure found him on a soft late-spring night in the Northern Kettle Moraine. Jim was snoozing in the state forest's Shelter Number 2 when he was rudely awakened by a loud rattling sound just outside the shelter's open window. Must be raccoons rooting through the metal garbage cans, he thought at first. But as Jim later wrote in the July–August 1980 issue of *Wisconsin Natural Resources* magazine:

> I switched on the flashlight expecting to see the bright eyes and bandit's mask. But the animal was huge with a long dark nose, large, glowing eyes and an unmistakable head. A black bear!

I got out of there in a hurry, didn't bother with the zipper but slid out of my sleeping bag quick, the long way. I dove out the other window and raced up the muddy trail.

About 200 yards away I found a large tree and scrambled up high as I could get. The garbage cans continued to rattle noisily. Suspenseful minutes passed. There weren't supposed to be any black bears within 40 miles, but there he was! He must have weighed 200 pounds and was as big as I. He seemed twice as big. Finally the noise stopped. Black bears are billed as shy and unaggressive but I was taking no chances. I didn't budge but sat cramped in that tree until dawn.

Jim spent a long time in that tree, painfully hunched some fifteen feet above the ground. The animal glanced at him now and then but was clearly focused on finding food—campsite goodies such as hamburgers, hot dogs, and marshmallows, not human flesh. Still, Jim was terrified and didn't want to descend until he knew the bear was gone for good. Later, after his article in *Wisconsin Natural Resources* was published, park rangers sharply criticized him. He must have made up the bear incident, they said, because there were positively no bears anywhere in the entire Kettle Moraine State Forest or they would have known about it. But others who read the article contacted Jim to say they, too, had seen that black bear. A rarity, for sure. But it was there.

As the weeks passed, Sarah Sykes tracked Jim's progress ever more closely, feeling somewhat responsible for his physical and mental health. As he called in his regular updates, she traced his route on maps, following his path as he traversed prairie and farmland, slipped through county forests, waded through lush spring wildflowers, and jogged along abandoned railroad lines repurposed into multiuse trails. She cheered when he climbed the tower at Lapham Peak; worried when she heard his tale of camping along the Sugar River and watching, fascinated and awed, as a tornado violently ravished the land in front of him; and smiled at the thought of him boarding the *Colsac II* to be ferried across the Wisconsin River. Sarah was the one who regularly mailed Jim his resupply boxes, packed by his parents, which typically contained a mix of food (rice, dried potatoes, honey, pasta), clothing, and miscellaneous items such as 35 mm film, batteries, and insect repellent.

Throughout all of these weeks following the new footpath, Jim found the Ice Age Trail signage varied widely. Generally, the markings on segments rolling through public land were plentiful, visible, and consistent. One small exception was in the Northern Kettle, home to some of the first officially recognized Ice Age Trail miles. Here the trail ran along portions of an older, blue-blazed path called the Glacial Trail; that path remained marked in blue until about 1999, many years after the rest of the Ice Age Trail had been consistently flagged in bright yellow. The biggest problem regarding signage in 1979, though, came on trail segments crossing private land. Many of these segments, created around 1976 via handshake agreements, were not being well maintained. Some parcels had even been closed to hikers after the land changed hands, without any notification to local trail volunteers or the IAPTF. This translated to slow going for Jim, who was averaging about thirteen miles per day.

⁓

Sometime after summer covered the state with a warm, sticky blanket, Jim had almost climbed his way to the trail's northernmost tier. And it was here, on an oppressively hot, muggy night, that Jim had what he would categorize three decades later as one of the most traumatic experiences of his life.

The day's hike was brutal. A storm front had passed through, and the trail was slick with mud, the streams rushing with water.

Biting deerflies were out in full force, and a wood tick hatch resulted in hundreds of the annoying pests latching onto Jim and
his gear. That night, setting up camp on a small rise in the Kronenwetter swamp fifteen miles from the nearest road, his sweat-
soaked clothing pasted to his skin, he was now chilled, wet, tired,
and miserable. Jim began building a fire to warm himself and to
use as a death pyre for the ticks; each night he carefully scraped
them off himself with a knife, then flung them into the flames.
Firewood was plentiful, as someone—hunters, he presumed—
had cut down the trees growing on this small rise and left them
on the ground. Jim lit his campfire and was just starting to chop
extra firewood when he saw them.

A pack of feral dogs.

Snarling, snapping, vicious.

All of the canines were large and muscular—German Shep-
herd and collie mixes, he thought—and all of them seemed to
have one thing on their mind: bloodshed. Before Jim could process anything more, the leader lunged at the heel of one boot in an
attempt to bring him down. Jim desperately scrambled for a piece
of firewood and lucked into a thick chunk with a small branch off
to one side that afforded him a solid grip. Fearing for his life—
feeling he had one chance, and one chance only, to survive—he
swung that chunk of wood at the charging dog as hard as he could.

And missed.

The dog had jumped back in the nick of time, the flying piece
of lumber merely grazing the fur on its neck. But rather than
bounding back off into the swamp, the dog, mad with rage, leapt at
Jim again. As Jim's terror intensified, a surge of adrenaline flashed
through his body and he swung again. This time his aim was good,
and the dog crumpled to the ground. Furious, indignant, in shock,
and still fearful, Jim continued beating the animal with the firewood to ensure he was truly dead.

When Jim's heart rate finally dropped and he calmed down, he realized the other canines had slunk off into the swamp. Now he took a good look at the dog that had attacked him, but it wasn't a pretty sight. The dog's dirty body was bloodied and broken, a symbol of everything the Ice Age Trail should not be. Jim picked up the carcass and flung it into the swampy wilderness with every ounce of strength in his body, hoping it landed somewhere far away from his camp. The rest of the night he huddled by the roaring fire, which he regularly stoked so it remained supersized. He was safe for now, but terrified and angry at the incident that marred his hike.

Thankfully, Jim made it out of the Kronenwetter swamp without further incident. About a week later, after Jim had shared the alarming tale with Sarah Sykes, Jim's dad showed up somewhere near Ringle in Marathon County and placed a .22 Magnum revolver and holster in his hand. That gun stayed protectively tucked against Jim's hip for the rest of his hike.

It wasn't until Jim picked his way through the Chippewa Moraine Unit of the Ice Age National Scientific Reserve on Plummer Lake, still some two hundred miles from St. Croix Falls, that he realized the length of the Ice Age Trail had been underestimated. Ray Zillmer guessed his proposed path would top out around 500 miles. Rep. Reuss's book said it was 830 miles. Jim guessed he would end up at the western terminus with at least 1,000 miles under his belt, based on the number he had logged so far.

All these weeks, Jim had been faithfully tracking his mileage on topographical maps using a "map measurer" his father had given him. Initially, Jim and Sarah thought a pedometer might be the best way to measure the trail, but when they tested a Cadillac version available at the time on a segment near Holy Hill in the fall of 1978, its margin of error was more than 20 percent. So the map measurer was the tool that got tossed into Jim's pack.

The palm-sized map measurer looked a bit like a compass, with red and blue concentric circles on its round face. The red circle converted centimeters to kilometers, while the blue ring transformed inches to miles. A tiny, black, rubber wheel was affixed to the device's lower end. To use it, Jim rolled the little wheel along his map, tracing the routes he recently hiked. He did this every few days, whenever he found a flat surface such as a picnic table where he could set down the map. If he placed the map on an uneven or bumpy surface, the instrument was not as accurate, and Jim was striving for accuracy. Now, here in Chippewa Moraine, he was pretty confident the trail would hit the thousand-mile mark. And that four-figure number seemed pretty darn cool.

On July 29, 1979, seventy-seven days after setting out from the eastern terminus, Jim's Vasque boots carried him into Interstate State Park. According to his map measurer, Jim had hiked 1,006 miles. Once inside park headquarters, he received a congratulatory phone call from Rep. Reuss. He was also congratulated in person by Sarah Sykes and her husband, Richard, park employees, some members of the IAPTF, and members of the media, all of whom had traveled to the western terminus to record this historic moment.

Jim's trip had been exciting, exhilarating, dangerous, tedious, and exhausting. Yet he ended it thrilled and fulfilled beyond measure. At age twenty-two, he had become the first person to thru-hike the 1,006-mile Ice Age Trail.

Unlike a record, his achievement could never be bested.

Unlike many distinctions, this was one that would always and forever be his and his alone.

CHAPTER NINE

Rough Waters

*Life is like the river. Sometimes it sweeps you gently along
and sometimes the rapids come out of nowhere.*
—EMMA SMITH, ENGLISH NOVELIST

The Kennebec River originates in Moosehead Lake, Maine's largest body of water. Flowing south for 170 miles, it winds through the state capital of Augusta before emptying into the Atlantic. The river's waters are quite placid south of Augusta. In fact, it was this stretch of the river that prompted the Algonquians to dub it "Kennebec," or "long, quiet water." But ironically, the bulk of the Kennebec River isn't placid at all. In many spots it's even roiling. One of those spots is Caratunk, where the river makes a little curve as it skirts around the town. It's right at this bend in the river that the Appalachian Trail crosses the Kennebec.

The Appalachian Trail leads hikers across innumerable bodies of water in its 2,100-plus miles. But the Kennebec is considered the most dangerous, bridgeless water crossing on the entire trail. At this particular spot, the Kennebec is about seventy yards wide. On a pleasant day, it's described as having a "swift, powerful current." One can only imagine the river's temperament on an unpleasant one—say, after a torrential rain, or when spring's snowmelt uncomfortably swells its belly. Complicating matters, the Harris Station Dam sits at the base of Indian Pond eighteen miles upstream. Harris Station is Maine's largest hydroelectric dam, releasing water as needed. This means the Kennebec's depth and speed can change dramatically in minutes, without warning.

In 1976, Alice and George Ference set out to hike the entire Appalachian Trail, a little at a time, starting in their home state of Georgia. Nine years later, they were in Maine, homing in on their lofty goal. Nearing Mount Katahdin, the trail's northern terminus, the couple stopped to rest at the Pierce Pond shelter, just south of the Kennebec. Alice took a few moments to scrawl this note in the shelter's trail register:

8/25/85—2 pm
Rain all day. Will go to river about dark. Wade across
tomorrow.
Alice & George
Brunswick, Ga.
S-K in 9 years

Alice Ference never made it to Mount Katahdin. Because Alice never made it across the Kennebec. The sixty-one-year-old hiker was killed trying to wade across its tempestuous waters. Shocked and saddened, trail backers promptly created a free canoe ferry service for hikers. Today, that ferry is the officially sanctioned means of crossing the Kennebec.

❧

Day eleven, and I'm facing my first two water crossings. There are only three on the entire Ice Age Trail—two in the Averill-Kelly segment, one in Parrish Hills—and none of the three are dangerous, Kennebec-esque fords. The crossing that's the most problematic is probably the first one, over the New Wood River in the Averill-Kelly Creek Wilderness segment. While the water here is typically just ankle- or calf-deep, hikers have occasionally been met by swirling, chest-deep waters. But deep water is more of an issue in spring, with its frequent rains and snowmelt, and not so much summer's end, although a violent downpour or string of rainy days can certainly cause trouble.

I'm not worried, though. It's been a dry summer, and when I checked in with a Lincoln County trail volunteer a few days ago she assured me the water wasn't that deep. What I *am* concerned about is my right foot, which is still a mass of puffy blisters and split, weeping skin that I'd prefer to keep dry. That same Lincoln County trail volunteer tells me her "MO" for these fords, when they're shallow, is to step into plastic bags before wading across. So I tuck two gray Walmart bags into my pack before leaving for the trailhead and hope for the best.

But the minute I walk up to the first crossing of the New Wood River I know the bags won't help. The water looks to be calf- or even knee-deep; there's no way two small plastic bags will keep my feet dry. But since I brought them along, I figure I might as well try. I ferret out the bags, carefully place a foot in the bottom of each one, then step into the river. Cold water immediately rushes over the tops of the bags and fills them, soaking my shoes and socks. The bandages I'd so carefully affixed all over my feet this morning promptly abandon their posts, sliding around in my socks until finally deciding to huddle together at the tip of my big toes. I usually carry a pair of dry socks in my pack, but of course today I'd forgotten to toss a pair in. Sighing, I slog across both river fords, then squish and slosh over the rest of the segment.

~

"Do you know how many miles you've walked so far? I calculated it out while I was waiting for you and it's 288! You'll pass the

300-mile mark by the end of the day. Woo hoo! Way to go, Mom! Do you want water? Snacks? Where do I need to go next? When do you think we'll need gas?"

As I peel off my soaking shoes and socks, Maura is rushing around, strawberry-blond curls bobbing, snapping photos of me and talking a mile a minute. My youngest child, and a college junior, Maura is leaving for New York in three days, where she has a contract job at the US Mission to the United Nations for the fall semester. She agreed to crew me during her last week at home, as Ed had to go back to work. A ball of energy and excitement, she swapped places with him last night. I try to soak up her verve. Maybe it will help me forget about my foot.

As the hours tick by, her cheery demeanor is certainly a blessing. Yet I can't forget about this foot. During the Turtle Rock segment, the path spits me onto a long jumble of rocky shoreline towering over the Wisconsin River. Balancing on rocky promontories, hopping from boulder to boulder, I might as well be stabbing my sore foot with a hot poker. The ensuing Grandfather Falls segment is kinder to my battered foot, but after its completion I'm faced with a several-hours-long hike along a hard-surfaced connecting road route. Each step feels like my foot is being whacked with a concrete club. By the time the day is winding down and I stumble into the Underdown segment, which runs through a popular county recreation area, I'm limping heavily and utterly miserable.

As the heavens open and rain pours down on my slumped, defeated frame, I decide to take that Eau Claire chiropractor's advice. As soon as I make it to the next road crossing, we're heading to see Dr. Draeger. He's the one recommended to help my knee, I know, but just maybe his supersonic laser can help my foot, too.

~

It's nearly 8 p.m. and pitch dark by the time Maura inches our car up the long, gravel drive. We're in the country somewhere south of Antigo, looking for Dr. Draeger's chiropractic clinic. This is supposedly the spot, according to the map on my smartphone. Yet when we finally reach the end of the driveway, it looks like we're at his home, not his clinic. I look at Maura uneasily.

"I'm not sure where to go. Do I go up to the house and ring the doorbell? This is weird."

Maura just shrugs as she stifles a tiny yawn. I open the car door and gingerly step out onto the gravel drive. I'd changed out of my soaking running shoes and into flip-flops—not a good choice on gravel—and slowly, painfully, gimp my way toward his front door. My right knee is still tender, the bottom of my right foot is killing me, and I'm just plain sore all over from hiking several hundred miles over the past eleven days. I also realize with dismay that I'm covered in dirt and burrs and don't smell so great. This doctor visit will be rather embarrassing. Halfway up the sidewalk, the home's front door swings open and a man emerges into the shadows.

"Hi! I'll go open up the clinic," he says, gesturing behind me.

I turn around and floodlights blink on, casting a warm glow into the chilly, dark night. The lights reveal an enormous white building squatting fifty yards behind us. We hadn't noticed it in the darkness. It looks like a big gym, or maybe a warehouse. There's no signage on the structure, just a set of double doors in the center and two small windows on each end, all of which are dwarfed by the height of the building. Maura and I glance at each other. This is not your typical chiropractic office. We reach the front door just as Dr. Draeger does. A short, compact man with a shock of neatly cropped, graying hair, he ushers us inside.

I don't know what I expected to see, but it certainly wasn't this. Dr. Draeger's chiropractic office looks like a luxury spa. A decorative stone floor in soothing mocha, charcoal, and tan tones spreads out before us in the spacious entry. The walls are painted a warm browned-butter, pleasingly set off by a wealth of recessed lights. Faux marble pillars flank a circular reception area, while an elegant side room with French doors holds a fancy beverage station. Beautiful floral arrangements, which provide a welcome pop of color, are tastefully placed throughout. When I duck into the restroom, I find another well-appointed space boasting handsome cabinetry, high-end plumbing, and plush hand towels. A large shower sits on one end; there's even a scale tucked under a small table.

I'm so confused.

We're in a cornfield south of Antigo in the swankiest chiropractic office—no, the swankiest medical facility—I've ever seen. Who is this guy, and who are his clients? Antigo, population eight thousand, is potato-growing country. The estimated mean household income is $34,634, well below the state average of $51,467. In 2012, only two building permits were issued for new construction, single-family homes. And the fanciest hotel in town is the one we'll be staying at tonight, a Holiday Inn Express.

As Dr. Draeger begins his exam, he fills me in on his background. A native of Antigo, he met his wife in chiropractic school and they opened a practice together in Schofield. In 2003, he began treating members of the US Olympic Decathlon and Heptathlon teams, traveling with them to the Olympic Games in Athens (2004), Beijing (2008), and London (2012). He also began treating some of the Green Bay Packers, including star players. But Dr. Draeger doesn't treat solely elite athletes. The bulk of his patients, who come to him from a mere one-hundred-mile radius, are seeking relief from chronic pain.

"There are that many people with chronic pain in this part of Wisconsin?"

"Yes," he says. "A lot of people are desperate for help."

I suppose I'm one of them. After he pokes and prods my entire body, adjusting not just my kneecap but also a tweaked shoulder and a few other hot spots I didn't even realize I had, I shuffle into the laser room. Dr. Draeger snaps on a pair of green-lensed goggles, then picks up a thick wand-type instrument. For the next several minutes he slowly moves the wand over my knee and the surrounding tissues, which become pleasantly warm. Maura is required to stay out of the room, lest a stray laser beam zaps her, I suppose. Similar to the cold laser treatment I received in Eau Claire, the high-intensity laser therapy I'm receiving here is supposed to reduce pain and swelling, soften scar tissue, and heal damaged tissues at the cellular level. But whereas the typical cold laser found at many chiropractic offices can penetrate your skin about a quarter inch, Dr. Draeger's laser, which he created with a physicist and a laser manufacturer, can sink four or five inches into your body. A souped-up laser sounds a bit dangerous, even futuristic. But if it's good enough for Olympians and the Packers, it's good enough for me.

Dr. Draeger does pass the laser over the bottom of my foot, too, but I can see in his goggle-clad eyes that he doesn't think it's the appropriate treatment for whatever ails it. When the laser session is over, Maura and I head into a dry hydrotherapy room, where we're both invited to climb onto adjacent tables, which Dr. Draeger sets rumbling into motion. For the next thirty minutes we lay giggling on the tables as we're treated to high-pressure massages with hot-water jets.

It's half past nine when we pull up to the Holiday Inn Express. I'm exhausted, but cautiously optimistic that I'll be feeling much better in the morning.

~

My eyes snap open. I'm freezing and have to pee. It's the middle of the night, and I need all the sleep I can get. I don't want to get out of bed. But my bladder is demanding otherwise, so I slip off the covers and pad to the bathroom. The entire way there and back I'm wracked with violent shivers. At first I think the air conditioner in our hotel room is set too high, but I soon realize what it is: I have a fever. And I never get fevers. If I have a fever, something is really, really wrong. It has to be that oozing foot. I'll have to take a "zero" day tomorrow and see a doctor, putting my FKT in jeopardy. I crawl back into bed and pull the covers up to my chin as a lone tear tumbles down one cheek.

CHAPTER TEN

A Bump in the Trail

Accept the challenges so that you can feel the exhilaration of victory.

—GENERAL GEORGE S. PATTON

The doctor gently touches my oozing foot, turning it this way and that. She blots up the sticky, brown substance welling up around the base of my toes, which now smells like rank goat cheese, and looks up at me calmly. "You have cellulitis," she says. "It's a skin infection. You could have picked it up from something you stepped in on the trail, or the bacteria that we all have on our skin could have gotten in from a small cut or scratch on your foot."

Cellulitis is pretty easy to treat with antibiotics, she says, although it also can get out of hand quickly. And if it does, it can be dangerous, necessitating intravenous antibiotics and other extreme measures. "Stay off your feet for the next few days. And certainly don't go running or anything like that."

I nod silently, but my brain is furiously calculating. It wouldn't be smart to try and hike today. It's already after 11 a.m., and it'll take a while to get my prescription filled. We're also nearly an hour from the trailhead in Underdown. By the time we got there,

I'd be able to hike only a few hours. And, of course, I'm not supposed to be hiking today. Or tomorrow, or the day after that. But lounging around in Antigo for several days is out of the question. I've got miles to get in. I'll be good and take today off, but that's it. My daughter Maura knows me well and can see how frustrated I am by this turn of events. So she ramps up her buoyancy. "This will be great!" she cries. "We can have a mother-daughter day! We'll rent a chick flick, eat some snacks, and just hang out. I can't wait!" Her excitement, heartfelt and real, brings a smile to my lips, previously pressed into a tight, angry line. If I have to be off the trail for a day, thank goodness it's with her.

Joe Jopek is tap-tap-tapping away at his computer, summoning up a wealth of photos. Maura and I scoot our chairs as close as we can get for the best views. Tall and kindly, a little fluff of white hair ringing his head, Joe is a bit of a legend in the Ice Age Trail community. When he and his wife, Peg, moved here in 1972, Joe was a county resource development agent with the University of Wisconsin–Extension system. His duty: attract jobs and tourists to the area. After Joe's first year on the job, Roger Drayna of the then-named Ice Age Park & Trail Foundation invited Joe and some folks from neighboring Lincoln and Marathon Counties to a meeting to discuss establishing portions of something called the Ice Age Trail in their counties. Although Joe had no idea what this "Ice Age Trail" was beforehand, he left the meeting excited and intrigued.

"I thought, part of my job is to bring people here to visit, and to provide employment," he recalls. "And this could do both of those things. Someday, this trail could amount to something." Forty-odd years later, Joe lives and breathes the Ice Age Trail. He's been volunteer chapter coordinator of the Langlade County chapter for forty years. He has led hikes, built trail, trimmed trail, signed trail. He's shuttled hikers, dropped water for hikers, and sheltered hikers. He's probably logged about ten thousand volunteer hours over the years, although he's too modest to track them or tell anyone the tally if he did.

I called Joe today on a whim. The Ice Age Trail Alliance encourages hikers to contact chapter coordinators before entering their area to get the latest updates on trail conditions. I had called one or two coordinators so far but hadn't made it a practice. Today, anxious and restive in my hotel room, needing to do something trail-related if I couldn't be hiking, I picked up the phone and dialed Joe's number. Pat Enright had mentioned getting lost in the Kettlebowl, one of the Langlade County segments looming ahead of me, and I'd read in the guidebook that the logging activity here can make navigating tricky. Maybe Joe could give me some tips. He immediately invited us over to his home so he could go over every inch of the Kettlebowl with me. So here we are.

The file Joe is seeking pops up on the screen. Soon dozens of Kettlebowl trail photos materialize before us. Most of the photos were taken in the spring, when the trees were bare and blazes glowed warmly in the dun-colored forest. I'll have a harder time spotting the trail markers now, he warns, with growth at its lushest and brightest, one hazard of hiking at this time of year. Still, it's not an impossible task if I keep a few things in mind.

Slowly, methodically, Joe spells them out for me. First, his chapter doesn't sign every intersection. "If you need to turn, we'll have a blaze. But if you're supposed to keep going straight, we don't mark it." Next, I need to be on the lookout for a wide variety of trail markers. They might be painted or plastic yellow blazes, or perhaps small brown signs with yellow arrows, the latter of which the NPS provides free of charge. Free is good for a small volunteer chapter that has to purchase its own signage, although the signs' brown background and compact size make them difficult to spot when they're nailed to trees. (I found *that* out back in Hemlock Creek.) The chapter also purchased six-by-six-inch yellow squares with black arrows to help out, so these types of signs are in the woods, too. There are a few places where the route is indicated by yellow metal posts, sometimes topped with an Ice Age Trail sign, other times not. Oh, and local ATV clubs also use yellow posts to mark their trails, plus yellow signs with black arrows, although the latter signs are long and rectangular, while the Ice Age Trail's are square. By the time he finishes describing all of the types of trail markers out in the woods, my head is swimming. No wonder Pat got lost.

All of the photos on Joe's screen are of the Kettlebowl. But Langlade County contains more than fifty miles of rugged trail. Another segment Joe warns me about is Parrish Hills. Sprawling twelve miles across hilly, hummocky terrain and extensive wetlands, Parrish Hills is the county's oldest trail segment. One of the first things I'll encounter about two miles in is a shallow ford across the Prairie River. That won't do with my infected foot, so Joe sketches an alternate route for me, where I'll head south on County Highway H after crossing State Highway 17, then take Five Cent Road to the trail. But entering the trail here means I'll enter near a section devastated by a 2011 tornado, then salvage logging. A reroute is in place, but even trail veterans have gotten turned around. If I'm at all in doubt about how to proceed, I should skip that section and hop onto Nelson Firelane, a gravel road that will take me to County Highway T and the end of the Parrish Hills segment. Clearly, I'll need to keep my wits about me on the trail here in Langlade County.

As Joe jots down some notes for me, I devise my short-term hiking plans. The doctor told me to take two or three days off, but I can't do that. I've got a record to set. Instead, I'll hike shorter distances for three days to give my foot a break and the antibiotics time to get to work. So tomorrow, Thursday, I plan to hike fourteen miles in Underdown, Alta Junction, and Harrison Hills.

Then on Friday, I'll finish Harrison Hills and hike Parrish Hills and Highland Lakes Western, about twenty miles. Saturday will be Highland Lakes Eastern, Old Railroad, and part of Lumbercamp, for about twenty-three miles. Sunday I'll try to be back around thirty-two.

Maura is leaving Friday around noon. My next crew member, Doug Erickson, won't arrive until the end of that day, so Joe agrees to drop a gallon of water for me at a small picnic area marking the end of the Parrish Hills segment.

"Good luck when you reach Langlade County," he says as we head out the front door. "And remember—if you're supposed to turn, it will be marked."

~

The next morning we sleep in an extra hour, since I'm going only fourteen miles. My foot is still sore when I wake up, of course; I've only taken one day's worth of antibiotics. But I feel much better psychologically. At least now I know what's going on with that foot. And while I can't test my knee out quite yet by running, it feels better as well. I carefully bandage my feet; with my ever-growing number of blisters and now this cellulitis, it takes fifteen minutes. Then I put my shoes on, step into plastic bags, and tie them around my ankles. After last night's rain the trail is likely to be damp, and I don't want my feet to get wet. At least not right away.

I head back into the Underdown segment in a great rustle of plastic. I'm not on the trail more than a few minutes when a flash of fluorescent yellow catches my eye, followed by a thick walking stick swinging slightly. Seconds later I'm facing a pleasant-looking man with a white beard. A navy bandanna is wrapped around his head, covering his ears; a cap is perched on top of the bandanna. Hanging around his neck is an Oklahoma City Thunder lanyard, from which dangles a small yellow whistle topped with a tiny compass. He has no backpack or hydration system like I have. Instead, a simple, black Kelty fanny pack is clipped around his waist, the pack resting lightly on his left thigh.

"Are you Papa Bear?" I ask, stopping and leaning on my poles.

"No," he says, looking at me curiously, and a flash of scarlet tumbles across my cheeks. "I'm Bob Fay."

CHAPTER ELEVEN

Bob Fay, Archaeologist

*If you don't know where you are going, you'll end up
someplace else.*

—YOGI BERRA, BASEBALL LEGEND

Date: 25 May 2012.

Locale: Sportsman Drive, northern Marathon County.

Bob Fay was on a reconnaissance mission. After spending the
day hiking the Ringle and Dells of the Eau Claire segments of the
Ice Age Trail, Bob, per usual, was out gathering intel in advance
of one of his next excursions. He had been working on his thru-
hike of the Ice Age Trail since 2009—checking off a section here,
a section there, instead of hiking the whole way through at one
time—a strategy that still counts as an official thru-hike of the
Ice Age Trail. His next hike would be a short one—the 3.3-mile
gravel connector between the Dells of the Eau Claire and Plover
River segments. His plan was to hike it on June 20, en route to
his home in Two Rivers, after tending to business in Madison
earlier in the day. But his current mission was to figure out where
he would stash his powder-blue 1976 Schwinn LeTour ten-speed
that day.

An unsupported hiker, Bob typically dropped off his bike at the day's planned finishing point, lashing it to a tree or trail sign with a cable, which he then secured with his trusty Master Lock, the same one he had used on his locker in Waukesha's Catholic Memorial High School in the late 1960s. He kept the lock not for sentimental reasons, but because he didn't think he could commit another combination to memory. Or he didn't care to try. After securing his bike, Bob would drive to the day's starting point, parking his truck on the side of the road or in the trail parking lot, if there was one. Then he would take off down the trail, or along the connecting route—whatever was on tap for the day. Once he arrived at his destination, Bob swirled the dial on his Master Lock just as he'd done for the past forty years, waiting to hear the familiar click as it gently slid open. Unleashing his bike, he would pedal back to his truck for the trip back home to Two Rivers, where his wife, Georgia, would be waiting.

Bob easily found a good spot where he could lock his bike— a sturdy tree right where the Dells of the Eau Claire segment intersected with Sportsman Drive. Mission accomplished. Then, while heading back east along Sportsman Drive mulling over trail details, two black shapes caught his eye: bears. They were slowly, nonchalantly lumbering across the gravel road, oblivious to Bob and his truck.

Wow, those are big, big boys, he thought, slowing down to watch as they completed their crossing and were swallowed by the woods. *They must be well over two hundred pounds.* After that initial flush of admiration at their girth, dismay washed over him. Bob had never really thought about the possibility of running into bears. Not once since Father's Day 2009, when he first began thru-hiking the Ice Age Trail. "This will be interesting," he mumbled half aloud, as the first seeds of apprehension planted themselves in the bottom of his stomach.

A few weeks later, on the day before his hike, Bob was in Prairie du Chien on business as president and owner of Old Northwest Research, an archaeological consulting firm. On an impulse, he ducked into the local Cabela's and asked the clerk to see what they carried to protect oneself against bears. All that was available were bear bells and a bear whistle, $3.99 apiece. He bought one of each. Interestingly, or perhaps unnervingly, the sales receipt described the bear whistle as a "kid's whistle."

On the day of his hike, Bob carefully hung the bear bell from his belt, then hooked the whistle, which featured a tiny compass and thermometer, to an Oklahoma City Thunder lanyard he placed around his neck. He didn't really think he would see a bear that day—he sure hoped he wouldn't see a bear—but he knew it was smart to be prepared. Still, he was pretty nervous.

Bob, you'll just have to "bear and grin it," he joked to himself. *It is what it is.* His humor-laced pep talk did little to calm his jangling nerves.

Now, rumbling along gravelly Sportsman Drive to his bike-drop site, his jaw dropped. The two bears he'd spotted last month were there again, this time in a little field opening up off the end of a grassy lane, not two hundred feet north of the road. It was roughly the same spot where they had crossed in front of him a month earlier. Incredible. Unbelievable, really. The duo had their snouts buried in a raspberry patch or something equally absorbing. Well, maybe they were fast eaters and would have moved on by the time he passed by on foot. Ten minutes later, driving back to his day's starting point sans bike, he saw the pair was still there, clearly in no hurry. Bob tried not to think about the two, nor the fluttering in his stomach. He was going to hike this connecting road and tick it off his Ice Age Trail checklist if it killed him. Which, hopefully, it wouldn't.

Soon Bob was jingling and jangling along Sportsman Drive, now worrying that his protective accessories were a mistake. *Those bears will hear my bells and think, "Here comes lunch!"* he mused ruefully. Why had he thought their noise would protect him? As he neared the grassy drive leading to the field, Bob picked up the whistle—which he really hoped was for bears, not kids—and began blowing a rhythmic stream of staccato notes, matching each blast to a footstep.

I'm-com-ing. I'm-com-ing. I'm-com-ing.

He threw in a few long blasts for good measure. As Bob tooted past the grassy field, the bears were indeed still there. But no big, brown eyes rolled toward him to ponder the possible edibility of Bob Fay; they were totally absorbed in their meal. Exhaling quietly, he let the whistle fall from his lips.

For westbound hikers such as Bob, this section of the Ice Age Trail in Marathon County is roughly the start of bear country. Before his thru-hike was completed, he would encounter eleven more of the furry beasts. All, thankfully, without incident.

~

It was a pleasant Sunday morning in the spring of 2009. Bob was plopped in his big easy chair, coffee cup in hand, perusing the *Manitowoc Herald Times Reporter*, when an article caught his eye. It said the Ice Age Trail was opening its new Mishicot segment in Manitowoc County. Bob didn't know anything, really, about the Ice Age Trail. But the idea of a hiking path based around Wisconsin's glacial geography piqued his interest. Bob, then fifty-six, was an archaeologist. Previously, he had worked for Wisconsin's Department of Natural Resources and had served as executive director of the Manitowoc County Historical Society for fourteen years. Exploring the Ice Age Trail segments here in Manitowoc County surely would be interesting.

The Point Beach segment was the closest to Bob, so he decided to tackle that first, on Father's Day. As its name implied, this segment was largely tucked within Point Beach State Forest, an expansive arc of greenery hugging a little bulge in the

Lake Michigan shoreline. The segment's southern tip abutted Two Rivers just past Neshotah Park, then stretched 10.1 miles north, passing through both the state forest and the adjacent Rahr School Forest. Point Beach State Forest's claim to fame was the Rawley Point lighthouse, a reconstruction and enlargement of the predecessing beacon, which once regularly beamed over the Chicago River. The 113-foot-tall steel structure was the tallest octagonal skeletal light tower on the Great Lakes at the time of its installation.

Bob thoroughly enjoyed his Point Beach hike, so he moved on to segments in Manitowoc, Mishicot, Tisch Mills, and Two Rivers. Then he hiked the connecting routes, completing all of the trail miles in Manitowoc County on August 16, 2009. This was supposed to be the end of his Ice Age Trail exploration.

Except it wasn't.

Studying the maps and guidebook he had purchased from the Ice Age Trail Alliance, of which he was now a member, Bob noticed the trail flowed through the northern unit of the Kettle Moraine State Forest. He'd taken his daughters, Meghan and Erin, to the Northern Kettle years ago and fondly recalled hiking along some of its picturesque eskers and kames. Why not hike there, too? So he did. Then he picked up some other nearby segments.

Throughout these early hikes, Bob's wife, Georgia, helped with shuttles. The two would drive to Bob's endpoint for the day—Bob in his truck, Georgia in her van—so Bob could drop his vehicle. Then he would hop in the van and Georgia would deposit him back at the trailhead. When he reached his truck later in the day, he would drive back to Two Rivers. Once back home, Bob would open a one-and-a-half-inch yellow binder—yellow to match the Ice Age Trail's blazes, with the trail logo neatly inserted on the cover—and log the number of miles he walked that day, plus the segment name, county, and date.

With well over one hundred miles under his belt, Bob's hikes were now taking him farther and farther from Two Rivers. It really wasn't fair to make Georgia spend several hours in her van every time he wanted to go hiking, especially since she didn't share his passion. He needed a new plan, so he came up with the biking system. No, it wasn't the most efficient way to thru-hike the trail. And it meant that by the time he finished the entire trail, he would have covered it twice—once east to west on foot, and once west to east by bike. But he didn't mind. Because he was hooked.

On a warm spring night in 2010, or maybe 2011, Bob was in his upstairs study—once a small tower bedroom in the Victorian home he and Georgia shared—hunched over his drafting table. The drafting table was carefully placed in the room's alcove, whose three long windows provided a wealth of natural light perfect for studying maps. Bob had a handful of Ice Age Trail maps spread before him as he carefully plotted his next hike. Georgia walked by and saw him there—*again!*—and chided him for spending so much time with his nose buried nostril-deep in Ice Age Trail maps and that yellow binder.

"But, Georgia, I have to do this," he said. "I can't just drive three hours and start walking. I have to figure out where to park, where to leave my bike, where the water is. There's a little bit of logistics involved, you know."

Georgia just shook her head. His wife thought he was being anal and compulsive about his hikes, and Bob readily admitted to himself that he was. But Bob liked to be prepared. He needed to be prepared.

Over the next few years Bob continually honed his hiking system. Generally, he hiked one day at a time, going in segment order, east to west, although sometimes he skipped around some, especially if he was traveling for work. He made several business trips to Madison each year, for example, so he started adding another day or two to each trip to pick up segments in that part of the state. He ticked off about eighty miles' worth this way, hiking the trail from Belleville to Lodi from his Madison base.

Although Bob had initially started his Ice Age Trail adventure during the summer, he didn't care for those days when its crushing heat and humidity could make the strongest man buckle, especially if the day called for hiking an asphalt connecting route. The mosquitoes were often nasty, too. He tried spring, but the ticks were horrendous. During one hike in late May 2012 near the Dells of the Eau Claire segment, he emerged from the woods and followed a short, one-hundred-foot grassy strip—a powerline right-of-way—and 107 ticks hopped on for a ride. (He counted them later as he pulled them off.) September and October, with their cool temps and bugless atmosphere, quickly became his favorite months to hike, so he started to limit his saunters to that time of year.

Bob also continually tweaked his hiking attire. He knocked off the early miles with his feet covered in cheap, thin, cotton socks, then shod in the heavy John Deere boots he wore when performing his archaeological fieldwork. But that ill-suited combo spattered fat blisters across his feet and robbed him of three toenails, including those on both of his big toes. He tried taping his heels and doubling up on the socks, with no luck. Finally, he ponied up for some thick, gray-wool Wigwam socks, plus a quality pair of hiking boots from The Shoe Box in Black Earth, purchased when he was hiking in the Cross Plains area. Voilà—happy, healthy feet.

Operating counter to conventional wisdom, though, he still hiked in cargo shorts, even in cool weather; he was more comfortable in shorts than pants. Completing his hiking ensemble was a thick walking stick he crafted in 2003 from a small maple sapling he found in Brown County. The stick was four feet, four

inches long, with a diameter of one-and-one-quarter inches—
perfect for helping him pick his way across uneven, cultivated
fields when he was working on his archaeological surface col-
lections, and for turning over rocks and artifacts he wanted to
inspect. Although most hikers would likely find the stick too
heavy and cumbersome, he tried it out on the trail and deemed
it quite useful in helping him keep his balance and in crossing
streams and beaver dams.

During his first year of hiking, Bob thought he was fueling
well. But when leg cramps began gripping his calves post-hike, he
realized he wasn't drinking enough water. His daughter, Erin, ran
out and bought him a two-bottle, navy-and-gray Mohave hydration belt so he could carry more. (Erin's gift to her dad was a gift
to herself, too; the hydration belt replaced an outdated fanny pack
her dad had been wearing when she accompanied him on hikes,
much to her mortification.) If the day called for extra mileage,
Bob strapped on a backpack and tossed in a third bottle of water,
frozen, to keep his food from spoiling. By the time he was ready
to drink it, the ice was transformed into cool water. Eschewing
large meals, Bob nibbled on finger foods throughout the day:
energy bars, cheese for protein, carrots, apples. Often a banana
for its potassium, which supposedly helped prevent cramps. His
one meal was a peanut butter and jelly sandwich, which he always
ate around 2:30 p.m.

Perhaps the biggest lesson Bob learned over time was to pace
himself, because hiking the Ice Age Trail was not a casual walk in
the park. Hiking the Ice Age Trail was not for wimps.

᠁

Bob was about halfway through his adventure, somewhere in the
Marquette/Waushara County area, when he had a revelation. The
biggest danger in thru-hiking the Ice Age Trail was not a bear,
or high heat and humidity, or encroaching raspberry bushes, or

dehydration. No, it was the farm dogs. To be fair, most of his farm-dog encounters had been when he was biking back to his truck and not on the trail proper—like the time when he was cycling back to his truck in the mid- to late afternoon and a farm dog flew off its property and began nipping at his heels. Bob was biking on the shoulder of the road and couldn't veer away from the dog because a car was puttering along next to him and a school bus was approaching. Trapped on the narrow shoulder, all he could do was bike as fast as possible and try to ignore the dog's hot breath on his ankles. Another time while he was hiking a connecting route, a farm dog flew at him, barking furiously. Bob impulsively jumped into a steep, grassy ditch and hiked along its bottom, the dog following on the road above, barking at his head until he was past the property. Given the choice now, he'd rather face that pair of black bears on Sportsman Drive than a farm dog any day.

~

On October 2, 2012, Bob's itinerary called for him to hike the Kettlebowl segment, 9.5 miles. The day was pleasantly warm, just a hint of autumn in the air. He entered from Oak Road at the southern trailhead and almost immediately noticed the signage was sparse. It would be a difficult trek. At an unmarked intersection Bob turned right, thinking he was turning onto Burma Road. Ninety minutes later, having hiked who-knows-where within the bowels of the Langlade County Forest without seeing a single blaze, he stopped, realizing he should never have hiked that long without spotting some kind of trail marker. There was no way he was still on the Ice Age Trail.

Discouraged and frustrated, Bob retraced his steps all the way out of the segment, deciding to try tackling it from its northern entrance off State Highway 52. He successfully navigated his way from the Kettlebowl's northern entrance all the way down to

the Big Stone Hole landmark and beyond, finally reaching what
he thought was that elusive Burma Road. Not so, said a hunter
who happened by on an ATV. Now out of water, dehydrated,
and rather dazed, Bob realized he had absolutely no idea where
he was on the map. Once again, it was time to turn around and
retrace his steps. Back at his vehicle, Bob admitted the Kettlebowl
had kicked his arse. The following day, Bob could have given it
another go. Instead, he opted to hike the Old Railroad and Highland Lakes East segments before heading home to Two Rivers,
feeling somewhat defeated.

Six weeks later, with fall winding down and winter looming, a
reinvigorated Bob Fay determined to finish what he had started.
His fingers were itching to open his yellow binder—he was on
his second one now—and mark the Kettlebowl finito. A success.
This time he entered the trail via Kent Pond Road, which should
absolutely, positively intersect with that #$@* Burma Road he
could never seem to find. Today, he found it. Yes! Bob was so
excited, so relieved, to have reached this spot that he didn't even
mind when he made yet another wrong turn in the Kettlebowl
before finally—finally!—completing this devilish segment.

A few years later, after Bob completed his thru-hike, he would
declare the Kettlebowl one of his favorites. It was challenging,
undoubtedly, but the scenery was spectacular, especially the segment's deep kettles.

~

On Thursday, September 12, 2013, Bob's eyes snapped open,
sensing his Panasonic radio alarm clock was about to sound. He
quickly switched it off before strains of classical music awakened
Georgia. Yawning, Bob stumbled out of bed and pulled on the
hiking clothes he'd set out the night before. It was 5:30 a.m. and he
wanted to start hiking Underdown by 10 a.m. at the latest. Tucked
into the Lincoln County Forest a little northeast of Merrill, it was

about two and a half hours away. Jumping into his truck, Bob stopped at Kwik Trip for coffee—a tradition—and rumbled west.

Bob made it onto the trail at 9:50, jotting down his starting time in the tiny trail journal he kept. The day was warming up already, and the mosquitoes were out in force. For September, anyway. He paused to wrap a navy bandanna around his head, making sure his ears were covered—he hated it when mosquitoes buzzed in his ears—then replaced the cap on his head.

The Underdown segment is named after Bill Underdown, the property's original homesteader. The trail here rolled through the popular Underdown Recreation area, a four-season playland crisscrossed with innumerable trails for hiking, mountain biking, cross-country skiing, snowshoeing, snowmobiling, and horseback riding. Just after crossing Loop Road, Bob paused to investigate the crumbling foundation of Bill Underdown's cabin, then snapped a photo. A few steps later he rounded a curve in the trail and was startled to see another hiker. She appeared to be thru-hiking. Since he started hiking the Ice Age Trail more than four years ago, Bob had never run into another thru-hiker, and very few casual hikers. Well, not counting those in the handful of popular parks, such as Kettle Moraine and Devil's Lake.

The woman smiled, then asked him a very odd question.

"Are you Papa Bear?"

"No. I'm Bob Fay."

~

My face reddened at my error, and words tumbled out of my mouth as quickly as the water rushing out of an open spigot. "Sorry, I heard there's a Papa Bear hiking on the Ice Age Trail, and I should be running into him right about now, so I thought you were him. Have you run into a guy named Papa Bear?"

Bob said no, that I was the only hiker he'd seen all day and the first thru-hiker he'd met on the trail. I told him about Pat Enright, the only other distance hiker I'd encountered so far. Flicking a hand toward his cocooned head, Bob warned me Underdown was full of mosquitoes. As we chatted, I surreptitiously glanced down at my feet, which caused Bob to do the same. The faucet opened again. "I'm trying to keep my feet dry from the morning dew. I was just diagnosed yesterday with cellulitis on the bottom of one foot, but I figured I might as well put bags on both feet and not just one." He clucked sympathetically, and we exchanged a few more pleasantries before he continued heading west, and I headed east, my bagged feet crinkling with each step.

◦∽

That evening, up in his study, Bob pulled out his binder containing the most current Ice Age Trail Atlas, thumbing to the page with Map 29f. Grabbing a pen, he jotted down in red ink: *Met thru-walker.* Then he carefully drew an arrow from the words to the Underdown homestead site marked on the map before snapping the binder shut.

CHAPTER TWELVE

Love Is a Many-Splendored Thing

The earth has music for those who listen.

—GEORGE SANTAYANA, SPANISH
PHILOSOPHER, POET, AND NOVELIST

I'm in love.

The realization pops into my wandering mind, unbidden. I giggle. A flush of excitement warms my body, and I feel like hugging the tree up ahead of me, that shaggy evergreen with the drooping boughs. Yes, I have cellulitis on the bottom of one foot. Blisters galore. Several toenails that are hanging on for dear life, although they know, and I know, that they won't make it. The late-summer heat and humidity double-team me daily, sapping my strength. And those mosquitoes buzzing around my ears and eyes, trying to get in their last few licks before summer fades away? They're as annoying as a little brother. Yet I'm struck with an intense love for this trail. Every sensuous curve, every burbling creek, every picture-perfect vista. I embrace her rocks and thorns and bramble; everyone needs some protection. Even the unsightly patches, like the moonscapes of cutover trees so common up here in logging country, I now view as handsome battle scars, proof that the Ice Age Trail is a tough old bird. And that no one's flawless.

I still have plenty of miles ahead of me, but I know this to be true: I won't be ready to stop hiking when I reach the eastern terminus. The Ice Age Trail has awakened something deep within me. When I stroll through its dancing grasses, I feel like a rock star being greeted by my adoring fans. When I'm cocooned in luxurious, emerald tunnels, it's like being embraced by a lover. When I splash through the trail's creeks and sink into its marshes, I feel like I'm being baptized into an intimate faith. Right now, breathing in the fresh, clean, pure scent of the trail, as heady as a lover's perfume, my heart is so full, it aches. I don't understand this swell of emotions at all. But I can't get enough of it.

～

At fifteen miles, Harrison Hills is one of the Ice Age Trail's longest segments, unfolding in a northeasterly direction through the Lincoln County Forest until petering out at the Lincoln/ Langlade County line. The remote, rugged segment is known for the sparkling blue lakes dimpled along the trail, some named, some incognito. It's also famed, not surprisingly given its name, for its hilly terrain. The highest point on the entire Ice Age Trail is here: Lookout Mountain, 1,920 feet above sea level. A radio tower and old fire tower are perched on the mountain. While the cabin sitting atop the fire tower is usually locked, if you're able to climb partway up you may be treated to some impressive views of the surrounding area.

I hope to climb the old fire tower today. We'll see. I have to get there first. For several hours now I've been huffing and puffing my way up innumerable hills, although occasionally the trail flattens out and leads me across wide, soft ATV and logging roads. These roads are pockmarked with tread impressions, indicative of recent traffic. Heavy traffic. But everything is quiet and still in Harrison Hills. No one appears to be enjoying the woods but me.

Then, a small crack.

It sounds like a branch being snapped in two by a foot. Or a paw. I pause. Why, when nothing ever sticks in my memory, do I suddenly recall reading in the guidebook that Harrison Hills supports a "thriving" wolf pack? I'd never thought about the possibility of encountering gray wolves when I decided to do this thru-hike. So I did no research on the storied canines, removed from the endangered species list in 2011. I have no idea if they're nocturnal, generally risk-averse, or aggressive bullies. I fear it's the latter. Before I can decide whether to proceed with caution or continue standing still, a figure pops into view. It's a younger man with a thick, brown beard. Clad in long, tan pants and a gray pullover, a shock of his hair is comically pushed straight up by a wide, red-white-and-blue headband. He looks tired. And hot; he's pushed up the sleeves of his pullover clear to his elbows. His face is also a pinkish hue, as are his hands, which look swollen with the heat. Clearly, he's wearing too many layers, and it surely doesn't help that an enormous black pack is strapped to his back. But I'm thrilled to see him. I can tell by his looks—the bushy beard, a body that looks a bit soft and cuddly—that he must be a certain elusive hiker.

"Hi!" I call out, this time quite confidently. "Are you Papa Bear?"

I'm sure I've finally found him.

CHAPTER THIRTEEN

Adam Hinz, Seeker

We see in order to move; we move in order to see.
—WILLIAM GIBSON, AMERICAN-CANADIAN NOVELIST

Twenty-eight: a pretty impressive blister count for one day of hiking. But even a couple dozen blisters couldn't top the back of his right heel, which had been rubbed completely raw; a patch of angry, red skin about the size of his palm sprawled nearly ankle to ankle. No wonder his socks were soaked in blood. He was in trouble. Big trouble. How could he possibly hike the trail's remaining eleven hundred miles if this is what his feet looked like after walking a mere twenty?

Any normal, intelligent person would call off this quest, he thought. But he'd promised himself before setting one boot-clad foot on the trail that he wasn't quitting, no matter what. Not for anything. Well, he'd actually given himself two outs—one, if he broke a leg, and two, if he was eaten by a bear. He'd have no choice but to quit in the latter scenario, of course. But a couple dozen blisters and a patch of raw skin? Nope. He couldn't quit because of that, even though the pain was incredible. So he huddled in the tent he pitched in Algoma's Ahnapee River Trails Camp, just steps off the Ice Age Trail, then opened his medical kit. First, he carefully drained his blisters, then he bandaged his heel. Tomorrow, he would take it more slowly. This first day had beaten him up pretty badly, but there was no way he was quitting.

⁓

Adam Hinz was working for a lawn-care company in Illinois when he dropped everything—his life, really—to help out his cousin, Andrew, who had a house to sell in Wisconsin. Four months later, the house sold, Adam now working as a screen-printer in West Bend, he felt like his life was in a holding pattern—like he was piloting a plane in a slow, endless loop around the vast sky, desperately waiting for someone to tell him it was clear to land. He prayed that when someone did beckon him down from the skies, he would know exactly what he was supposed to do with his life. Then one day, sudden clarity. He needed to make a change in his life, and not something little, like getting a haircut or moving, but a supersized change. No, that wasn't quite it. He needed to do something big. Something life-altering.

For years, Adam had joked to family and friends that one day he was going to wake up, toss some things in a sack, then walk across the country. He'd stop endlessly chasing his tail, working just to make ends meet and never really getting anywhere. Surely there was more to life than that. The idea crystallized in his mind one day when Andrew handed him a book called *A Walk Across America* by Peter Jenkins. In the book, Jenkins described the six years he spent walking from New York to Oregon after becoming disillusioned with life. Adam loved the book. Now, restless and unsettled, he knew it was time to shake things up. To undertake a colossal endeavor that would finally change his life. Although his long-standing talk of a cross-country hike had been mostly a joke, Adam realized the seriousness of the underlying dream. And it was time to make that dream become reality.

But as he started really, truly pondering such a journey, he quickly realized a trek from the Atlantic to the Pacific, or vice versa, was not in the cards for him. It was just too dang far and would take years of commitment. Plus, he wasn't sure he could even do it, physically or mentally. Adam confided in Andrew about his dilemma.

"Why don't you hike the Ice Age Trail instead?" offered Andrew.

Adam snorted. "That's just Devil's Lake!" he said. He might not want to tackle walking thousands of miles across America, but he needed something infinitely more challenging—more life-altering—than hiking ten or twelve miles at a state park.

"No, it's not," said Andrew. "It's, like, twelve hundred miles long."

A twelve-hundred-mile footpath in his own backyard? Surely his cousin was mistaken. Logging onto his computer, he typed "Ice Age Trail" into the search engine and discovered Andrew was right: There was a twelve-hundred-mile hiking trail coiled within Wisconsin. It was a prestigious National Scenic Trail, too. And, even better, only a handful of people had ever hiked the entire thing in one attempt. Adam thought he could walk twelve hundred miles, and he liked the idea of a challenging adventure that would still keep him pretty close to home. And although he had always enjoyed being out in nature, he was excited to see the trail regularly passed through towns, because he wanted his adventure to include climbing out of the little box he'd been in and meeting new people. Lots of them. Especially people who were different from himself. So in April 2013, after discussing his idea with his brother and sister-in-law, he decided he was going to thru-hike the Ice Age Trail starting on June 17. He was thirty-three years old.

Stoked about his plans, Adam told his parents and a few close friends and family members. Many were very supportive, but most told him he was crazy. Nuts. Un poco loco. And maybe he was. But he didn't think so, and he didn't care. Adam quit his job. He didn't really do much planning for his thru-hike because there wasn't any time. He did invest in the latest Ice Age Trail maps and guidebook, but he gave them no more than a cursory look, preferring to play things by ear. He would decide what he would do each day that very morning.

The week before his departure date, he gathered the gear he thought he would need: a little blanket, a two-person dome tent, some dry soup, Clif Bars. He also tossed his dad's old hatchet into the pile. He didn't know if he'd need it, but it was a pretty cool hatchet, so in it went. Then, on June 17, Andrew dropped him off at the eastern terminus and took off. Adam stood there all alone. Eschewing any kind of ceremonial beginning, such as touching the eastern terminus marker or climbing the tower, he quietly headed down the trail and into the woods, ready to be transformed.

~

When Adam awoke on day two, his feet were still killing him. Twenty-eight blisters and a skinless heel don't cure themselves overnight. He determined that morning the problem wasn't the miles he had put on or the weight of his pack (a hefty fifty-five to sixty pounds, a weight he would later determine was stupidly far too heavy). No, it was his boots. He thought he had done his due diligence. He thought he had been smart. Instead of purchasing a pair of the same comfy Merrells he'd worn for years, he had decided instead to go with the "Editors' Choice" pair listed in *Backpacker* magazine. This was a seriously long hike he'd be undertaking, and he figured he would need superserious boots. Surely the editors of *Backpacker* magazine knew their stuff. If they said these boots were good, they must be, right? But he hadn't really tested them out beforehand, let alone broken them in. And his battered feet were the result. Now he'd have to try and find a store along the way where he could purchase a more appropriate pair.

Bravely pulling on the offending hiking boots, Adam headed out from his campsite just north of Algoma. His feet instantly roared with anger. The pain was searing, intense, like nails being driven into his feet. Forced to stop every few paces, Adam wondered how he was going to manage. How in the world was he going to complete this hike? But he couldn't quit. Neither one of his legs was broken, and he hadn't seen anything remotely resembling a bear, let alone been eaten by one. And that was the deal he had made with himself.

Three hours later, Adam had managed to gimp through Algoma, a distance of just three miles. *Uncle!* He decided to throw in the towel for the day. After forcing himself to walk one more mile to Big Lake Campgrounds, a block southwest of Algoma High School, he pitched his tent, had a bite to eat, then promptly fell asleep.

The following day Adam once again pulled on his boots, those stupid Editors' Choice boots, and slowly made his way out of the campground.

Limp, limp, limp, curse.

Limp, limp, limp, grit teeth.

Limp, limp, limp, stop.

Limp, limp, limp, scream silently.

Sometimes the pain was so unbearable, Adam crumpled to the ground in tears. Other times, he ripped the offending boots off his feet and chucked them as far as he could. If he could have killed those boots, he would have. Eventually, he gleefully realized, he actually could kill them. To help forget the pain, he began crafting a plan, whereupon he would buy new boots as soon as he reached Two Rivers, the next sizable town, then mail these nasty Editors' Choice boots home. When he finished his thru-hike, he would celebrate by tossing them on a bonfire—a really big one—and watch them slowly burn. That would give them a little taste of their own medicine.

Several days later, Adam limped into Schroeder's Department Store in downtown Two Rivers, where he purchased a pair of lightweight Merrells. The minute he put them on, he could tell they fit properly. His feet were still terribly battered and painful, to be sure, but these boots would cradle his feet, not continually pummel them, as they recovered from their abuse. Before leaving town, Adam packed up his Editors' Choice boots and mailed them home as planned. They would get their due. They would get what they had coming to them.

It would take six weeks, until Adam reached Devil's Lake, before his feet were completely healed. Later, he would declare it the most challenging experience of his entire life.

⌒

Despite Adam's painful, tender feet, he soon was having the time of his life out on the trail. It was everything he hoped for, and more. He had no timetable for himself, since part of the purpose of his sojourn was to meet people and to savor the experience. So if he knocked off twenty-eight or thirty miles one day, fantastic. If the tally was eight or ten, perfect. If it was raining out and he would rather stay inside, he did. If he wanted to linger in a particular town for a few days to investigate its offerings, the backpack came off. It was so liberating to know his only job, his sole purpose, was to discover Wisconsin. To really see it for what it was.

One thing about this place, he was learning, was that it was filled with friendly, kind people—astonishingly so, especially the farther north he wandered. By now, not having shaven since June 17, and showering only every few days, if that, he realized he looked scruffy and unkempt and possibly even scary, yet complete strangers kept opening their hearts and homes to him. He'd gotten innumerable offers of breakfast, lunch, dinner, a place to sleep, a place to shower—so many offers, he'd lost track. And the offers came to him simply by sharing his stories of the trail. Everyone was excited about his undertaking, excited to hear about this eleven-hundred-mile trail snaking through their backyard, excited to share in his excitement.

This is not to say the tough days were behind him. Even though his feet had healed, hiking the Ice Age Trail was still hard work. He had to contend with ticks and heat and hills. Rocks and divots and tree roots continually tried to snag his feet. Some days, he just couldn't get into a hiking rhythm, stumbling and bumbling along the trail like a toddler taking his first steps. Other days he felt so tired, he wanted to let his legs fold under him like an accordion until he was lying quietly on a soft pile of leaves. Now and then the thought of quitting floated through his mind, but it was a decidedly fleeting thought. He never seriously pondered giving up, and that in itself always kind of amazed him. Because in the past, Adam had often had grand ideas and plans but never followed through. This time, though, was different. He knew it in his head and in his heart. He was not going to give up on the Ice Age Trail.

❧

You've got to be kidding me, Adam thought.

He had been on pace to finish his hike in September and was chagrined to find his plans derailing. And it was all because of his boots again. His Merrells, his sweet, sweet Merrells, were dying. He sure hadn't expected this, although he wasn't shocked, either. After weeks of hiking on the Ice Age Trail, he'd learned to expect the unexpected. But he was frustrated on many points.

When the trail led him past Madison a scant three days earlier, a buddy had driven him to the local REI to grab a new water filter. He could have easily picked up a new pair of boots, too, but he hadn't realized how worn out his were. It wasn't until he began frequently slipping on the trail these past two days that he stopped to inspect his footwear and discovered the Ice Age Trail had quietly erased their tread over the past several hundred miles. If he was reasonably near the western terminus, he would simply slip and slide his way there. But he was nowhere near that point— just around Devil's Lake. It was ironic, actually. His Merrells had lovingly cushioned his battered feet until they had healed, and it had cost them their life to do so. He certainly wasn't going to try to coax another 650 or so more miles out of them after what they had done for him. Even more frustrating than his boots' death, however, was that he had reached the point in the trail where he would start heading into Wisconsin's more remote northern stretches. It was not going to be easy to find good hiking boots way up in the boonies, far from any sizable town.

After much thought, Adam grabbed his smartphone and turned to the internet. He ordered a pair of his beloved Merrells from REI and had them sent to him on the trail: to Devil's Lake State Park, where he was camping for the time being. But he couldn't find the exact same pair of Merrells online, so he had to go with a pair that closely resembled them. When the boots arrived at Devil's Lake, via a two-day rush that cost him nearly as much as the boots themselves, they were uncomfortably snug. To be on the safe side, Adam decided to spend another two days at Devil's Lake, which had always been a favorite spot of his, and do some easy hiking to break them in. Then he would be on his way.

Two days later, he started in on the next trail segment. But after hiking several hours in his new boots, his pack weighing heavily on his back, he realized the boots hadn't stretched out. Not one bit. Instead, they began biting into his feet just like those cursed Editors' Choice boots.

Accepting that these boots weren't going to work either, Adam ordered yet another pair. Now camping near Cascade Mountain, still trying to inch his way up the trail, he had them sent ahead to the Portage post office. When they arrived he found, much to his chagrin, that this pair didn't fit well either. But they did seem to be slightly more comfortable than the Devil's Lake boots, so he decided he'd just deal with it. How bad could they be?

Bad.

Very bad.

After a mere day, day and a half, his feet were once again under a major assault. Grabbing his cell phone, he punched in the number of his cousin, Lisa. Lisa had kindly stashed all of Adam's belongings in her basement while he was on his thru-hike. He asked her to please, pretty please, dig out his old-but-not-worn-out Merrells and mail them to the campground at Hartman Creek State Park. It was quite a way ahead of where he was now, but he wasn't sure of his itinerary and wanted to play it safe. She acquiesced, and Adam slipped and slid his way another hundred miles in his worn-out Merrells, the latest pair of not-quite-right boots bouncing around the outside of his pack, where he'd tied them. He'd have to cart the stupid things, and their extra pounds, all the way to the Iola post office north of Hartman Creek before he'd be able to mail them back.

About twelve days since all of this nonsense with his boots began—a time frame that felt like years—he finally reached Hartman Creek. As the clerk at the campground office handed him the box in which his old pair of Merrells was nestled, he thought he might cry. The old boots were battered and torn, their insides rubbed to a raggedy softness from millions of footsteps, but when Adam pulled them on, his feet rejoiced. He felt like he was walking on pillows. No, on clouds. His feet felt so rejuvenated, he thought maybe he would *run* the rest of the Ice Age Trail. Even though he hated running.

Not too long after Adam's boots wore out, his backpack bit

the dust. It literally fell into pieces one day, shredding as he tried to pack it, pockets tearing, straps snapping, zippers sticking. Fortuitously this time, he had already made plans to be picked up in Hatley by Scott and Julia, some folks he'd met earlier in Wittenberg. The couple took him back to their home just outside Green Bay, where he logged a few zero days to purchase yet another pair of new boots—boots he could try on first—plus a new backpack. After careful consideration at the sporting goods store, Adam selected a pair of low-cut Keen boots and a backpack that looked reasonably similar to his old one.

When he got back to Scott and Julia's, he discovered his new backpack was noticeably slimmer than his old one. He was going to have to offload some items. By this time, August, he was well aware that the amount of weight he'd been toting for the past two months was too much for a long-distance hike. So Adam torpedoed some extra food and clothing, maps of segments he'd long passed, and, with some reluctance, a sleeping pad (which he'd later regret ditching, when nighttime temperatures tumbled). He also ditched his beloved folding bucket, which he'd been using for everything from washing his dishes and clothes to soaking his feet. The last item that he placed on the discard pile, slowly and with a twinge of sadness, was his dad's hatchet.

Man, that was really one sweet hatchet.

It was a warm September day, about 2:30 in the afternoon. Adam was enjoying a pleasant hike through the Harrison Hills segment, his pack now a much more manageable thirty-five pounds, when he heard noise along the trail up ahead. He couldn't figure out what the noise was—if it was an animal or if maybe he was hearing sounds from the highway, although he was pretty far from any roads. He wasn't worried, just curious. The sounds were getting louder now, so he'd soon discover their source.

When Adam saw the source of the noise, he was shocked—dumbfounded, actually. It was another thru-hiker approaching. In the three months since he walked out of Potawatomi State Park and began his adventure, he hadn't met a single other thru-hiker.

"Hi. Are you Papa Bear?"

He raised his eyebrows at the strange greeting. "No. I'm Adam Hinz."

~

Chagrined, I quickly explained that I had heard there was a Papa Bear thru-hiking the trail and that I'd been dying to meet him. Because his hiking name seemed kinda cool. Because I had read some entries on his blog—actually, the blog kept by his trail partner, Hiking Dude—and it sounded like the two were having interesting adventures. And not least of all because I'd been out here all alone for thirteen days and had only seen two other thru-hikers. Well, now three.

As we discussed our experiences, Adam mentioned his blisters and the hiking boots that had declared war on his feet, and I bemoaned the cellulitis attacking my right foot. I warned him of the perils awaiting on the Bear Lake segment, and he told me Parrish Hills wasn't too difficult, but to take care navigating Kettlebowl, where many of the blazes were hard to spot and it was easy to get turned around.

"Kettlebowl! Everyone keeps telling me how difficult it is!" I fretted, as the Kettlebowl was a mere two days ahead in my journey.

Adam was curious about my late start date. He'd already put about 750 miles of trail and blacktop behind him; I had those same arduous 750 to go.

"Wow—so you'll be hiking into winter then," he said with a hint of trepidation on my behalf.

"Oh, no, I plan to be done in early October," I said, explaining my FKT attempt.

After mentioning the FKT, I realized I'd better get going, and we parted ways. I was happy with my decision to try and set a women's record for innumerable reasons, but I also envied Adam and his leisurely pace.

～

Adam listened as the sound of my footsteps faded away down the trail. He enjoyed meeting someone else out here and wished we'd had more time to chat. But he was also fine being out here by himself. It no longer felt strange to be alone in the woods. In fact, it felt like home.

CHAPTER FOURTEEN

Now Entering Langlade County

Once you make a decision, the universe conspires to make it happen.
—RALPH WALDO EMERSON, AMERICAN POET

Langlade County, population 19,997, is true Wisconsin North-woods territory. More than a quarter million acres of forestland dominate the landscape—impressive stands of maple, birch, and hemlock. Within these acres lie innumerable miles of trail, tying together every corner like a giant cobweb and leading the county to bill itself as Wisconsin's "County of Trails." The recreational trails here were created so people could enjoy horseback riding, ATV-ing, mountain biking, snowshoeing, cross-country skiing, snowmobiling, and, yes, hiking.

Langlade County helped pioneer development of the Ice Age Trail. In early 1975, five or six people gathered at the Langlade County University of Wisconsin–Extension to form the Ice Age Trail Alliance's first chapter, led by Extension agent Joe Jopek. In its inaugural year, the scrappy group mapped and marked an astounding five segments of trail: Parrish Hills, Old Railroad, Lumbercamp, Kettlebowl, and Highland Lakes. Today 51.9 miles of the Ice Age Trail wind through the county, basted together with 28.1 miles of connecting roads. The route through the county looks a bit like the profile of a dog's forehead and snout, with the trail entering the county near Parrish in its northwest corner, gliding southeast to Polar with a little bump, then making a wide, rounded, 180-degree about-face (the snout) to usher you out through the county's southwestern quadrant and into neighboring Marathon County.

Since day one, Langlade County has been looming in my mind as a major destination point. Once I'm through this county, I'll have completed the Ice Age Trail's northern tier—a little more than one-third of the trail—leaving a steep plunge south to Janesville, and then a steep climb north to Sturgeon Bay and the eastern terminus. In addition to the thrill of completing one major stretch of trail, this particular portion of the Ice Age Trail is considered the toughest because it's the hilliest. It's also the most isolated and the most bear-filled. Once you make it through Langlade County, I'm told, you'll be on Easy Street. The trail will flatten out, open up, and overall be more pleasurable.

The trick is making it through Langlade County.

All of the thru-hikers I've met so far have warned me the trails here are sparsely marked and confusing. All of them have told me grim tales of getting turned around, spun sideways, and knocked off-balance while following the Langlade County trail's seductive curves and bulges. It now dawns on me that I'll be all alone the first time I place a running-shoe-clad toe on Langlade County soil. Maura heads home around noon on the day I enter Parrish Hills, the first segment coming in from the west, and her replacement, my good friend Doug, won't arrive until that evening. If I get turned around, injure myself, or run out of food or water while picking my way along the perilous tread, no one will be around to help me.

For a short while I pout about my situation, deeming it

patently unfair that I have a bum knee and an infected foot and now must plunge into Langlade County solo. Why, the very first bulleted item on the IATA's safety list proclaims, "It's best to hike with a partner." I'll be a miserable, vulnerable hiking party of one. But then I snap out of it. I've been hiking the Ice Age Trail for two weeks now, and I'm still standing. Langlade County will be challenging, yes—a true test of my trail-worthiness. But I *am* trail-worthy. I boldly proclaim to Maura and the cosmos that I'm going to conquer Langlade County. I will make it through all of its trail segments, including the Kettlebowl, without getting lost. I will succeed where the boys I recently met had failed. Although I'll be flying solo my first day, I do have two big advantages: I've got Joe Jopek's bits of wisdom tucked in my back pocket, and I've got my own determination.

Langlade County, watch out. Valderi is coming.

Maura bids me adieu on First Lake Road, a gravel scar bisecting the Ice Age Trail right where Lincoln County's Harrison Hills segment ends and Langlade County's Parrish Hills segment begins. She points to a spot on the trail atlas map where she'll drop a bottle of water for me. That extra bottle of water, combined with what I'm carrying now in my hydration pack, should be enough to tide me over until I make it through the twelve-mile segment and pop out at the wayside at Townline Lake, where Joe promised to stash a gallon of water for me.

"Mom, promise you'll call me when you find the water," she says protectively.

"Don't worry about me. I'll be fine."

"Mom!" Maura peers at me over the top of her oversized sunglasses, a stern look on her face. "Promise me. It's hot out again today, and I'll worry about you the whole way home if I don't know for sure you found the water."

It's that moment when the child becomes the parent.

"I promise I'll call you, Maura."

We embrace, then both set off on our new, couldn't-be-more-different lives: hers assisting senior advisors during the United Nations' General Assembly, mine walking seven hundred more miles through Wisconsin's countryside.

I quickly fall into a pleasant hiking rhythm. A slight breeze begins blowing through the trees, so I pause and listen for their response. Sometimes the trees answer the wind with soothing creaks, like the gentle rocking of a chair or a boat rubbing against a dock. Older trees often moan as they shift their thick, aged limbs, emitting sounds akin to a heavy door slowly opening. Once in a while, if the wind is playing a little too roughly that day, the trees will toss a few branches down to the ground in frustration. Today the trees are answering the wind in sad, raspy, end-of-summer whispers.

Crossing State Highway 17, one Parrish Hills mile under my pack straps, I turn right onto County Road H instead of continuing along the trail. This is Joe's suggested detour so I can avoid the Prairie River ford. Maura's water is waiting at the intersection of H and Five Cent Road as planned. I toss it into my pack, text her that her drop was successful, and head down the road, eventually picking up the trail. After walking a scant mile along the path, a pretty little bright-green ribbon of tread, I pop out into an enormous clearing. A wide logging road lies off to the left. The rest of the circular space is tightly ringed with thick vegetation.

Slowly, carefully, I walk around the edge of the clearing. The trail must resume somewhere across it, or off to one side, but I'm not seeing any blaze or arrow. It must be obscured by the dense foliage. But no matter how closely I peer, no matter how imaginative I try to be as to what might constitute a trail, I see no trail signage nor anything that looks like a footpath. Perhaps I missed a turn before this clearing. I retrace my steps and find the last marker, but as I thought, the blazes clearly point me here.

Perhaps this is where the tornado went through. If so, Joe encouraged me to detour around this area via Nelson Firelane. But I haven't seen Nelson Firelane, either.

I spend the next half hour going round and round the clearing, hoping an opening into the woods or a yellow blaze will magically appear. But neither one does. I pause and glance skyward, where the sun sits high in the sky, relentlessly shooting down sharp, hot rays. Two drops of perspiration glide down each arm, hang at my elbows a moment, then plop onto the ground.

A long, flat sigh escapes my mouth like the air coming out of a worn bellows. I don't want to give up, but I can't waste any more time in this crop circle of a clearing. I need to think strategically. Doug will be waiting for me at the end of the following segment, Western Highland Lakes, at 5:30 p.m. That's probably a good ten miles from here, or several hours' worth of hiking. I've got two options: I can go back to Highway 17 and skirt around the entire remainder of the segment, ending up at Townline Lake and Joe's water-drop, or I can take a chance on that logging road to my left. I should be very close to the tornado-ravaged section that Joe told me to avoid by hopping on Nelson Firelane. Maybe, just maybe, this logging road will lead me to Nelson Firelane. It's a gamble, and I'm not usually a gambler. But today, for some reason, I am.

Fifteen minutes later the logging road makes a gentle curve and deposits me neatly onto Nelson Firelane. I breathe a sigh of relief and consult my map. Looks like I've got about five miles on roads before arriving at Townline Lake. Hopefully I can make up some time by jogging.

Ten minutes later, as I'm shuffle-jogging down Nelson Firelane, wild yelping pierces the still, summer air. Then tires slowly crunch on gravel. Several trucks bump along the road toward me, each containing several hunting dogs baying excitedly from crates in their beds. When the trucks are nearly at my side, all abruptly stop and three men hop out, quickly opening the crates. Dogs spill out of the truck beds and begin trotting all over the roadside, snuffling in the dirt, panting, whining, and . . . jingling. Bells. The dogs all have bells hanging from their collars. I'd forgotten all about Pat Enright's bear bells and my lack of them. I feel a slight pang of fear.

"Hey!" I call out to the person closest to me, an orange-capped, leather-faced man clad in a green flannel shirt and dusty jeans. "Are those bear bells that are attached to all of the dogs' collars?"

"No. Well, yes."

"What do you mean?"

"Yes, they're bear bells. But the dogs aren't wearing them because of bears. Bears generally won't bother dogs."

"Then what are they for?"

"They're to scare off the wolves. The wolves around here are far more dangerous than the bears. Wolves will attack dogs when they're hunting or training."

I want to ask if the Parrish Hills wolves ever come after people. Like, say, people hiking the Ice Age Trail. But I'm afraid of his answer. So I wish him good luck on the hunt and continue on my way.

An hour or so later, hot and coated in a fine layer of Nelson Firelane dust, I finally spot two signs tucked under a canopy of green: "Townline Lake Wayside" and "Ice Age Trail Parrish Hills Segment." Just in time, as I've depleted my water supply. As I turn into the wayside, I hear voices. Two men are sitting at a picnic table set in a small clearing in the woods, relaxing. Two enormous backpacks are set on the ground near their feet, listing slightly against the wayside's weathered picnic table. They're distance hikers. Maybe even thru-hikers.

"Hey, do either of you guys happen to be Papa Bear?"
"Yes," says the one on the left. "I'm Papa Bear."

~

Papa Bear looks nothing like I imagined. Actually, I didn't have a sharp image in my mind of what he'd look like. It was more of a feeling. He'd be a bit squishy like the Pillsbury Dough Boy, yet strong, too. Congenial. Smiling and bubbly, with a hearty laugh. A tumble of thick, dark hair would top his head, and he'd have a full beard. Or maybe be clean-shaven. He'd be wearing heavy hiking boots and thick socks, and definitely a plaid shirt. His calloused, hardworking hands would be gripping a sturdy walking stick that could double as a weapon against threatening bears or wolves. Because no wild animal was going to get the best of Papa Bear. When we met, he'd know everything about the trail, and hiking, and the woods, and their creature-inhabitants. He'd be father yet friend, wise and fun, calming but full of exciting traveler's tales.

The Papa Bear I meet appears kind, yet soft-spoken. He's wearing a sensible tan button-down shirt with lots of pockets. There's not a whiff of plaid on him. He has neatly combed graying hair and a bushy beard, but he isn't squishy in the least. He has neither hiking stick nor trekking poles, at least not that I can see, just one large backpack. The man is hiking with a companion, whom he introduces as Hiking Dude. The name pings in my brain. Now I remember. Shortly before I'd left on my trek, Sharon Dziengel of the IATA had sent me an email listing the other thru- and section-hikers currently on the trail so I'd know who I might run into. She also gave me their blog addresses. The hikers were Pat Enright, Mother Goose and Joseph, Kehly Johnson, and Hiking Dude and Papa Bear. Only the names "Mother Goose" and "Papa Bear" had stuck in my jittery, pre-thru-hike mind, even though I read a little of Hiking Dude's blog on the drive up to St. Croix Falls.

The two invite me to sit down and join them. Hiking Dude,

also known as Paul Kautz, is lean with a similarly graying beard. He's dressed in a white Boy Scout T-shirt, a tan Boy Scout ball cap pulled over his balding head. Hiking Dude quickly snaps my photo for inclusion in his next blog post.

"So what's your name?" Hiking Dude asks, ready to jot it down on a small notepad, also for the blog.

"Melanie McManus. I mean Valderi. I'm thru-hiking the trail west to east. I started August 31. How about you guys?"

"We're thru-hiking east to west. We started August 3. But we took ten days off because it was so hot. You're not camping, are you?" he says, warily eyeing my compact hydration pack, which is a fraction of the size of his backpack.

"No, I'm not. I stay with family or friends at night, or else in a hotel or B and B. I can hike and run all day, but at night I like to have a clean bed and a shower."

"Oh, you're one of those kinds of hikers."

"What does that mean?" I ask, a tad sharply. I may not sleep in a sleeping bag at night, but I'm still working pretty darn hard out here.

"It's nothing negative," he says. "Just that you're a supported hiker. Meaning you don't have to support yourself overnight on the trail. Some thru-hikers frown upon that kind of thing because they think you should be carrying all your gear and camping if you're thru-hiking. But I don't think it matters."

Good answer, Hiking Dude. Because the important thing is to be out here hiking. The details aren't important. Everyone has to hike in a way that makes sense for them.

The men tell me Highland Lakes West, the next and final segment I'll be tackling today, is pretty flat and easy. Yes! But then I have to inform them that Parrish Hills, their next segment, is difficult. I'd just gotten lost. And the Langlade County chapter coordinator advised skirting around an area ripped apart by a tornado. The men immediately decide to hike around the entire portion of the segment that lies east of Highway H—the vast majority of its mileage—which flabbergasts me.

"You won't even try a little of it? Aren't you curious as to what it's like? And, well, you sort of have to do it, or at least try, if you're trying to officially thru-hike the trail."

"Are you one of those hikers who has to hike every step of the trail exactly as it's shown?" Hiking Dude says, a bit bemusedly it seems.

"Well, yes," I say, puzzled. "I want to be official. And I want to see everything."

"We don't do that," says Papa Bear, whose off-trail identity is Drew Hendel. "I've hiked the Pacific Crest Trail, and the basic philosophy there is that if you walk the whole way and don't hitchhike, you can take the official route or an alternate. The main thing is, did you walk the whole way? So that's our mind-set."

Fair enough, especially since they're toting around many more pounds than I am.

The afternoon sky is almost imperceptibly darkening as we visit, but I notice the change. Night is coming. And I still have 5.8 miles of Highland Lakes West to complete. I'd better get going. But first I need my water. Joe said he'd leave a jug by the boat landing under some spruce trees, but I don't see a boat landing or dock. I poke around the picnic table and behind some trees but find nothing. Ditto for the area around the pit toilet and the trail sign. Where could he possibly have set it? The men say they never saw a water jug, or any other people at the wayside who might have helped themselves to its contents. With the clock ticking, I decide I can knock off the last segment with the dribbles left in my hydration pack. Because I really have to get going.

As I turn to leave, Papa Bear asks if I want some of his food. He's carrying more than he needs and would like to lighten his load. I thank him but decline. Whatever he's got likely wouldn't fit into my small pack anyway.

"One more thing," he calls out. "Tomorrow is the start of hunting season. I went into the Walmart in Antigo and bought blaze-orange hats for us. They were just three dollars. You might want to buy one for yourself."

Hunting season. Huh. I never thought about that, either. A blaze-orange hat seems like a wise idea. I thank him, and we wave good-bye. Then I slowly jog down the wide, sandy, gravel path ushering me into Highland Lakes Western.

⌒

A piano riff sounds on my phone. It's Doug. He is supposed to be waiting for me at the end of this segment, a dead-end on the western end of Kleever Road, at 5:30 p.m. He's calling to say he's there already, about thirty minutes early. His promptness is rather unfortunate, as I'm running late.

"I'll run as much as I can," I tell him, "but so far it's been really rocky. It might take me two hours to get there."

He kindly says not to worry. But I do, and pick up my pace. It's not that easy. Every time my infected foot lands on a rock, which is pretty much every step, I feel a sharp pain, like it's being stabbed with a spike. I should be appreciating my surroundings; this segment traces, and sometimes travels within, the Parrish Terminal Moraine, which is a ridge of sand, gravel, and stone thoughtfully pushed here by the glacier, then abandoned when it melted away. But I can't appreciate my surroundings today, not when they're hurting me. I step squarely on another rock, right on the infected patch of skin, and curse under my breath. These antibiotics had better kick in quickly.

Thankfully the path changes from rocky to smooth as it plunges me into an especially scenic stretch of the Langlade County Forest. One of the Ice Age Trail's earliest segments, Highland Lakes Western initially followed narrow fire lanes carved into the earth in the 1930s. The lanes allowed the passage of logging equipment as well as firefighting equipment, forest fires always being a danger. But in the 1930s, the equipment was small, at least compared to today's logging and firefighting vehicles. In the 1990s, the fire lane I'm now jogging along was widened considerably so the modern, beefier vehicles could easily roll through the forest on their way to work. Today, no more logging is being done in this corner of the Langlade County Forest. At least for now. As I jog along the road, I notice hundreds of saplings silently rising up from the earth along the edges of the path and smile. These slender foot soldiers are stealthily stealing back an inch of trail here, a foot there, working diligently and efficiently to erase the ugly scars left by the musclebound mechanical harvesters and firetrucks that once regularly rumbled through the forest. I'm jolted out of my reverie when a dark vehicle appears on the road ahead, slowly inching toward me. Is it a hunter? A law enforcement officer? Some weirdo looking to harass women hiking solo on the Ice Age Trail?

A horn lightly blasts, and then an arm shoots out the window, waving wildly.

"Hey! I found you!"

It's Doug.

"What are you doing driving your car on the Ice Age Trail?" I say, astonished. "This is a hiking trail!"

"There was no trail sign at the end of Kleever Road where you told me to meet you, so I didn't know where you'd be coming out. I saw this gravel road and figured I'd drive down it and see if I could spot any trail markers. Or you."

Fortuitously for Doug, I've just passed a spot where a smaller logging road intersects with this one. He'll be able to drive up there and turn around. If not for that road, he'd have to back his car all the way out. Not an easy thing on a small road in the darkening woods.

"Gosh, I never thought about that," he says.

Doug turns around and drives back out to Kleever Road, while I continue jogging down the trail behind his vanishing vehicle.

Later that night, after completing the segment and settling in at the Holiday Inn Express in Antigo, we head out for a fish fry at Heart Breakers, a squat, gray bar on the southern edge of town. A young waitress bops up to our table, ponytail gently swinging. She takes our order—deep-fried cod for Doug, an enormous seafood medley for me—then pauses before heading back to the kitchen. "So what are you two up to this weekend?" she chirps.

"Well," says Doug, sitting up straight and clearing his throat. "We are thru-hiking the Ice Age Trail. We're hiking the *whole thing.*" He says this slowly. Importantly.

"Oh, how fun!" Beaming a megawatt smile on each of us in turn, she grabs our menus and zips away.

Doug and I stare at each other for a second. "She has absolutely no idea what the Ice Age Trail is!" he fumes, miffed at her lack of knowledge about the trail and the enormity of the venture he had so proudly proclaimed.

"I know. But why did you say 'we' are hiking all of the Ice Age Trail? You are not thru-hiking it! You can't horn in on my accomplishment by crewing me for a few days!"

Doug laughs, looking only a tad guilty. "I didn't mean to say that," he says. "It just sort of slipped out."

CHAPTER FIFTEEN

Drew Hendel and Paul Kautz, Explorers

A person does not grow from the ground like a vine or a tree, one is not part of a plot of land. Mankind has legs so it can wander.

—ROMAN PAYNE, AUTHOR, *THE WANDERESS*

The first time the black SUV glided past them on a quiet side street in Mishicot, they took no notice. But when it quickly turned around and slowly approached them, the men knew something was up. The driver's window glided down, and a woman's head poked out. She was middle-aged, pleasant-looking, with straight, dark hair smoothly pulled back from her face and held in a ponytail. Her bright red T-shirt cheerily proclaimed, "Love is a heaven!"

"I'm sorry to bother you," she greeted them politely, "but I just have to ask what you're doing."

Papa Bear and Hiking Dude looked at each other. They probably did look odd, two fifty-something men, each with a twenty-some-pound pack lashed to his back, walking down the streets of sleepy little Mishicot, Wisconsin, population 1,442.

"We're thru-hiking the Ice Age Trail," Hiking Dude said.

The woman introduced herself as Kathy. The two caught her eye because of their backpacks, she explained. Because, you know, she was quite the adventurer herself once. In her younger, wilder days, when she had done a lot of traveling around, backpacking and hitchhiking along the way. Now she was married and the mother of a preteen son, but she liked to help people who were out and about, who were on the road exploring.

"If you need a place to stay tonight, the town might let you camp in the park," she offered helpfully. "Check at the village hall. It's just one block away."

As Kathy drove away, the two conferred. They'd planned to take a rest stop here in Mishicot, then push on for a few more miles, eventually stealth-camping somewhere along County Highway V. But they didn't know what the roadside was like. They might have to set up camp in a ditch for all they knew. It seemed far better to stop now, a little early, if it meant they would be able to camp on a smooth, velvety park lawn. Hiking Dude offered to head over to the village hall to secure permission, and Papa Bear took him up on it, saying he would wait, oh, say, in this corner bar right here. As Hiking Dude neared the village hall, he spotted a black SUV parked in front that looked awfully familiar. Sure enough, as he climbed up the building's steps, Kathy emerged from the front door. She had impulsively driven there herself to ask if the men could camp in the park. The answer, unfortunately, was no.

"Thanks for checking," Hiking Dude said. "I'll ask if there are any other spots in town where camping is allowed."

"Okay. But if they don't have any spots, you can camp in my backyard," she offered, pressing a piece of paper with her phone number into his hand.

The clerk told Hiking Dude the village didn't really have any camping spots in town. That was actually totally cool with him, because he'd rather stay in Kathy's yard anyway. So he called

Kathy to say they were heading over, then collected Papa Bear from the bar. Later that evening, over a warm, home-cooked meal, Kathy's son regaled them with tales of his fishing exploits on the East Twin River, which neatly split the village. Papa Bear, spotting a mounted deer head on their wall, asked for the story behind it.

"Yeah, my husband got that deer," Kathy said.

"How?"

"He got it with a Buick."

Everyone laughed. Friends now, the men were invited to sleep inside Kathy's home rather than in their tents in the yard. Beds sounded mighty nice. In the morning, well-rested, the two filled their bellies with Kathy's French toast, prepared with her made-from-scratch bread, then bid the family a fond farewell before heading east toward Lake Michigan.

〜

In 2001, when Drew Hendel was forty-four, he hiked the Pacific Crest Trail. Well, 430 miles of it—almost all of the trail miles that pass through Washington, his home state. He was on the trail, in fact, when the Twin Towers were hit by Osama bin Laden's henchmen, so he would always remember the month and year of that trip, and he'd always remember where he was on 9/11. At that point in time, he was just Drew Hendel, not Papa Bear. Drew's section-hike of the Pacific Crest Trail, which he assumed would be merely a pleasant undertaking, got under his skin. So much so that in 2006, he drove down to Southern California, near the Mexican border, to attend the Annual Day Zero Pacific Crest Trail Kick Off—a.k.a. ADZPCTKO—a multiday educational event for potential thru-hikers and a place where alums gathered to fondly recall their time on the trail.

When Drew arrived, he was randomly assigned to a campsite with several others, including Chris, a graduate of the US Naval Academy, and Monica, a professor at the University of San Diego.

That night Drew was awakened by a harsh, snorty buzz. It was Chris, snoring so loudly his tent was practically levitating several inches with each raspy exhale. The noise was so loud, so grating, it kept Drew awake half the night.

"Oh, buddy, you've got to get that snoring fixed," Drew told Chris the next morning. "You snore like a chainsaw."

The name instantly stuck, and Chris's trail name became Chainsaw. Not too long after that, Drew commented on the sunglasses Monica was wearing, noting they looked like something from *CHiPs*, a TV show about California Highway Patrol motorcycle officers that debuted in 1977. Chris immediately seized on this, dubbing Monica "Ponch" after the show's dark-haired officer, Frank "Ponch" Poncherello. At some point after Chris and Monica became Chainsaw and Ponch, Drew can't quite remember when, Monica declared Drew's trail name to be Papa Bear. Drew wasn't sure if it was because of his size—six feet, two inches and 220 pounds—or if it was because he traveled to the kick-off in a car stuffed with every item a hiker could possibly want or need, sort of like a protective father, ready to take care of any emergency. Whatever the reason, just like that, Drew became Papa Bear. And he kind of liked it.

Papa Bear began chipping away at the Pacific Crest Trail's mileage that year, and again the following four years, until he finally completed the whole thing in 2010—along with Turbo, Grinder, Sparkles, HotMess, Balls, the Stumbling Norwegian, Trashpocket, Milk Sheikh, NoPants, Gangles, the Soft Chew Kid, Motor Giggle Bootie Butt, Hui Humuhumunukunukuapua'a, and 190 others. He was officially a "2,600-Miler." Papa Bear's only regret, if it was really a regret, was that he didn't thru-hike the trail. While there are pros and cons to both thru- and section-hiking a long-distance trail, and neither way is better than the other, a thru-hike is more of an accomplishment than a section-hike, he thought. He decided he'd like to thru-hike a long-distance trail.

Three months later, while doing volunteer trail work on the Pacific Crest near his home in Bellevue, a Seattle suburb, he was chatting with Dave, a fellow volunteer he'd seen a few times before at these events. Dave, also known as Saunter, told Papa Bear he was going to thru-hike the Arizona National Scenic Trail in March 2012. The Arizona Trail forms a jagged lightning bolt as it rambles slightly northwest from the Coronado National Memorial near the state's border with Mexico to the Utah state line somewhere in between Fredonia and Page. It's one of three National Scenic Trails located entirely within one state, the Ice Age Trail and the Florida Trail being the other two. At about eight hundred miles, it's considerably shorter than the Pacific Crest Trail. Papa Bear asked Saunter if he could join him on this adventure. It all seemed so perfect. He wanted to thru-hike a long-distance trail, and Saunter had already done all of the planning for a hike along the Arizona Trail, so all Papa Bear had to do was tag along. And be able to keep up, which he was sure wouldn't be an issue. Papa Bear refereed high school basketball during the winter, and the season ended the first week in March. He would be in great shape after running up and down basketball courts for months. Saunter said sure, Papa Bear could come along. Why not?

So in March 2012, the two drove from Washington down to Arizona to begin their adventure. But by the time they arrived at the trailhead, Papa Bear was a tad uneasy. He didn't really know Saunter very well, and he seemed, well, *different*. A few days of hiking on the trail confirmed Papa Bear's suspicions. Saunter was one odd duck. The two had agreed early on to hike separately during the day, maybe meeting up for lunch, but definitely hooking up again in the evening at their chosen camping spot. They also decided as a safety precaution that whoever was in the lead would leave a pile of four rocks at every intersection to ensure that, right or wrong, they would always be traveling on the same path. So one day when Saunter was in front, carefully leaving four rocks at every intersection per the plan, Papa Bear came to an intersection with just three rocks. Saunter must have miscounted. Surely this was the way he went. Another intersection, another three rocks. Papa Bear started to feel uneasy, but kept following the three-rock path, hoping it was Saunter's. Eventually he spotted him up ahead.

"Hey, did you realize you were leaving just three rocks at the last few intersections?"

"Yes," said Saunter, appearing surprised at the question.

"Well, *why?* We agreed our signal would be four rocks. I was confused and wasn't sure that I was following you."

"Oh, I just decided to change the signal."

"You can't just change a signal by yourself without telling the other person!" Papa Bear sputtered.

Saunter just shrugged.

Over the next few days Saunter's erratic behavior continued, and Papa Bear began worrying every day about what Saunter would or wouldn't do. Then, two weeks into their thru-hike, the men agreed to meet for lunch at the Pizza and Cookie Cabin in Summerhaven, a sleepy town north of Tucson in the Santa Catalina Mountains. They found each other as planned and were in the middle of enjoying their meal when Saunter abruptly set down his slice of pizza.

"Oh, by the way, I made arrangements with some people down the road, and they're coming to pick me up any minute."

"For what?"

"I'm quitting and going home."

"What do you mean you're quitting and going home?"

Papa Bear was dumbfounded. Saunter didn't seem to have any physical issues, and their hike hadn't been that strenuous so far. Plus, they'd been together here in Summerhaven for the past ninety minutes. Why hadn't he said something until now? As Papa Bear puzzled and fumed, a four-door sedan glided up to the door and blared its horn. Saunter looked up, grabbed his pack, and walked out the door without looking back. Papa Bear noticed he left his sit pad on the chair. He grabbed it and rose from his seat, about to call out to Saunter, then abruptly closed his mouth and sat back down. He was keeping Saunter's stinkin' sit pad.

-~

Once Saunter was gone, Papa Bear found he was actually relieved. He'd been going through an awful lot of mental gymnastics every day with that guy. Besides, he didn't mind hiking alone. About one-third of his Pacific Crest miles were logged solo—more miles than he had left to hike at this point. Hiking solo had its pluses. You could get up when you'd like, hike the speed that you'd like, camp where you'd like. The main drawbacks were safety and a lack of conversation. Papa Bear did like to talk, and especially to tell stories. Luckily, he'd have some company in a day or two, when he reached the Freeman Road water cache.

The Freeman Road water cache is an important spot on the Arizona Trail. Carefully set in the middle of a long, hot, dry, remote patch of desert, the cache is a large wooden cupboard snugged next to a spindly bush that's filled with a half dozen or so gallons of water. Some of the water is left by trail angels—hiker lingo for the kind folks, often trail enthusiasts, who leave food and snacks trailside for hikers, or shuttle them to and from trailheads, or perform any number of other helpful tasks—but hikers can also stash their own water and supplies here, too. When Papa Bear and Saunter had reached Tucson earlier in their hike, they stayed with friends who drove them to Freeman Road so they could cache food and water. Around this same time, Papa Bear ran into an elderly man who was section-hiking the trail. The two made tentative plans to hike together for a day on March 30, when Papa Bear reached the Freeman Road water cache. The plan was that if the man was able to hike, he'd be there by 10 a.m.

Papa Bear rose early on March 30 so he could hike to the Freeman Road cache before it got too hot. He arrived well before 10 a.m. and grabbed the food and water he'd stashed in the cupboard. He also helped himself to Saunter's goodies. Now all he had to do was wait until ten o'clock to see if his new friend would show up. The minutes ticked by slowly as Papa Bear grew increasingly uncomfortable in the desert's oven-like heat. The cache was surrounded by stubby, scruffy sagebrush and mesquite bushes—nothing that provided any shade.

Eventually he set up his tent and crawled inside, but it was just as hot in there, if not hotter. Sure enough, when he checked his high-tech digital altimeter (which also kept track of the time, temperature, and barometric pressure), it reported a stifling 107 degrees. Was it better to be sizzling outside under the harsh sunlight or baking like a turkey inside his tent? Hot and miserable, he kept ducking in and out, checking the temperature and time on his altimeter. Finally the appointed hour arrived. His friend did not. Papa Bear didn't blame him. Who wanted to hike in such hellish heat? He had already decided he was staying put for the day. Surely it wouldn't be this hot tomorrow.

Hours later, as the sun began to glide behind the Tortilla Mountains, casting a pearly hue across the desert, he spotted a twinkling on the horizon. Someone was coming up the trail. It was a man, fifty-ish like himself, trim and balding, with a graying goatee. Two six-hundred-milliliter bottles were inventively lashed to the front straps of the man's backpack, affording him easy access to his water. A small umbrella shielded his head from the desert sun, its slick, silver dome capturing each ray and flicking it out across the desert—the glinting Papa Bear had spotted from afar.

"Hey, do you need some water?" Papa Bear called out.

"Yes! Thanks so much. I'm Hiking Dude."

"And I'm Papa Bear."

The two began to chat. Hiking Dude, also known as Paul

Kautz, was also thru-hiking the trail alone. Paul grew up in the Rockies, where hiking was just what you did to get around, to play, to explore. But his parents eventually settled in West Bend, Wisconsin. And then, coincidentally and fortuitously, he married a woman whose parents also lived in Wisconsin. Once they had kids, the Kautzes relocated to the Twin Cities area to be closer to their folks and ended up in Eden Prairie, Minnesota. Paul became Scoutmaster for Eden Prairie's Boy Scout Troop 479, a position he held for seven years. Then, in 2011, a newly minted fifty-year-old, he turned over the reins to another fellow and quickly found himself with a bunch of free time on his hands.

Paul had heard about the Appalachian Trail before, and the idea of hiking it sounded intriguing. He did some digging but soon began to cool on the idea. At more than two thousand miles, it took most people five to seven months to thru-hike it. Even more unappealing to him was the "northbound hiker bubble," a sizable group of thru-hikers that sets out each year from the trail's southern terminus in Georgia in March and April. During this popular departure time, dozens of hikers step onto the trail every day or two or three. The group inches along the narrow trail like an overstuffed caterpillar, filling the woods with a symphony of clicking sticks, stomping boots, shouts, and grunts. At night, the hikers wedge themselves into far-too-small shelters for a fitful night's sleep before another day's noisy parade through the woods. At some point the caterpillar does slim down, as hikers abandon the trail due to its difficulty or their dwindling interest and ambition. And eventually this caterpillar transforms itself into a butterfly, light and airy, as the Appalachian Trail's thru-hike completion rate is only 25 percent. Still, the idea of spending weeks or months sealed within the stifling cocoon of the northbound hiker bubble sounded exceedingly unpleasant to Paul. But he wasn't discouraged, because his research unearthed something even more exciting.

The Appalachian Trail, he discovered, was a National Scenic Trail. He didn't know such a designation existed. Even better, ten others were scattered across the country. While all were considered long-distance hiking trails, they didn't all stretch two-thousand-plus miles. He fingered one called the Arizona Trail on the map. It was under one thousand miles, and Arizona sounded like an exceptionally pleasant place to be in March, when you lived in Minnesota. So here he was, exploring his first National Scenic Trail as Hiking Dude, a trail name he gave himself because, well, he was a dude who liked to hike.

Hiking Dude asked if he could camp next to Papa Bear for the night. He'd pushed himself that day, hiking thirty miles in the heat just to make it to the Freeman Road water cache, and he was exhausted. Papa Bear welcomed him to his rudimentary camp and offered him some of his Idahoan mashed potatoes. Inexpensive and easy to prepare, they were one of Papa Bear's go-to trail foods. A typical dinner for Hiking Dude was a pack of Knorr noodles or rice, coupled with a pouch of salmon, tuna, or chicken. After two weeks of eating the same handful of foods, mashed potatoes sounded downright exotic. He thanked Papa Bear and dug in. As he expected, the potatoes were exceptionally delicious.

The next morning the two decided to try hiking together. If it didn't work, they agreed, they'd go their own ways, no hard feelings. Of course, they'd really be going the same way and might keep running into each other, but they agreed not to take any possible hiking divorce personally. Thankfully, their hiking styles meshed. They both could hike three miles per hour, or slightly faster. They both liked to hike together, as opposed to hiking separately and meeting up only for meals or to camp. Hiking Dude was also a quieter person, a listener, while Papa Bear had loads of stories tucked into his backpack.

The two had a great time as they inched northward, trekking from the Gila River to Walnut Canyon, from Picket Post to

Roosevelt, from Black Bear Saddle to Sycamore Creek. Hiking Dude mentioned he'd like to hike the Ice Age Trail next. The Ice Age Trail was particularly appealing to him, he said, because it was so close to his home in the Twin Cities area. Plus he had relatives in two different areas of the trail who could help with lodging and shuttles. The more Hiking Dude talked about hiking the Ice Age Trail, the more Papa Bear decided he'd like to do that, too.

～

Friday, April 13. Papa Bear and Hiking Dude had been a team for two weeks when Papa Bear's chest started to hurt. He didn't take off his shirt to look at the painful spot because he and Hiking Dude were huddled in their sleeping bags on the floor of a cabin atop the Mogollon Rim, trying to stay warm. It was just twenty-five degrees in there, and a rare April snowstorm was raging outside. When he looked at his chest the next morning, a red rash sprawled from its upper right quadrant, under his right arm, and across his upper right back. The pain was sharp, searing. Luckily, someone had driven up to the rim that morning to hike, despite the inclement weather. When the man returned to his truck later that day, they were able to hitch a ride down into the town of Pine, where Hiking Dude had previously secured permission to stay in a fellow Scout's vacation home.

The men spent the weekend resting while Papa Bear's rash persisted, leaving its unsightly red calling card all over his chest and back. Thinking it was poison oak, he consulted the town's medical personnel when the clinic opened on Monday. But his red splotch stumped them. It could be poison oak, they agreed. Or poison ivy. Or poison-something-else. Or, maybe, shingles. Please see the doctor in Payson, they urged him.

The men now hitched a ride into Payson, but the town's good doctors weren't sure what was causing Papa Bear's painful rash, either. They handed him a sheaf of prescriptions for any and all possibilities, then pointed him to a nearby Safeway where he could get them filled. As the two headed into the Safeway, they noticed a sign over the entrance: Shingles Vaccines Here. An omen, perhaps? No matter what he had, Papa Bear knew his time on the trail was over, at least for now. The pain was simply too unbearable, no pun intended. Fortunately for Papa Bear, he had family in Phoenix. He would hitch a ride there to recuperate. Hiking Dude would again fly solo.

⌇

A few weeks later, a healing Papa Bear (who did have shingles) met Hiking Dude at the Jacob Lake Motel, two days from the end of the trail. He helped with shuttles and was waiting at the northern terminus when Hiking Dude arrived, successfully completing the Arizona Trail. A year later, in the spring of 2013, Papa Bear returned to the Arizona Trail with a friend and finished the remaining 350 miles of trail he missed. He had knocked off another National Scenic Trail, but once again via section-hiking. However, a chance at redemption loomed in Wisconsin. He and Hiking Dude were planning to thru-hike the Ice Age Trail, starting in August.

⌇

Stuffed with Kathy's French toast, Papa Bear and Hiking Dude headed for Lake Michigan and the Point Beach segment of the Ice Age Trail. The trail in Point Beach wound through a lush red pine forest. Gently undulating, with a cushy pine-needle base, it offered some of the most prime hiking on the entire Ice Age Trail. Except when it was mosquito season. Which it was right now, in early August. Hiking Dude talked Papa Bear into splurging on a bug suit—$28.50—before they started hiking. The lightweight suits—weighing a mere six ounces—consisted of a mesh pair of pants plus a pullover jacket with a fully enclosed hood; the hood zipped open a bit so you could eat and drink while wearing it.

The two quickly pulled their matching outfits from their packs and jumped into them while the mosquitoes swarmed, buzzing and biting. They weren't sure how well a bug suit worked, never having worn one before, but they hoped it would keep the mosquitoes at bay, especially because neither brought along bug spray. It was too much weight in the pack, too greasy, too smelly, too chemical-laden. For the next three hours, until the men emerged from the buzzing forest and out onto the breezy shores of Lake Michigan, the lightweight suits miraculously warded off the annoying insects. Definitely money well spent.

That night, the men planned to camp in the yard of a Scouting family living in Manitowoc. Hiking Dude, ever the planner and always a Scout (*Be prepared!*), had made the arrangements a month earlier. Just as he had done before hiking the Arizona Trail, Hiking Dude had contacted Boy Scout troops across the state in advance to say he and Papa Bear would be hiking the trail. He asked if anyone wanted to hike with them or hear about their adventure, or, ahem, let them camp in their yard or sleep in their home. This was a particularly useful strategy in Wisconsin, because camping along the Ice Age Trail could be problematic.

On the Appalachian Trail, more than 250 wooden shelters are perched trailside roughly a day's hike apart, ensuring hikers have a place to stay each night. On other National Scenic Trails, such as the Pacific Crest and Arizona Trails, the footpaths pass through vast swaths of public land, where primitive camping is allowed pretty much anywhere. Primitive camping is permitted in a large portion of Wisconsin's national, state, and county forestland, assuming you practice Leave No Trace principles. And the Ice Age Trail does pass through many of these areas. But they are concentrated in the state's northern tier. In its lower two-thirds, where Hiking Dude and Papa Bear were, there simply aren't any spacious tracts of public land. The Ice Age Trail Alliance is aware of this deficit and is working hard to dot the trail with DCAs, or dispersed camping areas, open to hikers. Yet as of the fall of 2013, only seven DCAs existed. Hence Hiking Dude's outreach.

His plan hit a snag that night, though, when the men learned a fierce storm was blowing across the state, homing in on Manitowoc. The Scouting family realized it wouldn't be safe for the hikers to be sleeping outside and invited them to stay inside their home instead. Thank goodness; intense winds, lightning, and heavy rain smashed through the area overnight, flattening buildings and downing trees. In the morning, the men awakened to tree branches littering people's yards, roofs, and all of the roads. If the two had been sleeping in their tents, it would not have been pretty.

Two days later Papa Bear and Hiking Dude stepped off the trail in the Northern Kettle, where Hiking Dude's parents collected them and brought them home to West Bend. The following day would be their first rest day. They'd covered about 175 miles in six days.

∼

Papa Bear and Hiking Dude were employing a semi-shuttle hiking strategy. When thru-hiking a long-distance trail, you can't tote all of the food and water you'll need for the entire trip. And you can't count on a grocery store or sporting goods shop to conveniently pop up trailside whenever you're in need of food or replacement gear. So many hikers carry what they can, then mail packages to a string of small post offices along the trail. The packages, which they address to themselves, are stuffed with additional supplies—trail snacks, extra socks, bandages, money—anything they might need to continue on their way.

Hiking Dude had mailed some packages to himself while hiking in Arizona, but he decided on a new strategy for the Ice

Age Trail. The men would use his Honda Odyssey as a mobile
post office of sorts, filling it with a few weeks' worth of food and
supplies. Then they would park it and hike for several days. When
they needed more supplies, they would find someone willing
to shuttle them back to the van. Then they would drive the van
back to their last stopping point, park it, reload their packs, and
be off once again. Hike. Shuttle back to van. Move van up trail.
Resupply. Repeat as many times as needed.

With Hiking Dude's parents now available to help, the two
decided to do some slackpacking. Slackpacking is hiking without
a fully loaded backpack. Out go all weighty, bulky items such as
a tent, stove, and sleeping bag; the only items that remain are
those needed for one day on the trail: some food and water, a
small medical kit, maybe a dry pair of socks and some sunscreen.
Slackpacking sometimes happens randomly, when hikers run into
friendly locals who offer to transport their heavy backpacks to
their day's ending point. Other times hikers arrange to be slack-
packed by family or friends.

People like me, who are trying to set an FKT, typically slackpack every day, as we're traveling with at least one other person
whose sole job is to assist us by hauling our food, water, and
supplies so we can travel as lightly and quickly as possible. But
not always. In the world of FKTs, there are actually two types:
supported and unsupported. A supported FKT is the type I'm
doing, where I have daily assistance. Hikers attempting an unsupported FKT carry their own gear and don't have any prearranged
assistance.

When thru-hiking the Ice Age Trail, it's actually pretty easy
to slackpack daily, since the trail passes through a fair number
of towns. Plus, many trail angels are willing to shuttle you on
and off the trail. But many people elect to camp anyway, because
they enjoy it or because it's cheaper than staying in motels every
night. For Papa Bear and Hiking Dude, hiking a long-distance

trail included camping at night. That was part of the experience and part of the fun. But if someone offered to help here and there, well, that was part of the experience and the fun, too.

~

After their rest day, the duo spent the next three days hiking from West Bend to Delafield with their nearly empty backpacks, which now weighed a scant pound, Hiking Dude's mom shuttling them to and from the trail each day. They ambled over boardwalks hammered across marshy ground, strolled along burbling creeks, and bumped across agricultural fields. Walking along a busy Dorn Road in between the Merton and Hartland segments, they passed two girls selling lemonade (50 cents per cup), plus "cokies and jewry," according to the sign. The men stopped to purchase paper cups of tangy lemonade and sweet chocolate chip "cokies," but passed on the homemade jewelry.

"We're hiking the Ice Age Trail," Papa Bear told the young entrepreneurs as he sipped his lemonade.

"Oh, that's nice," said the taller of the two. She appeared a little older and wiser, maybe because she was wearing glasses, although she was the one holding the sign with the misspelled words.

"It's a trail that goes across the *whole* state," Papa Bear continued, hoping to impress them. The two just smiled politely.

"They don't have any idea what you're talking about," Hiking Dude whispered, so they finished their treats and hiked on.

Not too long after their lemonade-and-cookie break, Hiking Dude's right shin began to twang with every step. Pain shot from the top of his foot on up the tendon running along his shinbone. A very similar shin pain hit him when he was hiking the Arizona Trail, only in his lower left leg. He was near the end of his hike that time, so he just gutted it out. Experiencing leg pain when you're not even two weeks into a seven- or eight-week hike isn't good. He decided not to think about it. Maybe it was just a fluke. But the next day the pain was still there, and now his shin was swollen, too. He carefully wrapped a compression bandage around the painful area and popped some ibuprofen. He was not stopping.

◞

August 18 arrived, a sizzling Sunday morning, the kind where heat radiates up from the ground in shimmering waves. The men had just ambled through the scenic Arbor Ridge segment, which winds through the Robert Cook Memorial Arboretum a little northwest of Janesville. Awaiting them was a 20.5-mile road walk out in the full sun. Hiking Dude snapped open the umbrella he carried with him on the Arizona Trail. This was no ordinary umbrella, but rather a GoLite Chrome Dome Trekking Umbrella, color chrome. The umbrella protected the user from rain, of course, but the reflective coating on its exterior also cast away the sun's rays, keeping the user ensconced in a cool, dark bubble. Some experienced long-distance hikers say using such an umbrella on a scorching day can decrease your water needs by a liter, plus lessen the need for sunscreen. And, of course, it makes you feel cooler. Hiking Dude carefully hooked the umbrella's handle and shaft under his backpack's shoulder strap in such a way that it shielded his head while allowing him the use of both hands.

Papa Bear didn't have a GoLite Chrome Dome Trekking Umbrella, color chrome. He didn't bring along any kind of umbrella. But as the temperature soared he purchased a cheap black one at the Walmart in Janesville. The pair realized they must look quite strange, two grown men walking along busy County Highway A on a summer day, packs on their backs and umbrellas held over their heads. So imagine their surprise when they saw another man walking toward them along A, a blue, lightweight backpack strapped to his back, carrying what looked to be the exact same umbrella as Hiking Dude. Once they were close enough, they saw that it was, indeed, a GoLite Chrome Dome Trekking Umbrella, color chrome.

"Hey!" Hiking Dude called out to the young man. "You must be hiking the Ice Age Trail. So are we!"

"I am. I'm Matt Kaufmann, and I work for the Ice Age Trail Alliance in Cross Plains. I'm section-hiking the trail."

Normally, Hiking Dude and Papa Bear would take a break and visit anytime they ran into a fellow hiker. But the air was so thick with humidity, so stiflingly hot, they wanted to keep plodding on to get this stretch over with as quickly as they could. Matt clearly felt no inclination to chat in this broiler, either. So after just a few minutes of chitchat, the three parted ways.

"Make sure you stop in and say hi when you reach Cross Plains!" Matt called out over his shoulder.

After six hours the two reached Albany, population 1,309. A local told the men they could get a cool drink at the Center, a tavern on the east side of the Sugar River. Pushing open the door to its cool, dark interior, the men blinked their eyes to adjust from the bright sunshine outside. When they could finally see, they were shocked. About forty or fifty people were stuffed into the tavern, and it was two o'clock on a Sunday afternoon. They had assumed they'd be the only patrons. Everyone turned and stared at the strangers blinking in the doorway. This was not normal. Something was up.

It turned out the Center was holding its monthly cash contest. Fifty people tossed twenty dollars apiece into a pot, and one person was selected to receive it all—one thousand dollars. The bartender immediately sized up the situation. Two strangers had walked into his tavern right when the raffle was about to begin. They didn't know a soul, so they would be impartial, the perfect people to select the winner. The bartender tapped Hiking Dude for the job, waving a white, plastic pickle jar under his nose. The jar was filled with numbered chips. Hiking Dude reached in, swirled the chips around, and pulled one out. The bartender took it from his hand and shouted, "Number forty-five!" Forty-nine people collectively groaned. Then silence. "Number forty-five!" All of a sudden a woman at the table next to them screamed. It was Tammy, who was now one thousand dollars richer. Tammy bought Hiking Dude and Papa Bear a pitcher of beer, which they enjoyed while the bulk of the crowd dispiritedly streamed out of the bar.

～

By day seventeen, Papa Bear and Hiking Dude were wilting. Each day the heat and humidity had been rising, as if each square on the calendar was in competition with the next to present the most brutal, the most hiking-unfriendly weather possible. Despite downing some frosty beers at both the New Glarus Brewery and Dot's Tavern in Basco, they were increasingly spent. Ironic, they thought, that the weather on the Ice Age Trail—the *Ice Age Trail!*—was so hot and humid. Why, it was much hotter, and certainly more humid, than their trek along the Arizona Trail, where they actually experienced a little snow. Go figure.

The two straggled up to the Ice Age Trail Alliance's headquarters in Cross Plains just as staff members were closing up shop. Matt, the staffer with the matching GoLite umbrella, was still there. He welcomed them inside, showing the duo the shower and washing machine in the building's lower level, which hikers are welcome to use. They made use of both, then took Matt up on his offer to shuttle their vehicle the next day.

The scorching weather continued the following day, the mercury soaring past the ninety-degree mark by midday and the humidity level reaching a tropical 95 percent. Papa Bear and Hiking Dude guzzled all of their water early on and had to stop at a farm to beg for more, which gave them pause. What if they ran out of water again, but couldn't find a farm or home with people around? Would they need to start filtering water? This was silly. They should stop hiking until the weather moderated. But they didn't want to seem like babies, so they came up with a list of why it was imperative, really and truly imperative, to take a break. The list, which Hiking Dude posted to his blog, included the following items:

- Our [upcoming] camping options in Lodi did not pan out so it looked like we might be stealth camping with a storm coming

- The Packers will play the Seahawks on Friday

- We've hiked twelve days without a rest day

- It's too hot!

It was hard to argue with that rationale. A quick phone call was made, and soon Hiking Dude's mother whisked them back to her cool, shady home in West Bend.

The men only planned to step off the trail for two days. But the jungle-like weather, which was supposed to drip and pant and puff its way across Wisconsin during those forty-eight hours, sat on the state, inert, refusing to move on. So they relocated to Hiking Dude's home in Eden Prairie for a week, where they restocked the Honda Odyssey and Hiking Dude treated himself to a haircut and pampered his aching shin. Finally, eleven days after they stepped off the Ice Age Trail in Lodi, they got back on.

Now the pair officially moved from day nineteen to day thirty in their travels. That's how thru-hiking works. You may spend sixty-one days actually hiking a trail, but if you step off for eight, your official thru-hike will be listed as taking sixty-nine days. It doesn't matter whether you leave the trail because of a medical emergency, a family wedding, to rest, or just for the heck of it. From the first day you place a toe on the trail, the clock starts ticking. And it doesn't stop until you've reached the opposite terminus.

For the vast majority of hikers, the total number of days it takes to complete a thru-hike is of little consequence. It's just a number. It's really a consideration only if you're trying to set a speed-hike record or if you have a limited number of days within which to complete your hike. For Papa Bear, it meant nothing. For Hiking Dude, it simply meant his hiking blog jumped from "Day 19, Wed–08/21/2013" to "Day 30, Sun–09/01/2013."

Over the next few weeks, the mercury glided up and down, sometimes flirting with the ninety-degree mark. But it never got quite as beastly as that last week in August.

~

At the north parking area of the Mecan River segment, the men spotted a trail register. Papa Bear and Hiking Dude had been looking for trail registers ever since starting in Potawatomi State Park weeks earlier. Common on long-distance trails, trail logs are often simple spiral notebooks set in a mailbox or handcrafted wooden holder. Though they may seem a bit whimsical, they're actually pretty important. They help trail stewards track trail usage and are important safety tools. If you go missing after signing five registers in a row, rescue personnel have some idea where to start searching for you. Registers also provide a means of helping your fellow hikers. Just waded through chest-deep water where a beaver dam broke through? You can jot that down in a register so hikers heading in the opposite direction know what lies ahead. They're also a means of hiker-to-hiker communication. Trail registers are especially legendary on the Appalachian Trail, where they're set in every shelter. Hikers typically write about what they've done the last day or two, but many also pour out their hearts in their notes.

Hiking Dude lifted a compact notebook and pencil from the box. His typical register entry was a simple "Hiking Dude was here," coupled with the date. But since this was the first register they'd seen on the Ice Age Trail, he scratched out a longer note on behalf of the two of them:

9/5/13
    Papa Bear & Hiking Dude thru-hiking W.B. Started 8/3 (inc. 10 day break). Awesome trail! Thank you IAT, Randy & everyone! On our way to St. Croix Falls! Halfway point is right about here. Great Trail and wonderful people.

Then, he couldn't resist a plug for his blog:

http://hikingdude.com

As he was about to replace the notebook, he remembered there was a young woman named Kehly who was also thru-hiking the trail, raising money for veterans. So he added:

Kehly—keep it up!

Papa Bear and Hiking Dude assumed they'd missed several registers by now, and they hoped that having spotted this one, they would find the rest. In reality, the only trail registers on the Ice Age Trail then were three in Waushara County, placed by the local volunteer chapter, plus three more at DCAs. The IATA is working on adding more.

↜

On the thirty-ninth day of their adventure, the guys entered Antigo. They downed some pizza, checked email at the library, and ducked into Walmart to purchase blaze-orange hats. From there on out, they'd be largely in the woods, and hunting season was about to start. The blaze-orange hats were tucked in their packs, awaiting use, when they entered the Kettlebowl segment two days later. They had covered a scant mile of trail when they bumped into another Ice Age Trail hiker, Steady Eddy.

Like Hiking Dude, Steady Eddy was from Minnesota. Unlike Hiking Dude, Steady Eddy didn't seem to be the most experienced hiker. A short man, sixty-ish, Steady Eddy had zipped his bulging belly into a long-sleeved, royal-blue sweater, despite the day's warmth. He was also clad in blue jeans, a major hiking no-no because cotton—and especially heavy cotton like denim—takes a long time to dry once it gets wet, whether from snow, rain, or sweat. In warm weather, jeans make you hot, and their stiff material can chafe. In cold weather, they offer little protection from the chill, and if they get wet, hypothermia can quickly set in. Steady Eddy's hiking system wasn't the most efficient, either. He would park his car at a trailhead, hike halfway, then return to his car. Then he would drive to the opposite trailhead, hike halfway, and return to his car. When he finished each segment, he'd actually hiked it twice.

The inexperienced-yet-amiable Steady Eddy joined the men as they wound their way north through the Kettlebowl. After an hour, the trail hit a T intersection.

"This is Burma Road," Steady Eddy said. "I hiked to this point yesterday from the segment's north entrance. You two need to turn right here." Wishing them well, he turned around and began the hike back to his car, per his system.

Hiking Dude consulted his map. A few miles from its start on Oak Road, the trail turned right onto Burma Road for a half mile or so before branching off to the left. Although the dirt logging road they were facing was unmarked, it must be Burma Road as Steady Eddy had said. The two turned right and continued on, but they didn't see any blazes. They weren't worried at first; signage might be sparse in this segment. But as the minutes ticked by, their anxiety ratcheted up accordingly.

"What do you think? Do you think this is the trail?" Hiking Dude asked.

"I don't know. There weren't that many blazes the first hour we hiked. We'd be really screwed if we turned around after hiking all this way, and the blaze was right around the next bend."

"You're right. But how do we know when we've walked far enough? At what point do we turn around if we haven't seen a blaze?"

Neither one had an answer for that.

The point came after they'd hiked a blaze-less forty-five minutes. This simply couldn't be the right way. Cursing, they did an about-face and headed back to the T intersection. Hiking Dude poked around in the brush, looking for clues to the trail, and came across an Ice Age Trail sign collapsed on its back in the tall grass. Its arrow pointed to the left, not the right.

"We're changing Steady Eddy's name to Crazy Eddy!" Hiking Dude said. But he knew the fault was as much theirs as Steady Eddy's. Lesson for the day: Never assume the trail heads in a certain direction without visually verifying. And don't keep hiking for forty-five minutes if you're not seeing any yellow blazes.

The men eventually found Burma Road another mile down the trail, then completed the remainder of the Kettlebowl without incident.

~

It was Friday the 13th. Papa Bear and Hiking Dude were resting at the small picnic area that served as the start of the Parrish Hills segment. The beginning of this segment skirted around the eastern shore of Townline Lake, one of only two natural trout lakes in all of Langlade County. After that, according to their notes, Parrish Hills was supposed to be a tangle of swampy, brushy scrub that was difficult to navigate. The perfect ending for a Friday the 13th hike. As the two discussed how to best tackle the segment, and where they might want to set up camp that night, a visitor hiked into the little wayside. Dressed in shorts and a bright red, long-sleeved technical T-shirt, she had a pint-sized blue pack strapped to her back. A pair of Keen sandals was lashed to the waist strap, as were a hand-held water bottle and camera.

"Hey, do either of you guys happen to be Papa Bear?"

"I'm Papa Bear."

The woman's face broke into a big grin.

"I've been looking for you for a long time!"

~

Elated at finally finding Papa Bear, I took a longer-than-normal break to chat with him and his partner, Hiking Dude. Then I headed south while the men shrugged their shoulders into their pack straps, turned their backs on the Parrish Hills trailhead, and headed west along Highway T, then north up Nelson Firelane. The sun plopped below the horizon while they were on Nelson Firelane, but the men were eventually able to spot an unlocked ATV club building, which they promptly decided would be their home for the night. The duo nearly whooped with joy when they saw a dry, clean floor, not to mention two honey-colored picnic tables and built-in bench seating. They would be sleeping in style tonight. The final coup: clean outhouses and a working well.

This was definitely a much better Friday the 13th than the one the two spent on the Arizona Trail, when a snowstorm raged outside and Papa Bear came down with shingles.

CHAPTER SIXTEEN

Conquering the North

Give a girl the right shoes, and she can conquer the world.
—MARILYN MONROE, ACTRESS

"Does my face look fat to you?"

I'm checking myself out in the mirror this morning, and my cheeks seem rather round, my eyes a bit squinched.

"I don't know," says Doug in typical guy fashion. "Maybe. A little, I guess."

I grab my hydration pack and thread my arms through the shoulder straps, but I can't snap the clasp around my waist without letting out the strap an inch.

"I'm gaining weight! I'm gaining weight! Who gains weight on a thru-hike?" My shriek reverberates throughout the hallway of the Holiday Inn Express in Antigo, where we're waiting for the elevator.

I thought my tummy looked a tad rounder the last few days, but I figured I was imagining it. Not that I'm obsessed with my weight—well, not that much, anyway—but truth be told, I was hoping to drop a few pounds on this adventure. My friend Jason lost five pounds when he ran the trail in 2007, and he was pounding down six thousand calories per day. He's bigger than I am and was covering forty-eight miles a day, but still, surely I'd drop a few pounds. And even if I didn't, *I couldn't possibly gain weight!*

I'd done the calculations in my head a thousand times while hiking. An energy bar and coffee to start the day: two hundred calories. One PBJ and six energy snacks during my hike: thirteen hundred. One candy bar sometime during the day as a treat: three hundred. A big dinner at night: about fourteen hundred. Daily total: thirty-two hundred calories. If I'm hiking thirty-odd miles per day with a pack, and jogging some of those miles, I should be burning off every one of those thirty-two hundred calories. And then some. How in the world can I be gaining weight? Yet the mirror and my hydration pack can't be lying.

I glare at my cherub cheeks in the mirror, then punch the elevator button twice for good measure.

～

Today's schedule calls for hiking a connecting road route, then tackling Highland Lakes Eastern, Old Railroad, and just under half of Lumbercamp, for a total of about twenty-two miles. This will be my last day taking it easy and letting the antibiotics kick in before resuming my thirty-two-mile-per-day pace. The bottom of my foot is still really tender, but every day a little less so. Thankfully, the sticky, oozing nastiness has stopped.

As I begin my hike along Kleever Road, a truck full of barking hounds appears out of nowhere, spraying me with gravel as it roars past. I unconsciously pull my new blaze-orange hunting cap more firmly over my head. Last night, heeding Papa Bear's recommendation concerning the start of hunting season, Doug ran over to Walmart and bought one for each of us. Not more than five minutes later, another truck rumbles down the road. This one stops next to me and a man unrolls the window. He's dressed in hunting attire and looks perturbed.

"Hey, did you happen to see a black Lab running around here, or in the woods?"

"No. Sorry."

"My dog got loose. She's wearing a red collar. If you see her, will you mind calling me?" He scribbles a number down on a scrap of paper and hands it to me.

"Sure." He heads off slowly down the road, his eyes methodically scanning right to left.

Clearly I'm in the middle of some hunting paradise. Thank goodness we have these hats. But I wish I knew what everyone was hunting. All I know about the sport is that gun-deer season is the end of November.

About ninety minutes later I turn into Highland Lakes Eastern on a wide service road. I'm looking forward to a pleasant hike, as this trail leads past numerous lakes and Camp Susan, a 4-H facility once used by the Civilian Conservation Corps. But after I have taken just a handful of steps, a yellow blaze abruptly directs me off the road and into a tiny opening in the woods, where I'm led a quarter-mile through the forest before being pushed out onto Bass Lake Road, which lies just north of the trailhead. What the heck? The map certainly doesn't show this route. Yet several blazes pointed me this way, and a yellow, metal Ice Age Trail sign is firmly planted into the ground right where I emerged from the woods and onto Bass Lake Road. As I'm puzzling over the meaning of this signage, a piano riff sounds on my phone. Doug.

"I parked along Highway B, where the trail crosses the road after leaving the Camp Susan area," he says. "I was going to jog in to meet you, but it's all flooded. Maybe up to my ankles. I'm not going in."

"Don't worry about it. The trail immediately led me back onto Bass Lake Road. Maybe it's a temporary reroute because of the water on your end. I guess I'd better hike around on the roads. I'll meet you at Highway B."

Doug and I hook up at B and study the map. There's about a mile left of Highland Lakes Eastern. Then the trail crosses busy State Highway 45/47 before descending into the 9.5-mile Old Railroad segment. Doug doesn't want to park along a busy highway, so we agree he'll drop the car at the Jack Lake parking lot, about three miles into Old Railroad, and jog back in to meet me. I'll be on my own for the next hour.

Old Railroad got its name because the trail runs along a former railroad grade. Years ago, in the early twentieth century, trains steamed along this route hauling logs harvested from the local forests, plus lumber camp supplies and the lumberjacks themselves. As I make my way along the segment, old, wooden railroad ties and iron spikes occasionally poke their heads up from the soft earth, struggling to catch my attention, as if to say, *Hey, I was pretty important back in the day. Don't forget where you're walking. Remember the past.*

I do start to think about the past. Not about logging and railroads, but about people trekking long distances. Although I'm only a few hours into the day's hike, and I'm not going all that far today, my cellulitis foot is already sore. I've got blisters upon blisters on both feet that, no matter how smartly I think I've bandaged them each day, always hurt. The sun is climbing ever higher into the sky, clearly planning to overheat yet another September day. So before I start pitying myself for the seven hours or so I have left to hike, I twist things around and acknowledge how grateful I am that I'm hiking because I want to, not because I have to.

How many millions of people over time—billions, maybe?—have had to flee from their homes and countries because of war, famine, or natural disasters? These people weren't used to distance running or other athletic endeavors when they began their treks, like I am. They weren't clad in technical wear that wicked away moisture and kept them appropriately warmed or cooled.

They didn't have someone waiting to give them water and food. And they often had no idea where they were going.

How did they do it? How did they walk day after day after day? Most of these people weren't walking with a small backpack, either. Many were toting squirming, squealing babies or terrified young children; some were pushing their most precious belongings in a wheelbarrow or handcart. What would I grab if I suddenly had to leave my home? What would I leave behind? I picture myself trying to push a cart full of my most cherished stuff through Old Railroad's knee-high grass, its dirt trails pockmarked with old railroad ties. That would be a heck of a lot harder than what I'm doing, that's for sure.

My mind wanders next to a magazine article I read years ago, back in 1997, that for some reason permanently lodged itself in my brain. It was the story of Lewis Shankle, a forty-seven-year-old from Tucker, Georgia. Lewis was married with two young children when he was laid off from his job. Desperate to find employment, he applied for a custodial position at Brookwood High School that a woman from his church had told him about. Lewis got the job and was ecstatic. There was just one problem. Brookwood High was twenty miles from Lewis's home, and Lewis had no car. The only way to get to work was to walk. So he did.

Lewis would leave his home every day at 3:30 a.m. and walk twenty miles along back roads and highways so he could arrive at Brookwood by 8 a.m. He'd spend the next eight hours working— probably pushing a broom around, emptying garbage cans, washing windows or cafeteria tables, all work that required him to be on his feet—before leaving Brookwood at 4 p.m. for his second twenty-miler of the day. When Lewis got home around 9 or 10 p.m., exhausted to the core, his work was still not done. His wife worked the graveyard shift at a nearby business, so Lewis would make dinner for his kids, hastily scarf some down himself, then help with homework. Sometime around midnight, Lewis was finally able to collapse into bed. Three hours later, he'd get up and do it all over again.

With no physical training, no proper footwear, no smartly wicking clothing, Lewis Shankle walked forty miles per day, five days a week, for three or four months. On just three hours of sleep. And he worked eight hours in between, at a job that required standing on his feet. Eventually a colleague noticed Lewis's tireless trekking and alerted the school; shortly after, Lewis was presented with a used car, courtesy of his colleagues and some parents of Brookwood High students.

As I walk and jog my way through Old Railroad, and then Lumbercamp, I think of Lewis Shankle every time I begin to tire, or I feel a new blister puffing up, or my cellulitis foot twangs in pain. Could I do what he did? I'm not sure. I don't think so. But I do know this: I hope I never have to find out.

With about two hours left in my hiking day, I enter Lumbercamp. Here in its western end, the trail runs through part of the Peters Marsh State Wildlife Area, a 1,687-acre swath of land that's home to innumerable species of animals such as deer, black bear, beaver, snowshoe hare, and ruffed grouse. I love the segment from the start, with its wide, grassy paths and sweeping vistas. The sun has slid halfway down the sky when I step into a spacious clearing thick with clover. A sudden movement up ahead on my right catches my eye, even though whatever moved is quite a way in the distance.

It's an animal, something larger than a dog but smaller than a horse. Sort of like a miniature horse, actually. It even has a blond mane, or so it looks from here. The creature stares at me for just a second, then darts off into the woods. What in the world was that? A wolf? I think they're nocturnal and don't like to be seen. Plus they don't have blond manes. Was it some kind of wild llama? A

Shetland pony? Perhaps a tiny unicorn? I suppose I'll never find out, unless it trots back onto the trail.

Now a bright orange cap is bobbing in the distance on my left, on the opposite side of the trail. It's Doug, coming to run me in. As he nears, I see he's limping.

"Are you making fun of me?" I demand, conscious of my own gimpy gait.

"No! I was jogging back to meet you and stumbled on a rock and hurt my ankle."

He pulls his sock down and I see a soft, fleshy mound where his anklebone should be.

"Oh, no! I'm really sorry. But you still have to wait on me," I say, hoping to inject a little humor into the situation.

Later that night, despite his throbbing, swollen ankle, Doug hobbles over to a nearby self-service laundry to wash my stinky duds, and he even runs into the adjacent Walmart to buy some scented Epsom salt so I can see if a hot soak at night will ease my various aches and pains.

I doubt anyone ever did that for Lewis Shankle.

~

My eyes flutter open. A soft rain is gently tapping on the window. Today's agenda calls for fifteen miles on grassy, shaggy trails before hitting a long road route. When you're hiking in lightweight running shoes, even a gentle morning dew clinging to putting-green grass can immediately soak your feet. When the grass is up to your ankles or knees or even higher, you've got a problem. I have a raincoat with me but not waterproof pants. Just one more thing I never considered.

"Hey, I hear rain," says Doug, now awake as well. "This isn't going to be a fun day for you."

"Thanks for the encouraging words."

We both get up and start preparing for the day, which will be

Doug's last day crewing me for a while. I pull on my usual hiking attire—shorts and a short-sleeved, wicking shirt—then go to work on my feet. Every morning, preparing my feet for the day is a fifteen-minute process. I drain any blisters that need draining, then carefully cover them with bandages. I look for any hot spots that formed the day before, proactively covering them with a thick layer of moleskin. The last step is to check out the cellulitis to make sure the angry, red splotch is shrinking and fading (it is), and that the oozing hasn't returned (it hasn't). Then I need to put a protective covering on it. Since it's a large area, about the size of a deck of cards, and in a terrible spot, just below the toes, I can't simply slap a bandage on it. So I take a rectangular piece of gauze and cut an arch on the top, gently place it over the entire bottom of my upper foot with the arched portion tucked at the base of my toes, then tape it into place with a large piece of red duct tape that I wind around my entire foot. Once all of that's done, I gingerly pull on my socks. The worst part is next: putting on my calf sleeves—compression garments I wear to keep my lower leg muscles loose and warm, plus protect them from the ravages of the trail. Being compression garments, they're small and tight. Really tight. Pulling them on over a healthy foot is no big deal. Squeezing your aching, oozing, bandaged feet through tiny, tight tubes really hurts. I take a deep breath and pull them on as quickly and seamlessly as I can, whimpering softly.

As we carry all my gear down to the car, I glance in the hallway mirror again.

"What do you think about my face today? I still think it looks fat."

Doug mumbles something noncommittal. I glance down at my tummy, and I swear it's a little puffier than yesterday. But I'm too worried about the rain to get annoyed about my weight.

Driving back to Lumbercamp, it's obvious that it has been raining all night. The trails will be a mess. Then, just as we pull up to the spot on County Highway S where the trail crosses, the rain stops. I take it as a positive sign. Stepping out of the car, I tie a white plastic bag over each foot. So far when I've employed this strategy, the bags have lasted about two miles before shredding off my feet. That's not a lot, but keeping my feet dry for two miles is better than nothing. Next I pull out a black plastic lawn-and-leaf bag and tie it around my waist like a skirt. This will hopefully keep my shorts and calf sleeves dry for a while. I raise the hood on my bright blue raincoat and, grabbing my trekking poles and hydration pack, prepare to step on the trail. Then I hear a soft snicker, which turns into a loud snort.

"You look ridiculous!" Doug says. "I have to get a picture of this."

"Go ahead and laugh, Chuckles," I say, turning and giving Doug a winning smile as he snaps a few photos on his phone. "But I'd rather wear this and be dry than get soaked in two minutes."

And with that, I step onto the trail in a thunderous crackling of plastic.

～

As its name implies, the Lumbercamp segment runs through an old lumber camp. The Norem Lumber Camp, to be precise. Operative from the 1920s to 1938, the camp contained numerous log buildings such as a bunkhouse, hay shed, stable, kitchen, mess hall, and root cellar. If you search for a clearing just before you reach Norem Camp Road—which the map helpfully notes might be called Otto Mauk Firelane instead, but in either case is the only primitive dirt road crossing the trail—you can still see some of the camp buildings' log foundations and one intact structure: the root cellar.

At some point, two local sportsmen renovated the root cellar as a hunting shelter for themselves, tricking it out with wooden sleeping platforms, a small table, and shelving. The guys affectionately dubbed it the Hillbilly Hilton and, being friendly folks, placed a journal inside welcoming others to this fine accommodation in the woods. Soon it became a popular stop for Ice Age Trail hikers, mostly just to look at and photograph, although a fair share do spend the night there. I have no desire to spend a night in the rustic Hillbilly Hilton. But much like the name "Papa Bear," the moniker "Hillbilly Hilton" captivates me, and I'm determined to check it out. So my two goals for the remainder of Lumbercamp are to stay as dry as possible and to stop in at the Hillbilly Hilton.

Despite the inauspicious start to the day, things go well in lumber land. The segment is a dream of wide, sandy logging paths. The sand and lack of rocks and roots along the trail allow my plastic bags to remain intact for almost the entire remainder of the segment, some six miles, well past their average longevity, meaning my feet remain dry. And since I'm not walking on narrow footpaths swallowed by soggy vegetation, my lower body stays dry as well. The only disappointment is that I fail to spot the Hillbilly Hilton.

Due to my fixation with the rain, I overlook the fact that this is the day I'll be traversing the Kettlebowl, the infamous segment that has bamboozled every hiker I've met thus far. It's not until I emerge from Lumbercamp and cross State Highway 52 that I realize it's next. Doug and I take a moment to confer about my hiking strategy and what to do if I become lost in the bowels of the Kettlebowl.

The segment is another long one at 9.5 miles. He can only access the trail and meet me at two spots—along Kent Fire Tower Road and Kent Pond Road—so I'll mostly be on my own for about three hours. The first portion of the trail winds up through the Kettlebowl Ski Area, beginning near the chalet and bottom of the south ski run, quickly piggybacking on its wide, grassy cross-country ski trails: portions of the Kettlebowl Classic, Cutoff Canyon, and Plum Creek ski loops. Once past the ski area, the trail runs by something called the Big Stone Hole, a large kettle filled with granite erratics, or chunks of rock, large and small, dragged and dropped by the glacier. ATV trails and logging roads then become intertwined with the path, and the guidebook warns of patches of rough, overgrown terrain due to a recent clear-cut logging operation.

"Why don't you hike with me for a while, at least through the ski area?" I suggest to Doug. "If there are two of us looking for signs, we shouldn't get lost."

"No," he says, without hesitation. "I'll hike with you up to the chalet, but then I'm going back to move the car. I think it's more important that I get to Kent Pond Road and wait for you there. If I spend too much time hiking with you, I might not make it in time, and then you won't be able to resupply. Plus my ankle is still sore."

When Doug makes up his mind about something, you can't change it, so I don't bother to try to convince him of the wisdom in helping me get off to a good start. Instead, I channel Joe Jopek. Joe told me I'd find few markers here. But he said that if I'm supposed to turn, a blaze will point the way. If there's no blaze at an intersection, I should stay on the trail. I just have to remember that. A surge of optimism suddenly flows through me.

"You know what? I'm going to rock the Kettlebowl. I'm going to beat all of those male hikers who got lost. Valderi is *not* going to get lost in there. Valderi *will* prevail!"

"Why are you speaking in the third person?" Doug says, just to irk me. I stick out my tongue at him and begin marching down the gravel road leading to the ski chalet.

↷

As everyone warned, I don't see many markers here. But every time I approach an intersection without a blaze indicating that I should turn—nor a "reassurance" blaze just past an intersection, indicating I should continue forward—I move ahead anyway.

"Think like Joe. Think like Joe," I chant to myself. Somehow, saying his name out loud is reassuring.

I spot a sign for the Big Stone Hole and peek through the trees. It should be just off the trail. There's a cleft in the earth several yards away, but all I see on its bottom is a tangle of wet, green vegetation, which I assume is smothering the erratics that are supposedly nestled in the bowl. I continue hiking along wide, easy-to-navigate paths when I come to a large wooden sign. The sign, half covered in greenery, is just like those found at trailheads and proclaims this the Kettlebowl segment. I recognize this particular sign from the photos Joe showed Maura and me a few days earlier. The bottom of the sign is deeply scalloped; the word *Segment* appears to have been nearly eaten away. The top of the support post on the left sports similar wounds. Bears and porcupines gnaw on these wooden Ice Age Trail signs because they like the salts used in the signs' paints and stains, Joe had told us.

I snap a picture of the sign, charming in its disfigurement, then pause as a small piece of gray metal catches my eye. It's nailed to the sign's opposite side, the side facing the brushy scrub. It looks an awful lot like the back of one of the Ice Age Trail's four-by-four-inch metal arrow signs. Pushing aside the thick vegetation, I step behind the half-eaten wooden sign and see that there is, indeed, a small Ice Age Trail arrow nailed here. If a trail arrow is on the back of this sign, it means westbound hikers are coming from this direction and are being pointed onto the wide path I was just traversing. This means that there's a trail somewhere right here, behind the sign, where I'm standing. And that's the trail I need to take.

I look down and see a shadow of a path pressed into the ground. So that's why the large wooden sign was here, in the middle of the segment. I thought it was just a sign confirming I was in the Kettlebowl, but it was telling me I needed to step off the main trail I'd been on and take this smaller one. In spring or fall, the path would have been easily visible through a denuded landscape. Not so in the lushness of late summer. If I hadn't paused to take that photo, I would never have noticed the tiny metal sign on its backside. I would have kept walking and gotten lost, just like Pat Enright, Bob Fay, Papa Bear, and Hiking Dude.

Patting the deformed sign, I push aside the vegetation and continue my journey.

꙰

If you look at a map of the Ice Age Trail, you can see that making it through Kettlebowl and Langlade County is a huge coup. Reaching this point means I've put behind me all of the Ice Age Trail's northernmost paths. They're the toughest ones, the most remote, the most tangled, and the paths filled with the most wildlife. Get through Langlade County on an eastbound thru-hike, I've been told, and it's smooth sailing from there. Get through Langlade County, and more than one-third of the trail is behind you. I feel lighthearted as I begin skipping southbound, angling out of Langlade County toward the Stevens Point area. The only thing bothering me is this puffiness. Every evening, it seems as though my abdomen is a little more swollen, my face more pinched.

A night or two later, staying in the Plover home of friends BobbieJoy Amann and Patricia Gates, I ask Patricia, a nurse practitioner, if she has any idea what could be going on.

Patricia takes one look at the medicine I'm taking, which apparently is one of the earliest, harshest antibiotics created, and tells me I need to be taking probiotics. The antibiotics I'm on are so powerful, they've been killing all of the good bacteria in my gut, which is causing this bloating. Since my foot is nearly 100 percent healed, and I only have one pill left, she tells me to skip it. The next morning, she hands me a cup of probiotic-laden yogurt for breakfast.

"How long will it take, now that I'm off the medicine, for this bloating to go away? A day?"

Patricia laughs softly. "No. It will probably take a week or two."

"A week? Or two?!" I want to stop letting out my pack strap every morning. I want my cheeks to stop looking like I'm gathering nuts to stash away for the winter. But at least I know what's going on. At least I'm not going to be the first thru-hiker who gains twenty pounds on the trail.

It's day nineteen, and Phil Brinkman meets Patricia and me on County Highway A, just south of Rosholt. Phil is going to crew me today. I know Phil because he's a member of a book club Doug and I created. We're friends but don't know each other all that well. I remind myself I can't just drop my shorts and pee if I'm too tired to seek out a sheltering tree, like I've been doing with my family and Doug. Or change clothes out in the open.

Phil had emailed ahead of time, asking if he can bring me a treat—something special I've been craving. I spent hours upon hours pondering his question these last few days. What *am* I craving out here? When you're hiking all day, every day, food is pretty much all you think about. There are so many things I'd love to sink my teeth into. But I can't ask for something warm, such as a thick slab of pizza or a juicy hamburger, nor something cool, such as an ice cream cone. I settle upon a scone, one of my favorite coffee-shop splurges.

As we pull up to our meeting spot, Phil is waiting. The minute I step out of Patricia's van, he holds out his left hand toward me. A paper bag is cradled in his palm, its top carefully rolled down to reveal the treasure inside: a freshly baked raspberry scone. The berries are so plump, their heads are poking out of the top of the round cake, and so juicy, each one is encircled with a delicate pink stain. The scone's pièce de résistance: a generous handful of fat, square sugar crystals that wink at me with delight. Even though I just ate breakfast at BobbieJoy and Patricia's home, I immediately break off a moist, flavorful chunk and pop it into my mouth. I've always thought Phil was very nice. But now I really like him. A lot.

I give Phil basic crewing instructions and my binder of trail maps, then send him down the road. It's not too long before I reach the next segment, the New Hope–Iola Ski Hill, which straddles the Portage and Waupaca County lines. The segment is a pleasant stroll through stands of red and white pine, birch, and oak—several of the oaks and pines are thought to be more than one hundred years old—plus some scrambles up and down steep ravines. Shortly before arriving at my rendezvous spot with Phil, the trail shoves me out of the woods and into an open meadow filled with tall, waving grasses. At that moment, nature calls. I promptly conduct my business in the meadow al fresco, glad I had to go now and not right when I met up with Phil. The second I finish adjusting my shorts, I hear a shout.

"Hey, Melanie!" I glance across the open meadow and see Phil slowly rise up from the grass, where he apparently had been crouching the entire time. His phone is in his hand, positioned like a camera. I freeze, unsure of what he—and his camera—had seen. Phil begins waving at me, a big grin on his face.

"I was just focusing the camera so I'd be ready to take a picture of you when you got here. You're here sooner than I thought. Smile!"

I smile weakly as Phil snaps away. Clearly, I'll have to be a little more strategic with my restroom breaks today.

The eastern end of the segment is a short roller-coaster ride on the cross-country ski hills of the Iola Winter Sports Club. When I emerge onto County Highway MM, a 13.2-mile road route leads to the next section of trail, Skunk and Foster Lakes. Phil patiently moves his car ahead two miles at a time, while I alternate walking and jogging toward him. What had been a cool, gray day abruptly transitions to blazing sunshine and heat. More problematic is the southerly headwind steadily blowing. I refill my hydration pack bladder again and again. Finally, around 4 p.m., I reach Skunk and Foster Lakes.

A compact two-mile segment, the trail here passes three kettle lakes—Skunk Lake, Foster, and Grenlie—as it rolls through a thick second-growth forest of sugar maple, red oak, big-tooth aspen, paper birch, elm, and white oak. Then a short, 1.3-mile road walk leads to the next segment, Waupaca River, which will probably be my last hike of the day. Phil is supposed to be waiting for me at the Skunk and Foster Lakes trailhead, but he's not here. I assume it's because this particular trailhead has no prominent signage. Instead of the traditional large wooden sign, a narrow, brown Carsonite post with the Ice Age Trail logo is inserted into the earth at the trailhead, which is just a slight hollowing in the thick roadside vegetation. As Phil has only been crewing for a mere eight hours, I'm sure he has no idea the trail is sometimes marked this clandestinely. I decide to start in anyway. If Phil couldn't find the start of the trail, he's most likely waiting for me at its terminus on Foley Road.

The lakes are quite beautiful now, the setting sun swiping them with bright colors. I barely notice the path's steep climbs until sweat begins dripping off my nose and elbows. I'd really like some fresh, cool water. I sure hope Phil is waiting at the end of this trail. I'm not sure if it's paranoia or prescience, but I become more convinced with every step that he's not going to be there. So when I step out of the woods' snug embrace onto a deserted road, I'm not surprised.

Grabbing my phone, I try calling Phil, but he doesn't answer. Our phones are powered by the same company, and the service today has been spotty, so the call might not have gone through properly. But I'm able to leave a voice mail message, so I leave a frantic one saying, *I need water!*

Sliding off my pack, I grab my map. Perhaps I can figure out where Phil is. At the very least, I'll know how to get to the next segment, Waupaca River; maybe he's waiting at that trailhead. I know it's quite close.

"Dammit!"

There's only one map in my pack, Map 46f, which ends in the middle of the trail section I just completed. I need Map 47f, which is with Phil, in his car. Without that map, I don't know if I should turn right or left here on Foley Drive—which just happens to be along a steep hill. I'd hate to turn right and climb this hill if I'm supposed to go left. But I don't want to turn left and go down the hill, only to discover I have to turn around and go back up it. This dilemma probably sounds ridiculous; when you're in the middle of an eleven-hundred-mile hike, what's the difference if you walk a few extra steps or miles or hills? Ask anyone doing it, however, and the answer is that it makes a huge difference.

How much of a difference? With nothing but time on my hands as I hike, I've already done the calculations. Let's say I meet the person crewing me ten times a day. If the car and my supplies are always one-twentieth of a mile away from where I emerge from the trail, I'll have to walk one-tenth of a mile, round-trip, each time I resupply. Take that tenth of a mile times ten pit stops, and I've walked an extra mile that day, not counting all of the extra mileage I likely also added due to wrong turns, double-checking blazes, deviating to check out interesting spots, and so on. One extra mile per day over the thirty-four days I'm hoping to hike is another thirty-four miles, the equivalent of a full day's hike. I'd rather use that energy to finish my hike in thirty-three days and set a more impressive female thru-hike record. And I'd rather not add any more miles than necessary on my feet, which are pretty annoyed with me anyway. So yeah, I'm cautious about taking even one more step than necessary.

But since I can't reach Phil, have no useful map, and can't

locate any Ice Age Trail signage showing me which way to turn, I head to the left, down the hill. A small home sits at the bottom, where Foley intersects with Indian Valley Road. If someone is home, I'm sure they'll know the way.

Luck is with me; an elderly man is sitting in a lawn chair outside the tidy home. "Excuse me! Excuse me! I'm hiking the Ice Age Trail heading south. I just came off the trail on Foley Drive. Which way do I go to pick up the next segment, Waupaca River?"

"You're hiking the what?"

"The Ice Age Trail."

"Ice Age Trail? Never heard of it."

"But it runs all around here! I just hiked on the trail around Skunk and Foster Lakes . . ." I wave my hand toward the woods behind me. "The trail starts right up the road from here. Now I'm supposed to walk a mile or so on another road around here to pick up the trail again."

I stare at the man earnestly, as if doing so will jog his memory. Surely he knows where the trail is. He's living in the middle of two segments. He must know the paths I'm talking about but just doesn't realize they're called the Ice Age Trail.

But he shakes his head at me stubbornly. "I've never heard of any Ice Age Trail."

"Well, can you think of any paths you've seen around here? There are all sorts of trails around here . . ."

He interrupts me, now a bit angry. "No! I don't know anything about any trails!"

I trudge back up the hill, hoping I'll spot a directional arrow I somehow missed, when a gold SUV comes gliding down the hill. I jump into the middle of the road and wave frantically. Mercifully, the driver slows down and stops. It's a woman, about sixty, dressed in office attire, likely on her way home from work. I spill out my dilemma, becoming more agitated with every word.

"I don't know where the Ice Age Trail is," she says kindly, ruefully, "but there is a parking lot just up ahead for some kind of hiking trail. It could be this Ice Age Trail you're looking for. If you want, I'll drop you off there."

Thanking her profusely, I open the door and climb in just as Phil drives up the road.

"Never mind! Here's my friend!" The car door slams, and she drives off with a cheery wave.

"Where were you, Phil?" I say shrilly. "I couldn't find you, I couldn't reach you by phone, there's no arrow showing me where to go, you have my next map, and I'm out of water."

"I was sitting in a parking lot that has a big Ice Age Trail sign— I thought that's where you would come out. I even hiked in a bit to find you. But then I got your voice mail—my phone never rang—and I've been driving up and down Foley and Indian Valley Road, trying to find you."

As if to prove his efforts, he adds, "I left a note and a big hank of chartreuse tape on the trail sign in case you showed up."

Calmed by the food and water I've been consuming while Phil spoke, reminding myself my distress is largely due to being dehydrated and low on calories, I thank Phil and pick up Map 47f, which tells me I need to head downhill on Foley, then turn right on Indian Valley Road, where I'll pass the spot where the elderly man became annoyed with me. With any luck, he's gone inside his home.

Before continuing on, I refill my pack with more water and snacks. Make sure I have the next two maps on hand just to be safe. Enlighten Phil about the occasional use of Carsonite posts at trailheads. And wonder how many Wisconsinites are like that old man, living within steps of our very own National Scenic Trail, yet having no idea it's there.

∼

It's day twenty. I wake up a little earlier than usual and start setting out my gear in BobbieJoy and Patricia's driveway to ensure I'm ready when my next crew member arrives to pick me up. I'll be starting at a spot just north of Hartman Creek State Park. I've still got a long way to go. There's the entire eastern stretch from Janesville to Sturgeon Bay. And on this plunge from Antigo to Janesville that I'm currently tackling, I haven't quite hit the half-way mark, still a day or two north of the bifurcation. What's so astounding to me when I consider where I am today is the fact that six years ago, when Jason Dorgan was setting the Ice Age Trail's fastpacking record, he was nearly finished on day twenty. On day twenty, Jason began in Slinger and made it through nearly the entire Northern Kettle. On day twenty, Jason had two and a half days of hiking and running left.

When Jason set the Ice Age Trail's thru-hike record, he was forty-one. I'm fifty-two now. I'm sure I could be making my way along the trail a little more quickly if I turned back the clock eleven years. But even so, I wouldn't be in Slinger today. Far from it. I'd most likely be a mere two or three days ahead of my current pace, maybe four if you give me back the day I lost due to the cellulitis. I'd still be a good week behind Jason, scrambling to make out his fading footprints on the trail.

I'm pondering all of this when a tall, lanky man comes to the door to collect me. It's Ice Age Trail legend Jason Dorgan himself, who will be crewing me for the day.

CHAPTER SEVENTEEN

Jason Dorgan, Speed Demon

The world needs dreamers and the world needs doers.
But above all, the world needs dreamers who do.
—SARAH BAN BREATHNACH, AUTHOR, *SIMPLE*
ABUNDANCE: A DAYBOOK OF COMFORT AND JOY

It should have been a celebratory day. It was day seven, meaning Jason had been on the trail one week now and was roughly one-third of the way through his mission of setting a speed record on the Ice Age Trail. But he was twenty-six miles behind schedule, he had just done a face-plant trying to maneuver around a fallen tree, resulting in a bloodied lip, and his ankles were killing him. Actually, it wasn't his ankles that were the problem, but those long, ropy extensor tendons that stretch down the front of your shins, over the ankles and tops of your feet, right on down to your toes. Whatever the technical term, they were pretty mad at him right now. With every step he took, it felt as though little knives were stabbing him, mainly right where the tendons curved from the shinbone over the tops of his ankles. Maybe it was a sign that he should just give up. Trying to cover the Ice Age Trail's eleven hundred miles in three weeks was an insane idea. A lot of people

had told him he was crazy. Yes, he *was* crazy. They were right. He
would quit. As soon as he saw Tom Bunk, the friend who was
helping crew him that day, he would stop, he decided.

No, you won't! You're tougher than that! Jason began arguing
with himself. He needed to stay positive. When things got rough
physically, he knew it became more of a mental game. He just
needed to reach Tom, because Tom would know what to say.
Tom would help him believe he could do it. Tom would be able
to make him feel more positive about today. So Jason continued gimping along the eastern edge of the Wood Lake segment,
carved into a remote slice of the Taylor County Forest. Although
the area had been extensively logged in the early 1900s, you'd
never know it now. Thick stands of hemlock, birch, and maple
crowded the segment's western end, alternating with soppy wetlands, before abruptly ceding the land to vast tracts of maple, oak,
and poplar. Wildlife was abundant, including black bears, which
was probably why one of the roads ribboning through the forest
was named Bear Avenue. Tom would be waiting for Jason shortly
after he exited the Wood Lake segment, crossed Tower Road, and
started in on the Timberland Wilderness segment, which very
quickly crossed Camp 26 Road, their rendezvous point.

Jason distracted himself by picturing his car, loaded with
everything and anything he might need: energy gels, Ensure, ibuprofen, Snickers and Payday candy bars, cold water, fresh socks
and a dry shirt, bandages, and petroleum jelly. The thought of
this waiting bounty rejuvenated him a bit, and he quickened his
pace. But when Jason skidded from the trail onto the soft dirt of
the unimproved Camp 26 Road, Tom wasn't there. Jason's slight
burst of energy hissed out of him like a popped balloon.

"Where is he?" A rather salty expletive escaped his mouth.

Jason bent down to shake a few tiny rocks from one shoe and
considered his options. On the one hand, Tom couldn't be that
far away. He'd last seen him in Wood Lake, where the trail crossed

Bear Avenue the first time. Or maybe it was the second time. But either way, from Bear Avenue, Tom just had to make three turns and drive about three miles to reach this spot. It wasn't a difficult drive. So why wasn't he here? Maybe he had car trouble. Or needed gas. Or had a medical emergency. If any of these was the case, who knew how long it would take Tom to get here? And Jason didn't have time. He needed to log fifty miles today to avoid falling further behind schedule. And fifty miles per day equated to perpetual motion. Sit down and rest for fifteen minutes? Lose a mile. Wait thirty minutes for your buddy to show up? Two more down the tubes. On the other hand, when you're logging fifty miles a day for days on end, refueling is mission critical. As an experienced ultramarathoner, Jason knew he could wait a little longer for more food, maybe an hour, but having adequate water was imperative. And he had just drained the last drop out of his black hydration pack.

Jason wasn't carrying a trail map; he was good with directions and had memorized his route for the day. So he knew this new segment was only a few miles long. Hopefully Tom would be waiting at the other end. Jason painfully pointed his right toe downward and etched a large *X* into the dirt, their agreed-upon signal to indicate that he had arrived at a particular trail crossing and carried on. Then he limped back into the woods, leaving a small cloud of dust in his wake.

～

For most thru-hikers tackling a long-distance trail, time isn't a major concern. In fact, many allow themselves plenty of it to take advantage of side trails, scenic views, and lazy picnic stops. But Jason, forty-one, wasn't your typical long-distance thru-hiker. He was a man on a mission. His task? To cover every mile of the Ice Age Trail, both official segments and connecting routes, in record-breaking time. Twenty-one days, in fact, largely because he only had three weeks of vacation to devote to the task. Since the trail at that point, in April 2007, was about 1,100 miles long—620 miles of trail, 460 of connecting road routes—that meant he needed to cover 50 miles per day, the equivalent of about two marathons. Jason planned to alternate running and walking to achieve his goal, spending about ten hours each day on the trail, from 7:30 a.m. until 5:30 p.m. or so. He hoped to average ten-minute miles on the roads and fourteen-minute miles on the trail.

Why put himself through such a strenuous undertaking? In part because Jason was a huge fan of the Ice Age Trail, which was struggling to grow. Few Wisconsinites had heard of it. And if they had, they typically thought of it as a small trail—say, three or four miles—winding around their locale. If he set a speed record on the Ice Age Trail, it would draw attention to it. And hopefully that attention would result in people donating money to build more segments or contributing their time to come out and help build and maintain the ones that were there. Besides, all of the famous National Scenic Trails—the Appalachian Trail, the Pacific Crest, the Continental Divide—had had people intentionally set speed records on them. Yet no one had ever set a speed record on the little-heralded Ice Age Trail. In fact, only fourteen people had ever thru-hiked it. Gary "Lindy" Lindberg, a sixty-five-year-old from Fridley, Minnesota, had the fastest time to date: thirty-two days. As a talented long-distance runner—he'd triumphed in the mercilessly hot 135-mile Badwater Ultramarathon in Death Valley, among others—Jason knew he could move faster than Lindy. As a lifelong fan of the Ice Age Trail dedicated to its completion, Jason wanted to take on that challenge. So he hatched this plan.

But a mere seven days in, Jason was already behind schedule. This endeavor was harder than he'd anticipated. Jason clicked on the digital voice recorder he was carrying to document his record-setting attempt. The recordings could also prove useful in case he ever wanted to write a book about it.

So I passed Tower Road. No Tom or Robert. So I'm hoping everything's okay with them. . . . But I'm out of water. So now I'm debating, do I find a stream and drink some? Because I haven't been able to take my ibuprofen because I don't have any water. So that's become an issue. But I don't want to have longer-term problems by drinking water laced with giardia. So I'll just keep going.

The recorder clicked off.

After an hour or so—during which time Jason fell again due to what he called "the trick stick between the legs," an annoying hiking phenomenon where a stick somehow thwacks the back of one heel while simultaneously striking the top of the opposite foot—the trail crossed an old logging road. A little bubble of hope rose in his chest.

No Tom. The bubble popped.

"Where is he?" Another expletive.

Jason had been reasonably calm this past hour, but now he was getting panicky. *Calm down, calm down!* On the positive side, Tom was a seasoned ultramarathoner himself, holding many age-group records. He wouldn't lose Jason for good. He would know how to find him. And he'd know, he'd expect, that Jason would carry on. In the meantime, Jason just had to keep moving forward. The trail led Jason across Knob Creek, then rolled over another old logging road.

Still no Tom.

He dipped back into the woods for a short bit, not quite a quarter mile, then popped out onto Tower Road as the segment sputtered to an end.

And there, finally, was Tom. The two had been separated two and a half hours.

"Thank goodness! I am so sorry!" said Tom, a wiry sixty-five-year-old with a shock of thick, white hair and a neatly trimmed beard to match. "I got twisted around on the park roads back in Wood Lake."

Standing next to Tom was Robert Wehner, another experienced ultramarathoner and trail hound. Robert was a slender-yet-muscular man, standing five feet, eight inches, with a headful of thick, blond hair parted far to the left. He had driven up from his home in Hubertus, near Holy Hill, to swap in as Jason's support person so Tom could return home for the weekend. He hooked up with Tom on Tower Road, shortly before Jason popped out of the woods. He didn't actually know Jason all that well; their common denominator was Tom Bunk. But when Tom told Robert about Jason's attempt, and how he'd be crewing him, Robert quickly offered his services, excited to be part of such an epic adventure. So here he was, trying to quickly learn how Jason liked to be crewed.

Robert watched closely as Tom went to work like an experienced pit crew at the track. Tom slid the pack off Jason's back and refilled the hydration bladder with cold water while doing a quick assessment: Was Jason wearing the appropriate clothing for the current weather? How much had he been sweating? What were his likely nutritional and hydration needs? Did he appear to be holding up mentally?

"Here, you need to take in more calories. Drink this." He handed Jason a can of Ensure, a nutrition shake; Jason obediently began chugging its contents. Glancing at Jason's lower legs, Tom noticed they were inflamed in addition to being swollen. He handed Jason four ibuprofen, then ordered him to lie on the ground, whereupon he began massaging and stretching his legs this way and that, causing Jason to wince in pain. But it was a good pain.

The stretching session over, Jason rose from the ground. He shoved a few more energy gels into the pockets of his now-water-laden pack, strapped it on his back, and confirmed with Robert that he should meet Jason two miles down Tower Road, at the start of the pint-sized Camp 27 segment, right at a sharp curve in the road. As Jason trotted off down the gravel road, he glanced at his watch. He had been stopped a lengthy fourteen minutes and thirty-five seconds.

~

Jason's adventure began in St. Croix Falls on April 14, an ideal spring day, sunny with a light breeze and temperatures that topped out at fifty-five degrees. Most thru- and section-hikers in 2007 were starting from the eastern terminus in Sturgeon Bay's Potawatomi State Park—purely coincidentally, perhaps, or maybe peer pressure—but Jason selected the western terminus. Why? He couldn't recall. But he specifically planned to begin his quest in April for several reasons. One, the weather would be cool. Two, mosquitoes wouldn't be a problem yet. And three, in April spring was still struggling to shrug off winter's dreary gray-brown hue. This would make it incredibly easy to spot every yellow blaze and arrow and keep zipping along the trail. Jason could think of just two possible downsides to an April trek: precipitation and ticks. He decided a little rain and some ticks were far more appealing than battling heat and mosquitoes while searching for arrows hidden in thick vegetation. So, April it was.

His first few days went pretty much as planned. Wake up and get on the trail by 6:30 or 7:30 a.m. Run, hike, and walk for the next ten or eleven hours. Make sure Tom was waiting at every spot where the trail crossed the road. Or, if hiking along a connecting road route, have him drive just a mile or two up the road—close enough so Jason could quickly see the vehicle and use it as motivation to reel him forward. Eat and drink—a lot. The latter was stressed over and over by Tom, who became obsessed with making sure Jason took in enough calories. A tall, lanky man at six feet, two inches and 170 pounds, Tom calculated that Jason should be eating and drinking six thousand calories per day to fuel his record-setting attempt, with about twenty-five hundred to twenty-six hundred of those calories coming while he was on the trail. So every time he met Jason at a crossing, Tom handed him something: a peanut butter and honey sandwich, a nutrition shake, some sports drink, a handful of energy gels. He also instructed Jason to take salt tablets, amino acid tablets, and an assortment of other items to bolster his system. Jason didn't question the master, ingesting everything he was given.

Once Jason decided he'd had enough for the day, he downed a sports recovery drink. Then Tom drove them to a nearby motel for the night, where Jason immediately prepared an ice bath. Ice baths are supposed to calm the inflammation, soreness, and small muscle-fiber tears that occur when doing intense or repetitive exercise—such as jogging eleven hundred miles. The cold water is said to constrict your blood vessels, reduce swelling, and flush waste products from the body. So in he would go for fifteen minutes. After his ice bath and a quick shower, it was time for a hearty dinner, followed by a little blogging. During this time, Tom was still busy at work, washing Jason's sweaty duds in the motel room sink or a local laundromat and restocking his hydration pack for the morning, adding electrolyte capsules, gels, and a candy bar or two—always Snickers or Payday—and filling up the bladder. When both had finished their tasks, it was lights out. Jason slept with his feet propped on a pillow to help combat swelling.

It was on day four, when Jason pounded out more than fifty-one miles, that his tendons began to hurt. And it was on day five that Jason had a terrible, horrible, no good, very bad day. His lower legs both continually shot searing pains up his shins, then puffed out into unsightly cankles. It was tendinitis, Tom told him, a common ailment in the world of ultrarunning. Basically, his legs were telling him to knock it off. He'd been doing too much, too soon, too many days in a row. Luckily, Jason was traversing Taylor

County that day, a county rich in glacial largesse, namely in the form of lakes, rivers, and streams. Tom had Jason ice his legs and feet in the streams he crossed, then had him pull on ankle braces Tom purchased the previous evening as a precaution. Sensing Jason's sagging morale, Tom inventively tucked a can of chicken noodle soup next to the car's engine block; the next time Jason jogged up, he was handed a warm cup of soup rather than yet another energy gel or nutrition drink. But ankle braces, icing, and chicken noodle soup could only do so much. At the end of an eleven-hour day, Jason had logged a discouraging thirty-one miles, far from the fifty he wanted to fill in on his chart.

Day six wasn't much better. While both legs were still quite painful, his left foot was now exceptionally uncomfortable. He tried turning it in as he jogged, which alleviated the pressure for some reason. So for the next ten miles Jason adopted an awkward pigeon-toed shuffle. He wouldn't slow down and walk, though; he had tried that and found it hurt just as much to walk as jog, so he might as well jog to get in more miles. At day's end, despite another punishing eleven hours on the trail, he'd covered just thirty-eight miles. And yet Jason and Tom estimated that in these first six days, he'd already put almost one-quarter of the trail behind him. Incredible. Just as important, the word was getting out about his thru-run—and about the Ice Age Trail.

Tom Held of the *Milwaukee Journal Sentinel* had been covering Jason's adventure in his blog "Off the Couch." A reporter from Luck took his photo. And Eau Claire's Channel 18 shot some footage one day for its evening news report. All of this publicity resulted in several strangers heading out to the trail just to try to spot Jason as he ran past and encourage him on. The support helped him endure and push on, even on days that tested his commitment, like the following one, when Tom lost him on the trail, his water ran out, and he stumbled twice, compounding his screaming leg pain. Somehow he knew he'd get through this.

Somehow he would find it within himself to soldier on. Somehow he'd complete the Ice Age Trail in the fastest known time.

~

On day nine, the trail sucked Jason into Langlade County. It was the only day he'd really get turned around during his entire adventure. The day dawned fresh and cool. The skies were leaden, the landscape still a dull palette of dove, dun, and sepia, the only splashes of color provided where evergreens dotted the earth. The forecast was for a warm day, so Jason donned black compression shorts, a royal blue singlet, gray socks, and a pair of running shoes, size 14. His shins were finally feeling better, but he still pulled on his black ankle braces to be safe; they stuck out several inches above the tops of his socks. Jason topped off his ensemble with a black compression wrap just above his right knee, a newly tender area.

After a few uneventful miles, the trail pushed Jason into Parrish Hills, a picturesque twelve-mile segment carved into the Langlade County Forest. Logging was still a major part of the economy in this region—the hardscrabble territory that helped birth the frontier legend of Paul Bunyan, giant lumberjack extraordinaire—and in the Langlade County Forest, which had seen continuous logging activity since the late nineteenth century. The Ice Age Trail here traced the Parrish End Moraine, a belt of rocks, sand, and gravel that the glacier shoved to this spot ten thousand years ago. As the ice sheet slowly melted, it also left its mark by dimpling and dampening the earth with extensive pockets of wetlands, plus a lake or two for good measure. As the path tumbled south and east, Jason made his way past scrawny spruce and pine, past barren hardwoods rising skyward like sentinels, along paths covered with last autumn's once-fiery-colored leaves, now soft and brown with decay. The bright yellow blazes easily winked at him in this dull panorama, luring him along the trail.

Then one marker seemed to say, *Hey, come over here and follow me!* But when he did, the path quickly devolved into a gauntlet of briars and downed trees. The briars sliced and diced his exposed arms and legs, while the trees' dense, sharp-clawed branches, much like bottle brushes, were nearly impossible to climb over without impaling himself. This could not be the Ice Age Trail, Jason thought, despite the blaze that had pointed him this way. Maybe it was the correct path at some point in time, but the trail must have been rerouted. When volunteers were removing the old blazes, it seemed someone had missed that first one. Heading back the way he had come, Jason quickly found the real trail. Scratched and bloodied, he considered it a lesson learned: No matter where a blaze points you, always confirm it's the correct way by the condition of the path you're on.

Shortly after Jason righted himself, the trail spit him out onto a hilltop and a true clear-cut zone. Sad and barren like a moonscape, the hill's mocha-colored earth was soft and worn from being continually massaged by the tread of heavy machinery, and it was littered with gray, brittle sticks and branches. Stumps rose out of the ground like headstones, while the few remaining trees, threadbare orphans, stood in scraggly clusters. No yellow blazes winked at him here. For thirty minutes, maybe more, Jason slowly jogged up and down the little hill, searching in vain for a sign, any sign, that the trail lay somewhere beyond. Clearly, it had to resume somewhere past this clear-cut. But he didn't see any trail, and he couldn't just start randomly bushwhacking when he had absolutely no idea where to go. He called out to Robert, who was now crewing him. But no matter how loudly he yelled, he heard no answer. There was no sound out here at all, actually. No wind blowing through the trees, since there were no trees. No animals scampering about, or brooks babbling. Just the sound of his own breaths, his own footfalls.

Jason could try hanging out here until Robert arrived. Robert's crewing strategy was to drive ahead to the next trail crossing, then jog back toward Jason. When he found him, the two made their way together back to the car. Using this strategy, Robert could multitask and get in his daily run while simultaneously crewing Jason. But this clear-cut section seemed pretty vast. Robert might not find him, and then they'd both be lost.

Jason returned to the trail that led him to this godforsaken spot and hiked backward until the path intersected with an ATV trail. Here, a small metal sign showed a map of Langlade County marked with the locations of both the Ice Age Trail and local ATV routes. At one point not too far from here, the trails were supposed to intersect again. Perfect. Jason snapped a photo of the sign so he now had a map with him, then headed down the ATV trail toward its next intersection with the Ice Age Trail. But he became turned around again and never found the Ice Age Trail, eventually exiting the forest directly onto County Highway T.

Soon he was at the trailhead, an hour behind schedule, catching Robert just as he was about to drive off. It turned out Robert had entered Parrish Hills after parking the car, per usual. But after running for quite some time without finding Jason, he realized something was amiss and booked it back to the car. Worried Jason had reached the car while he was on the trail searching for him, Robert was preparing to jump ahead to the next crossing when Jason showed up.

Both of these delays proved costly. Jason was on the trail eleven-and-a-half hours but covered only forty-four miles. That night, after Jason had blogged about his crazy day, Anne Riendl, one of a group of three female section-hikers, sympathetically replied, "We three ICE AGE CHICKS can relate to your experiences! Traveling the Ice Age Trail provides zillions of lessons on many levels of understanding or lack thereof!"

～

While Jason was tackling Langlade County, Rick and Roberta Bie were out tidying up the wooded Ringle segment in neighboring Marathon County, which Jason expected to reach in the next day or two. The segment staggered in a southeasterly angle from its starting point on County Highway N and Helf Road until it hit the Mountain-Bay State Trail, at which point it swooped due east along the recreational path right into the town of Hatley.

The Bies were members of the Marathon County Chapter of the IATA. Formed in the early 1970s, its first six miles of trail were laid in 1973 on what is now called the Ringle segment. True Ice Age Trail aficionados, Rick and Roberta, also known as Buzz and Frieda, had been section-hiking the trail since 2004. Trimming the trail to prepare for Jason's arrival was an incredibly kind thing to do. But amazingly, the Bies weren't doing this just because Jason was trying to set a speed record or because he was trying to raise money for the IATA. They did it for anyone who was heading their way, assuming they had the time. So would many other trail volunteers. No, they couldn't keep every inch of the trail perfectly groomed at all times. But if they knew someone was coming and they could get out there to spruce things up, they were more than happy to do so. Call it trail love, call it good old midwestern hospitality, call it whatever you'd like. Here in Wisconsin, we're darned lucky to have so many people who care so deeply about the Ice Age Trail.

Two days later, as Jason danced through much of well-groomed Marathon County, the Bies wished him well via his blog:

> We hope you enjoyed Marathon Co. today—we scouted our stretch of the Ringle Segment this weekend, cut back a few brambles and made sure the trail was well-defined. I would've left a bottle of Gatorade out for you but what sick freak drinks from a bottle they found out in the woods? You rock, man!

⤳

As Jason edged closer and closer to his hometown area, Madison, his running buddies eagerly awaited his arrival so they could sneak in a few miles with him. Cheer him on. Bring him a favorite snack. On day thirteen, friends Tim Goihl and Peter Wadsack couldn't wait any longer to be a part of his epic adventure. They hopped in the car and drove up to find Jason, who was somewhere north of Westfield in Marquette County. Jason had a lot of miles to hammer out on connecting road routes that day, and it was raining—the first real rainy day of his hike. Their presence should help.

Motoring along Dover Court, they spied someone in a red jacket running toward them in the rain. It had to be Jason. They backed their car into a driveway and climbed out, ready to say hey, you're doing awesome. Ready to clap him on the back and hear how things were going firsthand after reading his short blog entries. Jason cruised up and flashed his buddies a smile.

"Hey, guys! Great to see you!" Jason said, as he ran past the two and continued along Dover Court without so much as a backward glance. The two men looked at each other, dumbfounded for a second.

"Well, I guess it makes sense that he didn't stop," Tim said. "I mean, if he stops and talks to people all the time, he's not going to be able to cover fifty miles every day."

The two climbed back into the car and zipped down the road to catch Jason. When they did, Tim jumped out and began jogging with him. Peter would take over later in the day. Both men were experienced runners themselves, having done numerous marathons and ultramarathons. Tim even paced Jason twice in the Leadville Trail 100, a one-hundred-mile race that was one of the nation's premiere ultrarunning events. Yet Tim, for one, was surprised at how slowly Jason was moving out there. Sure, he knew he wouldn't be pounding out six-minute miles eleven hours per day for three weeks. But he didn't think Jason would be walking so frequently. Jason was only running a scant quarter-mile at a time before stopping to walk. And he was walking up every hill, even pint-sized ones that were little more than a bump in the pavement.

It wasn't this way initially, Tom Bunk later told him. At first, Jason was running much longer stretches. But after he began suffering from repetitive-motion injuries—his shin pain, some IT band issues—the two decided that if he changed his stride often, that should help greatly. And what about walking those "hills" that were really gentle rises? From the start, Jason walked up every sizable hill, a common ultramarathoning tactic that helps the runner save valuable energy and strength and often enables him or her to log a faster time than those who try to run every step. Jason initially cruised over these small bumps, but now, yes, he was walking them, too. Because, well, you try running eleven hundred miles and you'll quickly see how these gentle rises suddenly transform themselves into massive inclines. Thru-running the Ice Age Trail, as opposed to running a long race, even a hundred-miler, is all about pacing, conserving energy, and trying to keep your body healthy. Tim was a total believer in this strategy by the end of the day, when Jason entered his ending point in the Excel spreadsheet he'd meticulously been keeping. With the punch of a button, it revealed he'd covered 53.9 miles.

～

Day fourteen found Jason in his own backyard, finally tackling trails with which he was intimately familiar. The first of these trails was at Devil's Lake. Devil's Lake is one of the most important and impressive segments on the entire Ice Age Trail. The park is famous for the 1.7 billion-year-old quartzite cliffs that rise in its midst and form the sides of the Devil's Lake gorge. Part of the Baraboo Range, one of the most ancient rocky outcrops in all of

North America, older than the Rocky and Appalachian Mountains, the cliffs were once mighty mountains themselves that erosion slowly chiseled down to size. Then, some sixteen thousand to twenty thousand years ago, the glacier shot an icy finger creaking and groaning and lumbering toward the Baraboo Range. When it reached the range's eastern half, it abruptly stopped. Later, when the ice sheet finally began to melt, it carefully tucked a belt of its rocky, sandy debris at each end of the gorge, neatly sealing it up. Over time a lake welled up in between these two glacial plugs—Devil's Lake—as sort of an *I Was Here* piece of glacial graffiti. Today, those pretty, pinkish, 1.7 billion-year-old quartzite cliffs tower five hundred feet above the lake, and climbing up and down them is quite taxing, no matter what your fitness level.

Devil's Lake State Park sits at the base of the bifurcation. Hikers heading west to east, as Jason was, reach the top of the bifurcation bubble just south of Coloma, where they must decide whether to hike its eastern or western half. If they select the eastern path, they'll enter Devil's Lake from the Sauk Point segment, which lies to the east of the park. If they elect to travel along the western passage, they'll enter the park from the Baraboo segment to the north. Jason opted for the shorter eastern half, entering the park from the east, then traveling along its northern tier. He was joined by a running buddy, Matt Frank. The two climbed up the park's western bluff as the sun finally steamed through the gray curtain that had been hanging over the land all morning. They paused to snap a photo of the lake and eastern bluff at a particularly scenic spot where the vegetation had backed off, opening up the view, then pounded down its steep southern slope. As the men crossed over to the eastern bluff, they unwittingly marched right into an enormous swarm of mayflies.

Mayflies, or shadflies, are aquatic insects that innocently live most of their lives on the bottom of a body of water. Shortly before their time on earth is up, wings spontaneously sprout from their bodies. The insects rise out of the water in often colossal swarms, where they molt a final time, mate, lay eggs (the females), and then die, all within a few days. This mad dash out of the lakebed and the ensuing bacchanal is what Jason and Matt found themselves in the midst of. The insects, perhaps sensing death was nigh, were frantically, blindly whirring around the lakeshore, flapping into the men's noses, ears, and mouths, causing them to spit and sputter and curse and rage.

Thousands upon thousands of these insects had already met their demise and were piled up in a thick, slick layer over the grass and paved path. Climbing the super-steep Tumbled Rocks Trail leading up to the top of the east bluff now seemed rather appealing. The two jogged, slipped, and slid the mile around the lake and over to the bluff, then scrambled up and away from the madness. The park's steep terrain, and perhaps the mayfly mayhem, held Jason to forty-four miles that day.

∽

Jason passed the two-week mark, putting him in the final stretch. Still in the vicinity of Devil's Lake, it was almost impossible to conceive of someone getting from there to the Ice Age Trail's eastern terminus in a mere seven days. But that was the plan. Today five friends from the Madison area—Ann Heaslett, Timo Yanacheck, Dave Saroka, Brenda Bland, and Kevin Radel—were set to usher Jason in and out of his stomping grounds. Timo was on the scene first, waiting for Jason at 6:30 a.m. at the start of the Merrimac segment. Timo's nose was in the back of Jason's car, helping Tom take inventory of the day's supplies, when he heard a noise. Looking up from the trunk, he saw Jason trotting off down the trail without him.

"Jason does not wait for anyone," Tom said. Timo wasn't surprised. He was a good friend of Jason's and had run with him many times. He'd also crewed him in several hundred-mile races.

He knew it was his job to catch up to Jason, not call out for Jason to stop. So he left the final supply check to Tom and started running down the road.

The day was promising to be one of sun and warmth. Timo reached Jason and found him chatty and in good spirits. Even more impressive, his gait appeared fresh and productive. And while Timo could easily match Jason's nine-minute-per-mile jogging splits, he couldn't match his brisk fourteen-minute-per-mile walking pace. So he kept jogging.

Every once in a while Jason turned around, faced Timo, and began walking backward. Timo knew this meant Jason's hamstrings were bothering him, but Jason didn't mention it. Instead, he chattered on excitedly about the trail's beauty and its future.

The two reached the Wisconsin River and the obligatory ferry crossing on the *Colsac III*, which was being winched toward them along three submerged cables. A popular tourist attraction and part of the National Register of Historic Places, the Merrimac ferry is the last of more than five hundred such crafts that once ferried riders and vehicles across Wisconsin's inland lakes and rivers. It's also the only part of the Ice Age Trail that moves. The ferry takes about seven minutes to cross the river's roughly half-mile width, so Jason's feet were treated to a short respite, for which he was grateful. He'd heard some past thru-hikers illegally crossed the river on the railroad bridge sitting just upstream from the ferry because they felt it was cheating to take the ferry and wanted to walk every single step. Not Jason. The ferry crossing *was* the specified route. Plus it was a novelty among the eleven National Scenic Trails. Seven minutes after Jason walked onto the ferry, he began running again, Timo in his wake.

Timo tagged off to Brenda, Kevin, and Dave when he and Jason reached the Groves-Pertzborn segment just northeast of Lodi about 10 a.m. The three were supposed to have relieved Timo earlier, but Jason and Timo beat the trio to the agreed-upon meeting spot. And, well, Jason didn't wait for anyone. As Jason and his entourage jogged on, Timo hopped into Dave's car and caravanned behind Tom Bunk. The men continually hopscotched over the group as it rolled through Lodi, then Eastern Lodi Marsh, Lodi Marsh, and Indian Lake. As Jason & Co. were making their way out of Indian Lake along a connecting road route, Timo noticed a vintage pickup suddenly slow down as it reached the runners. Some type of exchange occurred, one that didn't appear to be all that friendly. So when the truck reached Timo, he slowed and unrolled his window.

"Was there any problem up there?" Timo asked the driver, a grizzled, elderly farmer dressed in faded overalls and a battered cap.

"Thou shalt not run on the roads," said the farmer sternly, as if quoting scripture. "Roads are the province of cars."

"Well, that's funny," said Timo, without missing a beat. "The New Testament says Jesus walked along the roads to Nazareth. But it doesn't say anything about cars."

Scowling disapprovingly, the farmer motored off.

⌁

Spring had definitely arrived in southern Wisconsin. A plush green carpet now covered the ground, instantly brightening the landscape. Dogwoods and wild plum were bursting into bloom, their white blossoms bobbing and waving in the breeze. Spurring this sudden rush of growth were the sporadic bursts of heat being emitted as spring properly calibrated its thermostat. The previous day, the mercury topped the eighties, a bit overboard for April 28, and the next few days looked to be nearly as steamy. But Jason wasn't worried. He was closing in on the eastern terminus, the hard stuff behind him. Nothing, and certainly not a little heat, could stop him now.

⌁

May 2. Day nineteen. The weather was balmy and pleasant, coax-
ing an increasing number of dandelions to pop their butter-yellow
heads out of the ground. Gauzy green curtains of unfurling leaves
were fluttering in every direction, as if they were the latest deco-
rating fad. The air swelled with a symphony of sweet sounds as
cardinals, red-winged blackbirds, sparrows, and other songbirds
tweeted and trilled and sang their pleasure with the changing
seasons, augmented by the staccato bursts of woodpeckers. The
previous day, Mike Sears from the *Milwaukee Journal Sentinel*
had tagged along with Jason all day, shooting video for the newspaper's website. Next up: The paper's Tom Held, who had been
blogging regularly about Jason's thru-run, would be running with
Jason for a few miles.

For Jason, it was a reflective day. He pulled out his digital voice
recorder.

> Had a nice group of people, four folks and one of their kids,
> come out just to say hi and wish me luck. That's always, that's
> so cool. And, uh, I didn't catch their names but I got a picture
> of them, so hopefully I can get their names sometime later.

Tom Held came and went. Jason buzzed through Lapham
Peak, including a climb up the observation tower, and was now
in Delafield.

> Well, it's about 10:00. Been a little low on energy. I've been
> taking in enough calories, but hard to say if I've got the
> right ones right at the moment. So I'm walking a bit. Going
> through a park in Delafield, Nama Nama Nawa—some
> strange name that I'm horrible at pronouncing. [It's Naga-
> Waukee.] And took some Jelly Bellies. They all tasted pretty
> good except for the popcorn. Had to spit that one out.
> Popcorn-flavored Jelly Belly right now—not good.

Later, in Waukesha County:

> There are two people hiking south . . . doing about, Tim said
> about eleven miles a day. They've got two dogs. So there is a
> chance I will intersect them some time during my second-to-
> last day. . . . So very cool. There's a bunch of crazy people just
> like me!

~

Sunday, May 6, 2007. A little south of Algoma, Wisconsin. The
Ice Age Trail speed-hike record would be set that day. As if ac-
knowledging the day was a special one, the sun rose in a blaze of
orange, sending a laser-like beam of light glittering across the in-
digo waters of Lake Michigan. It was crisp out this Sunday morning, so Jason donned a blue T-shirt proclaiming "Get Dirty," a
pair of black wind pants, and a gray jacket. Then he pulled on
a pair of white cotton gloves, perfect for spring runs when you
need just a little something to warm your hands and absorb any
nose drippings. Last came the cap. Normally, Jason did not run
with a hat on because hats made his head too hot. But sometime early on in this adventure, the continual exposure to the sun
began relentlessly baking the top of his head, burning through
his thinning hair. Tom removed his own cap and gave it to Jason,
insisting he wear it. A little gift. The hat appropriately proclaimed
"Trailbreaker" across its front and was colored Ice Age Trail blaze
yellow. Now, several weeks later, Jason couldn't imagine running
without it. At least here, on the Ice Age Trail.

   With a mere thirty miles to go, a little more than a marathon,
and much of it along flat, crushed limestone rail trails, Jason felt
confident he'd have no problem completing his journey that day.
In fact, he estimated he'd reach the eastern terminus sometime
between 12:30 and 2:30 p.m. Although several dozen family
members and friends were planning to celebrate with Jason once

he reached the eastern terminus in Potawatomi State Park, it was just Jason and Robert initially. Quietly, efficiently, Jason clicked off the miles like a metronome, as family and friends streamed northeast toward Sturgeon Bay, homing in on the state park from various locales around Wisconsin.

Soon a few friends surprised Jason by hopping on the trail with him. One here, another there, two more at the next crossing. Like followers of the Pied Piper, the line behind Jason grew longer and longer. Walking through the streets of town, a half dozen runners behind him, Jason couldn't stop grinning. Then, in some sort of cosmic alpha-omega moment, he spotted a young, bearded man walking toward him. The man had an enormous pack strapped to his back, complete with sleeping bag, and hiking shoes on his feet. No one would be strolling along the streets of Sturgeon Bay in such attire unless he was doing one thing: hiking the Ice Age Trail.

The two stopped and grinned at one another. The hiker was Chris, and he told Jason he knew Jason was out here. He was hoping they'd cross paths, but he wasn't sure. Chris was ad-libbing it out here on the trail. He didn't know how far he'd go that day, or where he'd stop and sleep that night. Jason silently shook his head, knowing he could never hike that way himself. He was a planner. He liked to know exactly where he'd be starting, stopping, and staying. Yet he admired Chris for his freewheeling hiking style, too. The men were both anxious to keep going, Jason being so close to the end, Chris so recently begun. So they wished each other good luck and hiked on.

When Jason and his entourage reached the entrance to Potawatomi State Park, Robert quietly stepped off the trail. With only a handful of miles to cover within the park boundary, Jason wouldn't need more food or water. It was time to savor his accomplishment with his closest friends and family. The excited, chattering pack moved up the trail, running alongside and behind Jason, always letting him set the pace and take the lead. Amazingly, the closer he got to the tower, the faster he ran. Even with nearly eleven hundred miles burnished into his apparently trail-hardened body.

Shortly before he popped out of the woods, applause and hoots rang out through the forest. And suddenly, there he was. At the end of the trail. Normally a reserved person, Jason started to get choked up. He thought he might cry, which would be embarrassing. But then his elation broke through, and the tears got sucked back into his eyes. He touched the terminus marker, affixed to a boulder, and then, to make sure his feat was official, he climbed the seventy-five-foot observation tower. Friends clambered up its one hundred steps with him and celebrated at the top by popping open a bottle of champagne and passing out brownies.

But Jason still wasn't finished. He wasn't positive what he needed to do to make sure he'd officially finished the Ice Age Trail. Was it merely emerging from the woods and standing near the observation tower? Did he have to touch the boulder? Climb the tower? He knew of one more Ice Age Trail sign about a quarter-mile down an access path to the parking lot. So he jogged down it and touched the large wooden sign proclaiming, "Trailhead. Ice Age Trail. Potawatomi State Park." A gaggle of friends and family members, including his parents, clustered around the sign with him, mugging for the cameras that magically appeared in several people's hands.

"Hey, Jason," his dad said. "Guess what. You finished in 1-2-3-4-5-6-7!" Jason gave him a puzzled look. "You finished at 12:34 p.m. And it's May 6, 2007. 1-2-3-4-5-6-7!"

Pretty cool, undoubtedly. But Jason loved these figures the best: 1,079 miles. Twenty-two days and six hours. An average of forty-eight miles per day.

Besting Gary "Lindy" Lindberg's pace by a whopping nine

days, Jason Dorgan now held the speed-hike record for the Ice
Age National Scenic Trail. He had completed the trail in the fastest known time.

~

That evening, back at home, Jason sat down at his computer and
tapped out his blog entry for the day:

> The sheer magnitude of what I have done is a jumble in my
> head. In one sense I wonder why it took so long to do and on
> another more sane level I wonder how it was ever possible
> in just 23 days. Driving back through some of the towns and
> roads I had just recently run the past 3 days made the task
> seem impossible, as the car miles seemed to take forever.
> Possibly what is most baffling is the body is probably ready to
> continue running as I just kept getting stronger as the last day
> approached and then today was a breeze. I of course still had
> to stretch out the IT band to prevent it from getting worse and
> the feet are pretty beat up (two toenails will be lost I suspect),
> but I think the body could probably continue to do more.

CHAPTER EIGHTEEN

Hitting Halfway Heaven

If you expect life to be easy, challenges will seem difficult.
If you accept that challenges may occur, life will be easier.
—ROB LIANO, AUTHOR AND LIFE COACH

Jason is looking at the pile in the driveway with a slightly shocked expression on his normally imperturbable face.

"This is all your stuff?"

I nod silently, a bit embarrassed.

"If I had known you had this much stuff, I would have left more room in my car."

I glance at my belongings, stacked in BobbieJoy and Patricia's driveway. I've never been one to pack lightly, even on an overnight trip. But honestly, I do need all these things. I have my two red suitcases, filled with a wide variety of hiking and running gear so I'm ready for all kinds of weather, from the endless days of heat and humidity I've been experiencing to drenching rains and plunging temps. The suitcases also contain my after-hiking clothing, pajamas, and toiletries. I also have two plastic bins stacked with energy bars, a large cooler filled with ice and anything that needs to be chilled each day, a case of sports drink, three one-gallon water jugs, a huge cloth bag filled with nine pairs of running shoes, which I'm alternating to prevent tendinitis, and a foot-tall cylinder of a sports recovery drink that I mix up at the end of every day. Oh, and my medical kit, laptop, camera, trekking poles, and hydration pack.

It's a lot, I know. But I'll be out here five weeks.

I did consider bringing just enough supplies for a week at a time. But then I'd have to make sure whoever was crewing me at the start of a new week collected resupply boxes from Ed before joining me on the trail. That seemed too complicated. It was far easier and more seamless to haul everything from one terminus to the other, transferring my suitcases, bags, and boxes from one person's car to the next. But as I peek into the back of Jason's compact Jeep Compass, I receive my own shock. His car is crammed floor to ceiling and front to back with stuff, save for one tiny space in the rear that he's carved out for my gear. It looks big enough to fit my smaller suitcase and maybe the bins of energy bars.

"Um, are you going somewhere?" I ask delicately. I don't want to appear rude when he's giving up time to help me out.

"Yeah, as soon as you're finished today, I'm heading over to Door County. I'm going camping this weekend."

And that explains it. Silently, artfully, Jason rearranges the items in his car, then manages to fit everything of mine inside. He does this without any shoving, squishing, grunting, or swearing. I even have the front passenger seat largely to myself. It's quite impressive, actually. Soon I'll be even more awed by Jason's crewing skills, which far surpass the creative car-packing I've just witnessed.

~

I'm in a trance, flying along the trails in the Belmont, Emmons, and Hartman Creek segment. The paths here are a runner's dream: soft, smooth, gently undulating. With my cellulitis finally gone and the painful freckling of blisters across my feet transitioning to hardened calluses, I feel one with the earth. I power across rolling forestland, stopping briefly to gaze upon one of the largest erratics on the entire Ice Age Trail. I dance along the middle of a browning prairie, still alive with the warbling of innumerable songbirds. I'm feeling strong. Happy. Alive. The only slight negative is the weather. Although the day began gray and cool, the sun has muscled aside the clouds, which responded by flinging every drop of moisture left in them into the increasingly humid air. Halfway through the segment, the thickening air is pressing against the back of my throat with every inhalation, so heavy, so ponderous, that it can't quite make its way down into my lungs. Sweat seeps out of every pore. By the time I reach Jason, I have sweat through every article of clothing I'm wearing.

"I need to change clothes," I pant, as he reaches for my water bottles. Since I'll be able to hook up with Jason every thirty minutes or so today, I've stashed my hydration pack in his car and am running with just two handheld water bottles. It's nice to lose the weight of the hydration pack, small though it may be.

"You're not drinking nearly enough water for today's heat and humidity," he scolds, filling the bottles with water and ice. "The next time we meet, these had better be empty."

I'm about to plop on the ground to change my shoes when I see Jason has taken my large cooler and set it next to his car, then draped a towel over the top to create a little sweat-proof seating area for me. Why hadn't I thought of that before? He's also set out everything I might need in a fan-shaped, Pinterest-worthy display: my medical kit, an assortment of energy bars, a chilled bottle of sports drink, my plus-sized bottle of ibuprofen, new shoes. Jason orders me to change my socks, which I don't think are all that wet, but he insists, noting it's the best way to prevent more blisters. Then, despite the day's heat, he commands that

I slurp at least a few spoonfuls of the chicken noodle soup he has warming on his car's engine block, a trick he learned from Tom Bunk.

"You'll really need the sodium in the soup on a humid day like today," he says, handing me the can and a plastic spoon.

I dutifully do everything he tells me to do. If anyone knows how to rock the Ice Age Trail, it's Jason Dorgan.

～

I'm humming along a fifteen-mile connecting road route that unspools through Waushara County in a southwesterly direction when I spot two royal blue signs carefully placed near the roadside for optimum viewing. They're the size of political yard signs. Both shout out in white, capital letters: MENARDS SUCKS. I laugh out loud as I snap a photo. Some people like to call it as they see it. Not my style, but the bold, brassy message distracts me for the next thirty minutes or so, allowing me to temporarily overlook the stifling heat.

Months later, while giving talks about my thru-hike to various interested community groups, the photo that always gets the biggest reaction out of the crowds, hands down, is this photo of the MENARDS SUCKS sign.

～

Later that night, with thirty-two miles behind me, Jason drops me off at the Mecan River House, my lodging for the evening. The bed-and-breakfast inn sits right on the Ice Age Trail; I'll be jogging past it tomorrow. The proprietor, Agnes Breitzman, is an eighty-four-year-old dynamo. Short and petite, with a fashionable red bob, she welcomes me into her home and shows me my room for the night, which is right off the kitchen.

"I have to say, I am just so impressed with you," she says, bustling around the kitchen in a pair of Gloria Vanderbilt skinny jeans. "What you're doing, hiking the whole Ice Age Trail, is just so impressive." I beam at her proudly.

Then she stops, fixes her gaze on me, and adds, "Because you're not that young, you know. You're no spring chicken."

～

The next morning at seven thirty sharp, Doug pulls up to Agnes's inn. He's crewing me one final time. As we begin loading up his car with my assorted bags and boxes, Agnes asks if he'd like a cup of coffee.

"No, thanks. I drank coffee on the drive up here." He glances around her countertop. "But can I have this banana?"

I shoot him a look of motherly disapproval.

"What?" he whispers to me as he begins unpeeling the banana.

"You didn't stay here!" I softly hiss. "You shouldn't be asking her for food."

"But she said I could have it," Doug says petulantly, shoving the banana into his mouth.

Agnes turns again to Doug. "Boy, I am really impressed with your friend here. Hiking that whole Ice Age Trail. That is unbelievable."

"I know," says Doug solemnly.

"Because, you know, she's not that young. She's no spring chicken."

"No, she is not," he says, and I can feel the smirk behind his serious mien. "She is definitely not a spring chicken."

～

Doug's ankle has healed from the spill he took on the trail the previous weekend, so he joins me on portions of the Bohn Lake and Greenwood segments, where we weave through a heavenly scented pine plantation, along rolling paths tucked into savanna forest and up to a one-square-mile restored prairie, the largest here in Waushara County. Carefully positioned near the prairie's edge for optimal viewing, yet sheltered under the broad, green arms of the fragrant pines, are a handcrafted log couch and ottoman. Doug immediately plops down on the couch and props his feet up on the ottoman.

"This is actually quite comfortable," he says.

"Don't get used to it. We have to keep moving."

"You're such a slave driver."

"You can't set a fastpacking record by stopping all the time. Now run ahead to the car and make sure some water and snacks are ready for me when I get there."

Sighing loudly and dramatically, Doug eases himself off the couch and trots off into the woods toward the car.

Waushara County sits squarely in Wisconsin's midsection, a little to the left of where its belly button would be if it had one. Home to some twenty-five thousand residents, it appears somewhat nondescript. Its largest cities are Berlin, Silver Lake, Wautoma (the county seat), Redgranite, and Marion, places little known to many Wisconsin residents. It also lacks the major businesses and tourist attractions that can give a locale some pizzazz. Yet the county, part of the state's Central Sand Hills region, is a picturesque mix of farmland and wetlands, such as tamarack swamps and sedge meadows, small kettle lakes, and a series of moraines the glacier deposited as it lurched back and forth during its final retreat. It's also home to the Mecan River.

The headwaters of the Mecan River originate on a patch of land a little northeast of Coloma that cradles the Mecan Springs. The river flows 48.7 miles in a southeasterly direction to a spot near Princeton, where it feeds into the Fox River. The Mecan is known for its crystal-clear waters, which support a naturally reproducing rainbow trout population—one of the few such streams in the state. It's also home to brown trout. In the fall of 1999, Perrier turned a watery eye on the Mecan. The bottled-water giant wanted to tap its rich spring waters for use in its Ice Mountain brand, one of the most popular bottled spring waters in the Midwest. It also wanted to locate a roughly $35 million bottling plant in the vicinity that would employ up to 250 people. The company had already drilled several test wells near the river, plus near the adjacent Wedde and Schmudlach Creeks feeding into the Mecan, when county residents discovered Perrier's plan. An uproar ensued, and Perrier left empty-bottled.

The Ice Age Trail winds throughout the Mecan Springs State Natural Area, where outdoors lovers often hike, snowshoe, hunt, canoe, kayak, and fish. The natural area is rich with oak woodland, prairie, grassland—where the federally endangered Karner blue butterfly lives—and pine plantation. Shortly after starting in on the 6.8-mile segment and traversing a hilly patch of forestland, I roll out of the trees and to the top of a hill. Stretching out before me is a vast, open field dotted with plump, rounded hay bales. A path has been carefully mowed into the grass to indicate the proper passageway, and when I see it, it takes my breath away. The path curves and tumbles its way down the hilly field, lined on each side with a soft shock of knee-high golden grass, which waves gently in the breeze. The effect of this rather simple setup is stunning. The path appears like a special passageway for royalty or VIPs, with the bobbing grass akin to a waving, adoring crowd. I slowly make my way along the path, feeling like a queen, or a bride walking down the aisle. It's as if the Ice Age Trail is applauding my efforts so far and encouraging me onward.

Later in the segment, I pass several piles of large rocks, cleared from farm fields long ago by rugged Wisconsin pioneers. Previous hikers have created dozens of cairns from the smaller bits of rock and carefully set them in rows atop the larger ones. The cairns similarly stand sentinel along the trail, as if saluting my passage.

A lump forms in my throat as I realize I'm right around the half-way point of my hike. I've endured scrapes, scratches, and bruises. A banged-up knee. Cellulitis and bloating antibiotics. The trail has turned me around more times than I care to remember. But I'm still here. I'm still hiking. And I know that no matter what I encounter along the Ice Age Trail's remaining miles, I'll be able to conquer it.

~

The day is drawing to a close. Ed will be meeting us somewhere on a connecting road route once I finish this last trail segment, Chaffee Creek. Doug is waiting for me at its terminus in a way-side off I-39, an odd spot for a trailhead. I don't often drive along I-39, and I don't recall ever stopping at this particular wayside. I wonder how prominent the trail signage is. I wonder if some-one ever got out of their car to take a short stroll, stretch their legs a bit, and ended up on the Ice Age Trail. And I wonder if someone ever accidentally started hiking the Ice Age Trail and got so entranced with it that they just kept walking and never looked back.

Soon the thrum of the interstate assails my ears. The sound feels quite foreign to me, and a little chilling. I've jogged and walked hundreds of miles along roads so far, so it's not like I hav-en't heard the sound of traffic in three weeks. Yet the steady whine of cars and trucks along an interstate highway is a much louder, much more citified sound than you hear on relatively quiet state highways and county roads. While I find the incessant rumbling harsh and grating, a small thrill accompanies the sound, too. It means I'm making progress. I'm leaving the real remote stretches of trail, the lonely northern reaches of the state where people and restaurants and motels are few, and entering the more populated portion of Wisconsin. This is the territory I know. This is in my comfort zone.

Just as I'm pondering how the trail will safely lead me across four lanes of traffic hurtling down the road at speeds topping sixty-five miles per hour, I'm led under a bridge, then slipped into a giant, metal culvert. Chaffee Creek is burbling along the culvert's bottom; thankfully, a spacious, raised concrete sidewalk is affixed to one side, ensuring a dry passage. At least for today. Later, at the wayside, I use the women's restroom. It's the first time in twenty-one days that I've used an actual toilet while on the trail.

~

Ed pulls over on the side of Highway E, also known as Seventh Court, which runs north-south along I-39 south of Coloma. The wayside I passed through late in the day yesterday marks the top of the bifurcation, that bubble in the middle of the Ice Age Trail where the path splits in two for some seventy miles before rejoining at Devil's Lake. When you reach the wayside, you have a choice: head west if you're following the western bifurcation, go south if you're entering its eastern half. Like most people, I select the eastern side. It's shorter and features more trail segments. I made it a few miles along the eastern bifurcation yesterday, here along Highway E, before calling it a day. Now I'm resuming my journey.

As I climb out of the car, a buck suddenly clatters down the paved road, startling us both. I'm plenty used to seeing deer crashing through the woods by now, but not so much galloping down a road next to an interstate highway.

"Did you see that?" exclaims Ed, with the excitement of someone rarely in close contact with wildlife. I smile at him like a doting mother watching her child exclaim over the wonder of, say, a large fire truck zooming down the road, lights flashing. I've been eyeball-to-eyeball with plenty of wildlife since August 31, but to Ed, it's still a novelty.

I gather my gear and send Ed ahead with a wave, only to call him back almost immediately. My right heel is in pain—a lot of pain. The kind of pain you know you won't be able to put up with all day. I check out the offending area and see an old, drying blister there. Why in the world does this hurt so badly? It makes no sense. A bandage does nothing. Neither do the various other running shoes I try on. I've got one choice left: hike the day in my Keen sandals. I've worn my Keens around the house for an entire day plenty of times before. But how many steps would that equate to? Two or three thousand, perhaps? I'm going to be putting some thirty thousand steps on each foot today. Will my feet like the Keens that much? There's only one way to find out.

Surprisingly, I'm able to walk and even jog in my Keens. I roll through Packwaukee, a small, downtrodden town perched on the north side of Buffalo Lake, then pull up short when I reach a farm field filled with sandhill cranes. The large, majestic birds are emitting their strange, prehistoric-sounding cries, an unearthly sound that, once you hear it, you never forget. I spot another flock winging its way across the leaden sky; it drops into the field to join the others. As I stand mutely before this impressive site, a middle-aged man with a pack on his back walks up. He's section-hiking the Ice Age Trail. I don't think to ask why he's hiking along this connecting route if he's section-hiking the trail; I'm too absorbed in the birds. Within seconds, he is as well.

"I wonder if they're migrating now," I say.

"I suppose so."

Unbeknownst to me, Marquette County is a popular fall staging area for Wisconsin's sandhill cranes, tall, statuesque gray birds with six- to seven-foot wingspans, long black beaks, and a cherry-red patch on the crest of their heads. When cranes "stage," they gather together in great numbers to prepare for their migration. Here in Wisconsin, home to some fifteen thousand to twenty thousand sandhill cranes, the majestic birds will gather in groups of about two thousand on up to fifteen thousand or so. In other areas of North America, the number is much larger; more than five hundred thousand sandhill cranes, 80 percent of the world's total, stage along the Platte River in Nebraska every fall.

The birds are restless, perhaps sensing the long flight that lies ahead, and hop about the field distractedly as more and more flocks join them. The cranes have probably been here since early March, when the first warm puff of air drew them back north. Depending on the weather, they head out of town anytime from October through early December, transforming themselves into snowbirds. Their destination varies, depending on the weather; they'll fly only as far as necessary to get a little warmth. A long-term banding project undertaken by the Baraboo-based International Crane Foundation has revealed that that could mean anywhere from northwestern Indiana (which doesn't sound all that pleasant for a winter escape) to Kentucky, Tennessee, Georgia, or Florida.

While the state's largest sandhill crane staging area is Crex Meadows in Burnett County, two popular spots are right here in Marquette County: White River Marsh near Princeton and Comstock Marsh north of Montello. The field filled with flapping sandhills I'm staring at lies a bit southwest of the White River and Comstock Marshes, so it may not be a true staging we're witnessing. But whatever is going on is mighty impressive. At one point in history, Americans would never have been able to witness something so magnificent.

In the country's early days, sandhill cranes were hunted for their meat. Written accounts suggest cooked crane may have been proudly set down on the Pilgrims' first Thanksgiving table. Between hunting and, later, the destruction of their natural wet-land habitats, the stately birds were nearly wiped out. Eventually Americans realized what was going on, and in 1916 the federal Migratory Bird Treaty Act was signed into law, which basically stopped the hunting of migratory birds. It was almost too late; the crane population continued to plunge, reaching its lowest levels most likely in the 1930s, when it was estimated only about twenty-five nesting pairs remained in Wisconsin, plus a smattering in other Great Lakes regions. But the sandhill crane population rebounded, soaring to about 650,000 today, making it by far the most populous of the world's fifteen crane species.

The section-hiker and I snap several photos of the field, which resembles a crowded runway with waves of birds continually flying in and out, then part ways. The birds' harsh clackety-clacking echoes across the field, following me for quite some time.

It's Sunday morning. Ed will be handing me off later today to my younger sister, Alison, for three days of crewing. As I patter around the bathroom getting ready for the day's hike, I frown. The bottom of my left foot is tender—quite tender. Probably another blister to bandage up this morning. As Ed goes into the kitchen to grab some breakfast, I drop onto the bed with a sigh, tossing the medical kit next to me, ready to see what I'm dealing with today. Turning my foot sole-side up, I stare in utter disbelief. A large patch of skin just below the base of my toes is an angry reddish-brown, and a foul-smelling, sticky, dark liquid is seeping between my toes.

"Ed!" I wail. "I have cellulitis again! On the exact same spot, but in the other foot!"

Silence.

And then I hear, "My toof fell out!"

"What do you mean, your tooth fell out?" I yell, confused.

"My toof fell out! My front toof!"

This has to be some sort of bizarre dream. We continue yelling back and forth, me from the bedroom, Ed from the kitchen.

"What were you eating?"

"I juss took a bite of hamburger leff from dinner and it pfell out!"

This is too much for me to comprehend.

"How can a bite of hamburger pull out your front tooth?"

Ed appears in the bedroom doorway, his front lip curled over, his right hand carefully cupping something.

"My toof didn't come out of my mouf. My crown pfell opf."

He extends his hand toward me. But before he can open it up to show me his crown I shout in alarm, "No! Don't show me your crown or your mouth!"

A lot of people have anxiety dreams where they're standing naked in front of a crowd, or suddenly realize they're late for class and there's an exam that day. My anxiety dreams are of the dental variety, and I have several of them. Like the one where I have my braces taken off and my teeth instantly crinkle back into their original crooked formation. But the main dental dream I've had for decades, the one that haunts me the most, is—unbelievably— one where my front tooth falls out during the weekend, when all dental offices are closed. I wander around the streets, my lip curled down like Ed's, my hand cupping the lost tooth in the exact same manner, desperately seeking a dentist who happens to work on the weekends. If I get a glimpse of Ed's crown, or his ruined smile, I'll be scarred for life, I know it.

So while Ed calls our dentist's emergency number, I find out when the urgent care facility opens here in Wisconsin Dells. And I wonder why all of this is happening. It's not fair.

～

Thirty minutes later I'm pacing outside the front door of the Dean Care urgent care facility like a Black Friday shopper, waiting for the clinic's 9 a.m. opening. I'm going to rush through that door so I can be the first patient to be seen. I need to get my official cellulitis diagnosis, grab my meds, and get back on the trail. I will

not lose any more time because of these stupid skin infections.
I step through the door the minute it's unlocked, and soon I am
seated in an examination room. A young, bearded man enters,
a physician assistant. I explain the situation, extending my bare
foot toward his face.

He bends to lift it up so he can get a good look, then abruptly
pushes it back down toward the floor, his nose wrinkling. "Whoa,
I can smell that from here. That foot is definitely infected."

The physician assistant is a hiker himself, so he doesn't tell me
to stay off the trail for three days. But he warns me to protect the
skin, take all of my antibiotics, and keep a close eye on it. Cellulitis
can get out of hand pretty quickly and become quite dangerous.
I ask for a different antibiotic than I was given in Antigo, noting
how bloated it had made me. He acquiesces and prescribes probiotics along with the antibiotic to help keep me bloat-free.

It's about 10:30 a.m. when I step back on the trail just south
of Portage, Alison now crewing me, and one foot again swathed
in bandages.

~

Alison helps me gimp my way through Devil's Lake, across the
Wisconsin River via the Merrimac Ferry, through the Lodi-area
trails, and into Cross Plains, where I duck into the Ice Age Trail
Alliance headquarters to say hello, fill my hydration pack with
cold water, and use the restroom, the second time I use a real
toilet while on the trail. The staffers have been following my progress on my blog, *An Epic Ice Age Adventure,* and two of them pose
outside with me next to a wooly mammoth sculpture.

Later, on the connecting road route to the Valley View segment in Verona, I'm struggling to finish the day strong. This road
segment is quite hilly, and my quads are trashed. As I slowly plod
up yet another hill, a splotch of yellow catches my eye. "Shut Up
Legs" is spray painted onto the blacktop. A smile creeps onto my

tired face. A few paces later another smudge of yellow draws my eyes downward: "Smile This Is Fun." My smile broadens. What a great idea! The IATA must have painted these messages here to encourage us on. It's only when cyclists on triathlon bikes begin zipping by that it hits me. These are not love notes from the IATA to hikers. No, I'm hiking along part of the Wisconsin Ironman bike course. The 2013 race was held a few weeks ago, which is why the paint is so fresh, so unblemished. Those pedaling by are already preparing for the 2014 competition.

No matter. I'm viewing the messages as personal notes of encouragement to me. And with that, I power my way up and down the hills, trekking poles clicking furiously.

CHAPTER NINETEEN

Home-Field Advantage

Life is either a daring adventure or nothing.
—HELEN KELLER, AMERICAN AUTHOR,
LECTURER, AND POLITICAL ACTIVIST

"So, do you regret starting this hike?" John says with a slight smirk on his face.

"No!" I say, startled at the question. "It's been challenging for sure, but I don't regret it at all. I'm having a good time."

"Well, I think you're nuts," he says good-naturedly.

I'm staying the night with friends John and Liz Senseman because their Verona home is just a few steps from the trail. And while it's only thirty minutes back to our own home in Sun Prairie, I know going there would be far too distracting. I'd start going through the stack of mail I'm sure is growing on my desk. Obsess about how the house needs a good cleaning. Start worrying about the nearing holidays. I don't want to do that. I've done it all my life. And that's one of the magical things about long-distance hiking: you can get away from all of life's petty annoyances and distractions and obligations. For a few weeks it's just eat, hike, sleep.

Later that night, Andrew Schupp stops over. A chiropractor and avid runner, he has offered to give me an adjustment and do some soft-tissue work when I pass through the area. John and Liz graciously agree to let him set up shop in their living room. As I lie on his portable table, Andrew says, "How much weight have you lost so far?"

"What? I haven't lost any weight." Although my stomach has stopped expanding and my cheeks are a little slimmer, I still look pretty puffy. Patricia told me it would take a few weeks for the probiotics to do their work, and she was right. I know bloating doesn't equal fat, but it's hard to think of yourself as losing weight when you're still sporting a pretty noticeable set of chipmunk cheeks.

"Yes, you have. I can see your sartorius and gracilis muscles. I could never see those before."

Both are superficial muscles in the thigh. I'm not sure I believe him, but it's encouraging to hear. It makes up a bit for this second case of cellulitis.

Earlier this year, in April, I drove up to Trollhaugen Outdoor Recreation Area in Dresser. It was the site of the IATA's annual conference, which Jason suggested I attend. Each year's annual conference is open to the public, and newbie thru- and section-hikers often find its hiker panel helpful. Typically the panel is composed of the previous year's successful thru- and section-hikers, who talk about their experiences on the trail and offer helpful advice. I eagerly signed up. During the panel, I jotted down all sorts of useful information dispensed by the panelists:

1. If you walk for more than fifteen minutes and don't see a
   blaze, you're probably going the wrong way.

2. If you don't see a blaze in a while and are starting to worry, try turning around. You might spot a blaze for hikers going in the opposite direction. If you do, you'll know you're on the trail.

3. During tick season, be prepared to brush hundreds upon hundreds of ticks off of your arms and legs every five minutes, or else leave them on all day and remove them every night. [This one nearly caused me to scrap my planned thru-run until I learned, mercifully, tick season is roughly April to June, not September to October.]

4. Make sure to stop in at Dot's for a beer.

When uttered, the last helpful hint drew hearty applause and more than a few cheers of "Yeah, Dot's!" Dot's, I learned, is a tavern in Basco, an unincorporated town in Dane County. But it's not just any old Wisconsin tavern. Dot's opened in 1948 in the basement of Art and Dorothea Northwick's small home. Only it wasn't called Dot's then; it was called Woody's, because it belonged to a guy named Woody, not to the Northwicks. The Northwicks were just doing their neighbor a favor by locating his bar in their basement. Woody and his wife, Marie, had been operating a dance hall across the street from the Northwick residence when a fire swept through the structure and destroyed it. That was bad enough, but it would have been even worse, in Woody's eyes, to lose his prized liquor license. If he were to keep it, he had to find a way to continue serving alcohol. Immediately. Hence his request of Art and Dorothea, or Dot as she was known.

Woody's was a pint-sized joint, because the Northwick residence featured only a partial basement; the space measured about ten by twelve feet, further compacted by a six-foot ceiling. But it served the purpose: Woody and Marie were able to keep their liquor license. But apparently Woody and Marie quickly tired of running a bar in someone else's basement. Or maybe the North-wicks figured if there was a bar in their basement, they should be running it. Just a few years later, the Northwicks purchased Woody's and renamed it Art and Dot's.

Art and Dot's was quickly embraced by the Basconians and their neighbors, who often stopped by for a beer or just to shoot the breeze. But the bar really developed its character and enduring legacy after Art died in 1959 and the place became simply Dot's. Dot hadn't really been that involved with the bar when Art was alive. She was too busy caring for the couple's two daughters, Audrey and Shirley. But when Art passed, the bar became Dot's livelihood.

Although Dot was a quiet, reserved woman, her bar developed a friendly, cozy feel. It was the place local farmers headed every Sunday to play cards and throw back a cold one, which tasted even better with some warm cashews from the "nut huts" she carefully placed on the bar. If you were hungry for something more, you could grab a sandwich; Limburger and onion was the favorite, made with fresh Limburger procured from neighboring Monroe. Kids were welcome at Dot's, too. They loved to stop in after school or on weekends for the ice cream and candy bars Dot made sure to have on hand, the latter carefully stacked on a shelf along the back wall.

Although involved in the tavern business, which can be a rough, crude one, Dot made sure her bar was on the wholesome side. If you cursed inside her tavern, she would wag her finger in your face and tell you those words weren't allowed in her base-ment. It was the one and only warning you'd get. If you swore a second time you'd be shown the door.

At some point Dot swapped out the card tables for a bumper pool table, where games cost twenty cents. And she installed a Wurlitzer jukebox that played 45 rpm records, even though the machine only accepted fifty-cent coins. Since people didn't typically have fifty-cent coins on hand, Dot kept a stash of them behind the bar. At some point the jukebox records began skipping. Patrons sometimes became angry and would pound on the Wurlitzer. Dot didn't like that. She would tell them to knock it off and then, like Fonzie from *Happy Days*, she would walk over to the jukebox and rap it just so, and it would resume operating smoothly.

During the early years Dot's had no restrooms. Men would have to go outside to urinate, while Dot would let the women use her own bathroom, accessed by climbing a small, wooden, rickety set of stairs leading from the bar into her home. By 1969, it was clear Dot's needed its own restrooms. More space would be helpful, too. So a group of friends gathered with their shovels and hand-dug an addition to the bar that roughly doubled its size, easily affording space for restrooms and a longer bar.

Dot continued running her basement bar as her hair grayed and her limbs began to stiffen and creak. Not one to complain or ask for help, she did it all, from purchasing supplies and bookkeeping to bartending and cleaning. Even when the bar flooded, a frequent occurrence after it rained, Dot soldiered on, resolutely using a shop vac to suck up the water, then hauling it up the stairs and dumping it outside. Around age eighty, her hands and wrists sore from years of pouring drinks, Dot had surgery for carpal tunnel syndrome. The surgery took the wind out of her sails and, following a subsequent stroke, Dot passed the bar to her daughter, Shirley, before her death in 1995. She was eighty-two years old.

Like her mother, Shirley was rather stern and liked the way things were. She wasn't a fan of changing things to suit modern times. Her passion for the past included a fondness for the old Illinois Central rail line that ran through Basco three doors down from Dot's. Once a bustling track whose trains regularly shuttled grain, livestock, freight, and people, its passenger service ended in the 1960s, before all service was shut down in 1993. In 1997, the Department of Natural Resources began studying the possibility of transforming the old rail line into a recreational trail, the Badger State Trail. The master plan for its transformation was approved in 2006 by the Natural Resources Board. Shirley was not happy about this change and had mounted a little protest beforehand, erecting signs inside Dot's saying, "No to Trail! Keep the Rail!"

Her efforts proved fruitless, much to the appreciation of the hikers and bicyclists who now use the Badger State Trail. Today, the Ice Age Trail piggybacks along a portion of this recreational trail, from just north of Monticello to County Highway W west of Dayton, and again from County Highway A just south of Basco to Purcell Road near Verona. So the Ice Age Trail runs right near Dot's.

Shirley ran Dot's for seventeen years, until 2012, when the business was purchased by Kari and Dave Ace; Kari is Dot's granddaughter via Audrey. By that time Dot's had become an old-timers' bar, creased and worn with time. A handful of regulars still faithfully descended the stairs to sit at the old bar, resting their feet on its weathered barn-beam foot rails that came from a farmer down the road. But sadly, the place had lost its cachet.

The Aces quickly breathed fresh air into the small space, keeping all of Dot's original charm while incorporating a few modern touches. You can still play bumper pool for twenty cents at the original table, now an antique. Glasses cradling butterscotch discs are set on the L-shaped bar because, well, Dot always had candy on her bar. The Aces are trying to find some nut huts, too, to revive Dot's warm-cashew tradition. The Wurlitzer is gone, however, replaced by flat-screen TVs. And while most of the beer is of the Miller-Budweiser-Pabst variety, Dave does keep some craft brews on hand.

Thanks to these updates, Dot's boasts a growing, devoted fan base. The tiny basement tavern is listed as a stop on the Dane

County snowmobile map. Patrons buy "Dot's Tavern" T-shirts, cozies, hats, and the like, then take photos of themselves in or with the item when they travel. Later, they send the photos back to Dot's, where they're taped to a back wall. The "Dot's Tavern" logo has shown up in places as varied as Dublin, Puerto Rico, the Boundary Waters, Wrigley Field, Lambeau Field, Amsterdam, and even Petra, Jordan. The friendly watering hole holds monthly meat raffles, hosts bands, prepares catfish fries and chicken barbecues, and, best of all, sponsors the annual Dot Fest the third Saturday in August, a customer appreciation fête with live bands and free food.

No wonder all of these Ice Age Trail hikers hooted 'n' hollered for Dot's. I quickly decided that, speed record be damned, I'm stopping in for a beer at Dot's when I reach Basco.

⌇

Today is the day I'll be passing through Basco. As usual on this trek, the forecast is for a sunny, warm day in the upper seventies to lower eighties. But today, I don't mind. It will make that cold beer taste all the better. I'm retrieved this morning by my friends Ann Heaslett and John Selbo, runners extraordinaire. John is tall and lean, with a thick head of graying hair and round, wire glasses. Today he's dressed in a white race T-shirt, royal blue short-shorts, and gray running shoes. A neon-yellow running cap is pulled over his head. John, sixty-four, puts other sexagenarians to shame. He can still pound out a twenty-minute 5K (that's about a 6:30-per-mile pace for 3.1 miles) and earlier this year ran 2:37:34 in his hometown of Stoughton's famed twenty-mile race, the Syttende Mai Run. Impressive as his running résumé is, Ann's easily tops his. Ann is a petite five feet, three inches and can't weigh more than ninety-eight pounds soaking wet. Always cheerful, with an infectious, bubbly laugh, she dances across the ground like a ballerina when she runs, although a fierce competitive drive belies her graceful stride. In 2002, Ann won two national running titles: the USA 50-Mile Trail Championship (8:13:17) and the 24-Hour Championship, in which she covered 128.55 miles in a day. One day. Those accomplishments led to a spot on the 2002 US women's 100-kilometer team, which competed for the world championship in Belgium. The team nabbed the bronze medal, thanks in part to Ann being the third runner to score for the United States. Today Ann is dressed in her signature bright smile, a pair of navy shorts, and the blue, American-flagged USA shirt that formed part of her USA Track & Field 100K team uniform. The two stash all of my food and gear in Ann's compact blue 2012 Prius without saying a word about the quantity. As we head out, John Senseman calls after me, "Watch out in the Valley View section. Liz walks there a lot and says it's pretty overgrown and wet."

The Valley View segment, where I'm starting my day, begins at an easy-to-miss wooden post sitting innocuously at the end of the aptly named Ice Age Drive. It's not that the post is hidden; it actually sports not only a bright yellow blaze, but also a small, metal sign with a hiker on it plus the Ice Age Trail's official triangular sign dominated by the picture of a fierce woolly mammoth. But Ice Age Drive is a residential street in a tony enclave filled with sprawling, swanky homes. The street ends at a black metal gate barring entrance to a long driveway whose endpoint is obscured from view. A square sign proclaims "Private Driveway" in case you somehow miss spotting the gate, which features one of those boxes where, if the gate is closed, you have to press a button to call and gain admittance. Or maybe it holds a spot for a key or entry card. I don't know; I don't inspect the box. I'm too nervous about walking on what appears to be private property. As it turns out, the trail is snugged against a brown wooden fence that parallels the private driveway. And while it consists of an inviting, neatly mowed path in the grass maybe four feet wide, another posh home lies not too far to the right. I feel like I'll be trespassing. But this is clearly the trail, so off I go.

This particular spot in Dane County sits along a true piece of the glacier's terminal moraine. The Ice Age Trail leads me first through a patch of woods that's part of the five-acre Noll Valley Conservancy, a town of Middleton park. This section is an oak savanna, once one of Wisconsin's main plant communities, along with prairie and oak woodland. But clearing, overgrazing, and invasive species wiped out virtually all of Wisconsin's oak savannas, along with those in the rest of the Midwest, where only 0.01 percent of them remain undisturbed. Next it's uphill to a slice of the terminal moraine, today a sprawling stretch of prairie. As John Senseman warned, dense foliage slumps dispiritedly over the trail in numerous spots, burdened by a heavy serving of morning dew. Clad in my typical shorts, T-shirt, and calf sleeves, I'm soaked from the waist down by the time I emerge not a half mile later. Luckily the day warms quickly, and I'm soon dry.

John and Ann have decided to alternate running with me, if that's what you can call what I'm doing today. It's a bit embarrassing, actually. They're so talented, so much faster than me when we're out together for group runs. And what I'm doing now only remotely resembles running. For some reason, I haven't been able to really breathe deeply since the first week on the trail. I feel constantly taxed and out of breath, which I've assumed is simply fatigue from this gargantuan endeavor. So I jog a pitiful tenth of a mile, then walk. Jog a tenth of a mile, then walk. My cellulitis foot is pretty painful today, too. But I receive a boost of sorts when I spill out my woes to Ann as she's effortlessly gliding alongside me at the start of the Montrose segment, which at this point runs along the Badger State Trail.

"You're short of breath because all of that bloating from the antibiotics is excess gas pressing against your diaphragm," she says. "That gas is preventing you from taking in a deep breath.

Once the bloating goes down, you'll be able to breathe better and run faster and farther. I'm actually still a little bloated, too, from being on antibiotics since spring due to an infection."

Ann pats her tummy in sympathy. But instead of sporting a faux baby bump like I do, her belly is only a shade rounder than washboard-ab status. Still, I'm heartened to learn there's a reason behind my less-than-stellar performance out here on the trail.

It's early afternoon, the sun a bright ball of merciless heat, when we reach Basco, where John is waiting with the car. I'm sweaty and hot, perfect conditions to throw back a cold one at the infamous Dot's. I can't wait. The three of us walk abreast down Henry Road toward the tavern. It's the third home on the right, a small, white house with black shutters. The house has three sections. The far-right section is a single-story structure fronted by a screened porch. The middle, two-story section is dominated by a red-brick fireplace that runs from the roof to the ground in between two sets of windows, neatly bisecting them. The third part is clearly an add-on, a small, rectangular covered entranceway stuck to the side of the home: the entrance to the basement bar. A small, black-shuttered window eyes us from its street-side perch on the side of the entryway. Wedged above the window and below the low-hanging eave is a plain, rectangular sign that reads "Dot's Tavern." A much larger, newer-looking sign for the establishment towers on the front lawn. The round sign proclaims "Dot's Tavern" in a flourish of orange and white; above the *o* in "Dot's" is a caricature of the grande dame herself.

I eagerly walk up to the entrance and tug on the screen door. It's locked. A sign on the door notes the establishment opens at 3:30 p.m., and it's 1:34. I didn't get to have Steve's pizza at the Mondeaux Esker. I didn't get to see the Hillbilly Hilton. And now I'm not going to be able to have a beer at Dot's. I slump dejectedly on the weathered picnic table sitting in front of the entryway on a concrete slab. A rusted coffee can sits in its center, probably for cigarette butts. Then inspiration hits. I've got a beer stashed in my cooler, left over from the weekend when Ed was with me.

I grab the beer, a Leinenkugel Honey Weiss, and run over to Dot's front lawn. I'm going to have a beer at Dot's, and that's all there is to it. No one can stop me. I pop open the bottle and take a long drink. The beer is lukewarm and doesn't hit the spot. And really, it's probably not wise to quickly down a beer on a hot day when I'm trying to run-walk thirty-two miles. So after John snaps a photo of me appearing to heartily chug the beer, I gently place it in the coffee can and jog back to the trail.

I'm worried anew about my feet. No, not the cellulitis. Everything else. All of this endless walking and running has turned them into pulpy shreds of their former selves. Nearly every toe sports a puffy, fluid-filled area, and several nailbeds are tender to the touch. Nickel-sized blisters adorn my heels, while the bottoms of both feet ache in pulsing flashes. I try my best to help them endure this sudden boot-camp experience, which they didn't ask for or expect. At the end of every day's hike, I immerse them in an ice bath, then gently pat them dry. I carefully drain blisters, dab on antibacterial ointments, and daintily prop them up on pillows. I've heard your feet protest initially when embarking on a long-distance hike, then toughen up and take the daily onslaught. But mine seem caught in a painful, rebellious loop.

Every morning I gird them for battle, applying more salves, bandaging tender areas, making sure dry socks and extra shoes are easily accessible in the car in case my feet tire of the originals. They squawk for the first mile or two, then seem to settle in. I think, "Yes! I've finally broken them in!" But at the end of the day, the minute I decide I'm finished hiking, they begin to wail, and they don't stop for the rest of the night. What if I'm ruining them for life? Is this possible? Can you hike your toes or feet into permanent deformity or pain? I don't know the answer to this, and it's making me nervous.

~

My friend Terie Cebe joins Team Valderi for two days, shepherding me from Albany over to Janesville. I hike the twenty-ish miles along the same connecting route where Hiking Dude used his GoLite Chrome Dome Trekking Umbrella to shield himself from the unrelenting sun and heat, Papa Bear following behind with his cheap, black Walmart version. The temperatures are in the low eighties, not the sizzling nineties Papa Bear and Hiking Dude faced, but still uncomfortably warm. And I have neither a GoLite Chrome Dome Trekking Umbrella nor a cheap, black Walmart imitation to shield me from this misery. I begin chanting a mantra I adopted at some point in this odyssey: *One day at a time. One hour at a time. One step at a time. One day at a time. One hour at a time. One step at a time.*

I smile only once during the five or so hours I inch along this road, when I see a sign near the Disch Family homestead, established in 1975, proclaiming it to be Belly Acres. Mostly I grimly chant my mantra and wonder why, oh why, did all of these property owners never once think to plant some nice shade trees right here, next to the roadside? Sure, the roads are mainly for cars. But you never know when someone might need to hike twenty miles out here in the heat and sun. And then, you know, it would be nice if they could rest for a bit in the cool embrace of a leafy shade tree.

At the end of the day I make it through the Arbor Ridge segment on the west side of Janesville. *Janesville.* Another milestone. Tomorrow, as I wind my way through the city, I will pass the southernmost portion of the Ice Age Trail before beginning the march up north to Sturgeon Bay and the eastern terminus. I'll be more than two-thirds of the way finished. The thought of reaching Janesville was what pulled me along the beastly hot road all day. Now, I'm here. I did it.

One day at a time. One hour at a time. One step at a time.

A small sob escapes my lips as I pull my tight calf sleeves over my battered feet. Definitely the most painful times of the day are pulling these compression garments on in the morning and pulling them off at night. I turn my left foot over and inspect the infected patch of skin below my toes. It should be healing now, after six days on antibiotics. But it's not. It's still an angry purplish-red, still sore to the touch, and it seems as if, maybe, it's starting to spread. It's certainly not receding. I don't think this new, non-bloating antibiotic is effective. And that's not good. I know the smart thing is to deal with this now, while I'm in Janesville—a big city that has a lot of pharmacies and is in my HMO network. Sighing, I gather my innumerable belongings at the doorway of the inn and wait for Terie to pick me up.

The Ice Age Trail winds roughly fifteen miles through and around Janesville. It enters the city of sixty-five thousand on the west via the Arbor Ridge segment, which rolls through the Robert Cook Memorial Arboretum, a beautiful nook where ancient bedrock hills poke their heads skyward, Marsh Creek merrily burbling at their base. From there the Devil's Staircase segment pushes hikers deep into a steep wooded path high above the Rock River. In the 1930s, Civilian Conservation Corps (CCC) workers built trail in this very spot, but it deteriorated over time until it was rebuilt by the IATA with assistance from dozens of other groups and individuals. Part of the trail here passes along a stone retaining wall, believed to be set by the CCC. The Janesville segment proper starts at the city's attractive Riverside Park, making a U-shaped scoop through the city as it follows the Rock River on the west, then runs along part of the city's extensive recreational trail system from the base of the U and up its eastern arm. Somewhere at the base of the U, shortly after the trail crosses South Main Street, is the southernmost portion of the Ice Age Trail. The segment ends after leading you over bustling State Highway 26 via a pedestrian bridge on the city's far northeastern edge.

Janesville must really love the Ice Age Trail, I decide as I wind my way through the city on yet another steamy late-September morning. I pass several large, wooden trail signs making various boasts: "Hike or Ski the Glacier Path of 10,000 Years Ago on Wisconsin's 1000 Mile Long Trail."

And: "Part of Wisconsin's 1200 Mile Trail." (A little mileage dispute here.)

And, helpfully:

"Potawatomi State Park 324 Miles →"

"← Interstate State Park 776 Miles"

Green street-sign-like "Ice Age Trail" signs also line much of the recreational trail on the path's eastern route. I feel so welcomed by the kindly folks of Janesville that I almost forget today's main mission: call my doctor. Pulling out my cell phone when I'm almost at the segment's end, I spill out my problem to the nurse who answers: "I'm hiking eleven hundred miles. I had cellulitis in one foot, and now I have it in the other. The antibiotics I had for my first round of cellulitis worked well but caused a lot of bloating, so I asked for a different kind for my current bout. It's not working, though. Will my doctor please call in a prescription for the original antibiotics I had? The Whitewater Walgreens would be great."

She agrees to inform my doctor of my request, but cautions that physicians normally don't prescribe antibiotics over the phone. I know this. But I've known my physician a long time. He's a runner and competitor, too. I'm hoping he trusts me and will prescribe the medicine. All I can do is cross my fingers and wait.

꘎

Milton is softly thump, thump, thumping. The beat pulses rhythmically, pulling me along the trail. Soon, strains from a brass section float across the still air, and I realize I'm hearing band music. And that this is the first music I've heard in twenty-eight days. The trail leads me past Milton Senior High School, the source of the music, just as my phone chimes. It's my doctor.

"I'd really prefer you have someone look at your foot," he says sternly. "Can't you find a clinic in Janesville?"

"I'm already past Janesville, and the clinic in Whitewater will be closed by the time I get there tonight," I say in what I'm hoping is my most pleasant, reasonable, persuasive voice. "I already lost a few days when I first got cellulitis in Antigo. I can't afford to stop hiking again. I only have one week left, and then I'll set the women's thru-hike record."

"You won't be setting any records if you've got something worse now, like MRSA," he retorts. "That can be life-threatening, you know."

I don't know much about MRSA, or Methicillin-resistant Staphylococcus aureus, but I do know it's considered to be a "superbug"—some mutant kind of staph infection that's resistant to many antibiotics. I'm pretty positive I don't have MRSA; if I did, surely I'd have a fever and feel tired and achy and things like that. The bottom of my foot just hurts.

In the end, he agrees to prescribe my initial, harsh antibiotic if I promise to see a doctor as soon as I can.

I promise.

But I don't add that my definition of "as soon as I can" is "when I finish hiking the Ice Age Trail."

～

Skritch, skritch, skritch, skritch. Someone's coming up behind me. Someone who's running. Being a runner myself, I know the sound. Being a runner myself, the sound makes me immediately want to start jogging. But I'm just getting warmed up for the day. Walking is better. Skritch, skritch, skritch, skritch. Someone is running along the gravel shoulder and glides past me on the left. It's a middle-aged woman dressed in a brightly colored running skirt and jog bra. We nod at each other and I watch her quickly, effortlessly float down the road. Just when she's about to fade from view, she makes a sharp turn to the right, crossing to the other side of the road. What is she doing? A few steps later I see—she's drinking from some kind of roadside fountain.

When I reach the same spot, the woman now gone, I see the "fountain" is actually a metal pipe driven into a pile of rocks, from which cool, crystal-clear waters are gushing. I drink deeply, then read the large, adjacent sign: "Flowing Well. In 1895 this well was hand dug by Adam Channing. The original depth was 55'. It has been flowing steadily to this day." A small shelter with two benches sits back in the shade, while a compact parking area is adjacent to the well. I soon see why, as a car pulls up and two young people hop out, empty milk jugs in hand, and begin capturing some of this bounty. I wish I could fill my hydration pack's bladder with the Flowing Well's pure waters—it appears it should be a mandatory rite of passage when you're on the trail—but since I've just started hiking, my pack is full. So I wave to the young folks and continue on. Minutes later, I'm ensconced in the Southern Kettle.

～

Created in 1937, Kettle Moraine State Forest stretches about sixty miles. But it's not one contiguous forest. Instead, it's composed of a Northern Unit and a Southern Unit, both about thirty miles in length, with a gap in between. The twenty-two-thousand-acre Southern Unit runs from just southeast of Whitewater to Dousman. The thirty-thousand-acre Northern Unit stretches from Kewaskum to Glenbeulah. Both areas are pitted with kettles and dimpled with lakes, studded with pine woods and hardwood forests, alive with the sounds of rustling prairie grasses, warbling songbirds, burping frogs, and more. Well over two million people come to the Kettles every year to recreate. This is where my family first hiked when we moved here from Chicago. This is where one of the first Ice Age Trail segments was built. This is where I collected mushrooms for an eighth-grade science project. Where I ran my first (and second, third, fourth, and fifth) fifty-kilometer trail races. Where I fell in love with hiking. Kettle Moraine, in a way, is home.

Maybe it's because I'm thrilled to be on my home turf, or because I have new antibiotics, or because I'm heading back north. Whatever the reason, I'm able to easily power through the Kettle's first segment, Whitewater Lake. Through Blackhawk and Blue Spring Lake. Through Stony Ridge, Eagle, and Scuppernong. Past scores of families, couples, and Boy Scout troops—it's a gorgeous early-fall weekend—and past a man clad in camouflage toting a rifle. I tug the brim of my blaze-orange cap absent-mindedly as he tells me he's hunting squirrels.

The Southern Kettle behind me, I race toward her Northern twin, rolling through Waterville, Lapham Peak, Delafield, Hartland, and Merton, before skidding to a halt before a concrete viaduct on Funk Road (today East Kilbourne). A colorful mural painted on its bottom half is obfuscated by angry swirls of harsh, black graffiti. But two messages worm their way out of the dark tangle and catch my eye: "Play Dirty!"—I recognize this as trailspeak for "Get your ass out on the trail!"—and "Don't Give Up."

᷄

My parents are picking me up tomorrow. They will be crewing me the next six days—my final six days.

Over the last week, the miles have suddenly flown by with terrifying speed. Where once I was excited to file away the day's completed Ice Age Trail Atlas pages—*Today I went through Maps 44f, 45f, 46f, and 47f!*—I now slowly, reluctantly place the maps I've completed in my folder. I realize with a sickening feeling that I don't want the trail to end. That is, I do and I don't. I certainly want to finish and to set the record. Not to mention, I want to be back home with Ed, to let my poor, battered feet heal, and to sleep in my own bed.

And yet.

I'm addicted to being outside every day, letting the fresh air infuse every pore, my heart, my soul. I love exploring Wisconsin on such an intimate level, admiring the state's fresh, supple beauty as well as its gnarled, aged charms. After a lifetime of deadlines and duties and worries and cares, it's so liberating to step onto the trail day after day and have one duty, and one duty only: to walk. So many people quizzed me ahead of time about this venture. *What will you think about all day? Won't you be bored? Lonely? Scared?* Now, I'm not even sure how I'll answer them when I get back home. I don't know what, exactly, I've been thinking about all day, every day, but my mind never has a chance to be bored or blank. There are always far too many things to see and ponder. To be in awe of and to salute.

No, I'm not ready to step off the trail. And yet, I must march on.

CHAPTER TWENTY

My Journey Ends

Returning home is the most difficult part of long-distance hiking; you have grown outside the puzzle, and your piece no longer fits.
—CINDY ROSS, AUTHOR, *A WOMAN'S JOURNEY ON THE APPALACHIAN TRAIL*

"Hi, sweetie pie!" My dad sweeps me up in a bear hug. "I can't wait to start hiking with you. I brought my trekking poles." Dad points to a set tucked carefully in the backseat.

As he begins loading my bags and boxes into the car, my mom whispers, "He thinks he's going to hike with you every day. He's been practicing for the last week."

A wave of panic washes over me. Although my father is in fantastic shape for seventy-nine, he certainly can't walk thirty-plus miles in a day. And he doesn't run at all. He might even be wearing dress shoes right now for all I know; I'm not sure he owns a pair of tennis shoes. Where did he get the idea we'd be hiking together all day?

I'd stayed overnight with my friend Laurie; she presses a few extra mini bagels into my hand as I climb into the backseat.

"Okay," says Dad, settling in with the maps while my mother points the car toward West Bend. "Where should we stop for breakfast?"

Another wave of panic.

"Dad, we can't stop for breakfast. I'm trying to set a speed record. Plus, I already ate breakfast. Didn't you eat something before coming here?"

"Your mother said there wasn't enough time."

"Well, as soon as you drop me off on the trail, you two can find a spot and eat breakfast. In the meantime, these should tide you over." I hand Dad the mini bagels.

This will be an interesting six days.

My parents are patiently sitting in their white sedan in the trail parking lot on Wildwood Road at the end of the Southern Kewaskum segment when I jog up to them, practically snarling with frustration.

"The grass was really overgrown in there, and it was really wet! All of my bandages came off!" I tear my shoes and socks off and rummage around the car for a new pair of each. "Where's the medical kit? I need the medical kit!" My parents scurry around, trying to help their child as any good parents would, ignoring my temper tantrum.

"Where are the water jugs? I need water!"

My mom quickly hands me a jug of water. I pour a generous portion of it over my head and can actually feel a cloud of steam escape into the air. It's only midmorning, but it's another scorcher; the forecast is for the temperatures to soar past eighty degrees. Not only that, but it's quite humid today. My face is beet red.

I spend more time than usual in this pit stop, rebandaging my feet, changing socks and shoes, chugging water and more water. Finally, ready to go again, I've calmed down.

"I'm sorry I was so crabby," I say contritely. "I'm just really sick of this heat. I haven't had one cool day yet."

"That's okay, dear," my mom says. "Where do you want us to meet you next?"

A major perk of having family crew you: even if you act like a jerk, they still have to love you.

∾

For the past month, I've been waiting patiently, and then not so patiently, for autumn to make her splashy appearance. I had envisioned watching a Technicolor movie playing out as I danced along the trail, with summer's rich vegetation fading into the background as autumn began to paint a canvas in fetching crimson, tangerine, and buttery hues. But for most of my journey, the landscape has stubbornly refused to shed its green coat. Its pigment has faded a bit, and the vegetation is emitting the dry rustling of the aged, but no striking pops of color have appeared.

Until today.

Climbing the hilly Kewaskum segment, I emerge atop a hill, part of the Roman and Mercedes Otten Preserve, which affords me sweeping views of the countryside. I'm supposed to be able to see Kewaskum and Campbellsport to the north and the Dundee Kame and Kettle Moraine State Forest to the northeast, but all I see is a beautiful palette of color. I snap photo after photo, then remember I'm on a mission. Placing my camera back in my pack, I skip along the trail, back into a heavily wooded stretch. A bit later the trail pushes me out of the woods and atop a hill—one of several gentle rollers forming Sunburst Ski Area. I barrel down the hill, past dry snow cannons pointing giant, unseeing eyes toward the sky. Past lifts baking in the day's heat, their red chairs empty and forlorn, longing for the day when these hills are covered in a blanket of white, and the air is ringing with laughter as they power skiers up the runs: White Carpet, Pussy Foot, Holy Moly, Four

Forty, Bull Run, Snow Bowl. A yellow sign quietly hanging from a black, metal post instructs "Prepare to Unload," so I do, jogging off the grass, across the parking lot, and onto Prospect Drive.

Less than ten minutes later I'm crossing thrumming State Highway 45 and about to enter a brand-new two-mile extension of the Milwaukee River segment. I'll probably be one of the first to hike it, which is rather exciting. But as I wander through the new addition's fields and snake through its tight forestland, I see a segment that appears to be in limbo. The path is freshly marked with canary-colored blazes, but the footing isn't uniformly well groomed, and a partially constructed boardwalk sits off to one side like a discarded puzzle piece, its naked top missing the majority of its two-by-eights. It's clear the extension was never finished.

After I complete my thru-run, I'll learn this Day of the Abandoned Boardwalk marked the start of one of the year's most noteworthy news stories, one of which I was totally unaware while on the trail: the federal government shutdown. The federal government shutdown of 2013, the first such shutdown in seventeen years, began on October 1, the day I passed through the almost-completed Milwaukee River addition. It would last sixteen days, during which time all 401 national parks were closed and more than twenty-one thousand national park staff members were furloughed. National Scenic Trails, however, remained open, so my hiking was legit. However, even if the National Scenic Trails had been closed, no government employees would have been around to kick us off the trails—if they could even locate us.

While the National Scenic Trails remained open, the IATA told its trail-building volunteers to please set down their saws and Pulaskis during the shutdown. Trail volunteers receive medical and liability coverage through Volunteers-In-Parks, a program run by the National Park Service. The program was not in effect during the shutdown, so it wasn't safe for them to be out there. But the trail-building that was affected by the shutdown was the St. Croix

Falls segment, not the Milwaukee River one. So what about that forlorn boardwalk I saw? Its abandonment was due to a local permitting issue. The boardwalk-in-progress would end up sitting there, half-completed, through the winter and into early spring.

I finish the day hiking the Parnell segment, part of which encompasses the Parnell Tower Trail I first hiked as a newly minted Wisconsinite in 1970. It was here that my mother had us belt out "The Happy Wanderer" as we marched through the woods. It was this spot that birthed me as a hiker. That birthed me as Valderi. When I step off the trail and into my parents' car, I quietly say, "Thanks, Mom." She smiles back at me, a bit puzzled.

&

The Parnell segment seamlessly transitions into the Greenbush segment, keeping me carefully sheltered in the Northern Kettle's green bosom the next morning. Then suddenly it ejects me from the woods and onto the Old Plank Road Trail fronting Highway 23. The Old Plank Road Trail rolls about seventeen miles from the city of Sheboygan to Greenbush along Highway 23. It was one of the first recreational trails in the United States to share the right-of-way with a four-lane divided highway. At one point the trail moves me from the paved Old Plank Road Trail onto a grassy patch immediately south of the highway; a neatly mowed path in the grass directs me onward. Soon I'm pointed north across the highway and back into the woods. For sixteen years I regularly traveled State Highway 23 from Madison to Sheboygan to visit my parents. Yet while I was aware of the Old Plank Road Trail, I never once noticed the Ice Age Trail quietly unrolling along its side.

&

I'm trudging up a steep hill just north of the Kettle's northernmost reaches, taking my own connecting road route to the next patch of trail, La Budde Creek east of Elkhart Lake, when I see it. "Camp

Evelyn. Serving Girls Across America Since 1912. Est. 1948." So this is where Camp Evelyn is. A series of painful memories cascades into my mind like a waterfall.

It was 1971. We had lived in Sheboygan almost a year. I desperately wanted to go to camp that summer—Girl Scout camp. The one nearby was called Camp Evelyn. I thought the name sounded just lovely. I didn't want to go to Camp Evelyn because I was excited by the idea of camping, swimming, and canoeing. I didn't want to go to Camp Evelyn because I'd always wanted to roast weenies over a campfire, stuff s'mores into my face, or earn a boatload of merit badges. I wanted to go to Camp Evelyn for one reason, and one reason only: to go horseback riding. I had never been horseback riding before, but it sounded like the most exciting activity in the world. Horseback riding wasn't a regular part of Girl Scout camp, but you could go if you paid a little extra. Our family didn't have much money, but for some reason my mother agreed I could go to camp *and* go horseback riding. It was a dream come true—or so I thought.

The much-awaited day finally arrived. I'd carefully packed my clothes, plus a new box of the prettiest pale-green stationery; it came with a colorful set of daisy stickers to help seal the envelopes shut. I planned to write a lot of letters to my parents and grandparents during my week at camp, telling them how much fun I was having. The drive to Camp Evelyn seemed to take forever as we wound along all sorts of small, country roads, but eventually we arrived. My mom unloaded my bag, gave me a quick hug, and vanished.

I found my tent, stretched over a dusty, wooden platform, which housed several girls plus a teen counselor. I picked out one of the empty metal beds and began to lay out my sleeping bag and pillow when I noticed a large depression in the center of my mattress. It didn't look very comfortable. Maybe they could find me another bunk, or at least a different mattress.

"Excuse me," I said timidly to the teen counselor, a stern-looking brunette with a long, sleek ponytail. "There's a big dip in the middle of my bed." I slowly extended my index finger toward the indentation to make sure she saw it.

She gazed at me a second, then narrowed her eyes as if I was already the most annoying camper of the entire summer. "Yeah, I see it," she said, then laughed harshly. "You're going to get sway-back after sleeping in that all week!" And with that proclamation, she abruptly walked outside, ponytail swinging.

I had no idea what swayback was, but I didn't want to get it. I imagined it as some Quasimodo-like hump that would slowly rise out of the middle of my back until it was the size of a basketball by next week's pickup date. Terrified, I headed out toward the baseball diamond, where we were told to assemble for our first activity: kickball. I loved kickball, and by the time I was up to kick I'd forgotten all about swayback. Thwump! My foot contacted the ball, which flew straight above the grass in a near-perfect line drive. I raced toward first base and easily got on.

The first baseman, a pigtailed girl with a smattering of freckles across her face, tapped my shoulder. "There is a worm on you," she said matter-of-factly.

"Help! Get it off! Get it off! Get it off!" I began flailing my arms and hopping and dancing all around first base. "Get it off! Get it off!"

"Well, hold still if you want me to get it off you," she said, unfazed at both the worm and my freak-out. I paused, my heart hammering, as she reached down to the hem of my T-shirt and pulled off a tiny green worm. Then she extended her hand toward me. "Do you want to see it?"

"No! Get it away! Get it away! Get it away!" And I began my crazy flailing again until I saw her flick it into the grass. But even though the worm was gone, the game was ruined.

That night, I scooted over to the very edge of my bed so that no part of my body touched the swayback-birthing divot in my mattress. Then I tried to go to sleep, despite my hammering heart. So far I really didn't like Girl Scout camp.

The following day did not go any better. We were told we'd be going canoeing, which initially excited me, but instead of paddling around Crystal Lake, all we got to do was perform a scary safety drill. We had to climb into the canoe in pairs, then rock our canoe until it dumped us into the lake. Treading water, we had to swim underneath the capsized canoe and pop our heads into the air bubble formed by the hull floating on the lake's surface. After the canoe stunt, I decided I was going home. I still desperately wanted to go horseback riding, but not if it meant five more days in this place. I slowly walked up to my counselor, then cleared my throat. She looked up from her book and glared at me.

"I want to go home," I said quietly. "Please call my mom."

"You can't go home!" she barked. "No one goes home. You have to stay all week. I am not calling your mom."

Somehow I made it through the next few days until Thursday. Horseback riding day! Those of us who paid to ride excitedly boarded a bus bound for the stables. I said a little prayer that I would get to ride a butterscotch-colored Palomino, my favorite breed of horse, although I would have been happy with any kind, really, except maybe an Appaloosa, the one breed of horse I thought was ugly. It always looked to me like someone dropped a can of paint on their backside. I also wished for a horse with a really cool name.

At the stables, the owners quickly paired girls with horses. Karen got a pretty chestnut horse named Hiawatha. Laura got a jet-black beauty named Geronimo. Susie got a white horse with a silvery mane named Chief. And I was given a sour-looking Appaloosa named Cochise. Cochise is the name of a brave Apache warrior who took on the American government in 1861. But I didn't know this at age nine. I'd never heard the name before, and I thought it was as ugly as the jagged patch of spots on Co-chise's rump.

Someone helped me into the saddle, and our little train of rid-ers set off, Cochise and I bringing up the rear. We weren't more than a tenth of a mile from the stable when Cochise abruptly turned around and began galloping back to the stable while I screamed and hung onto the saddle horn as tightly as I could. Our leader heard the commotion and came racing back to get us, pulling a sullen Cochise back into his place at the end of the line. The rest of the ride, I clutched the saddle horn in a death grip, petrified Cochise would again try to run back to the stable.

When our family's boxy, beige Ford Country Sedan pulled up Camp Evelyn's long, gravel drive Saturday morning, I jumped in before my mother could get out, declaring, "I hate camp, and I'm never going back!"

Today is the first time I've seen Camp Evelyn since my one-week incarceration here in the summer of 1971. It actually seems like a sweet little place.

~

Not too far past Camp Evelyn is the La Budde Creek segment, a dried-out tangle of vegetation today in late September, a month that is still belching oven-hot blasts of air across the landscape. I'm jogging strongly today and pass a few other runners out on the trail. One middle-aged man is running toward the La Budde trail-head as I'm coming off. Tanned and shirtless, with dark sunglasses shading his face, he stares at me a second longer than normal, then calls out, "How many miles have you done so far?"

I pause a second, confused. Does he know who I am? Has he read my blog? "About one thousand," I say.

"No, no," he says, a bit annoyed. "I mean today. I've seen you on another road earlier."

I toss off some random number, and we both continue on

our way. It's interesting that he gave no reaction when I said I'd run a thousand miles, surely an unusual response to his question. Perhaps he thought I was reporting my yearly or lifetime mileage. But clearly he never once considered I might be thru-hiking the Ice Age Trail. He probably thinks the Ice Age Trail is this 3.1-mile La Budde Creek segment here in his hometown. He doesn't get it. No one does.

~

The Ice Age Trail in Manitowoc County circa 2013 is mainly one long patch of asphalt. The only dirt paths here are in the Dunes, Point Beach, Mishicot, and Tisch Mills segments—some 13 miles out of the county's total of 68.6 Ice Age Trail miles—although another 12 or so miles of urban trail run through Manitowoc, Two Rivers, and Mishicot. Because of this, most Ice Age Trail hikers think of the county as one long road walk. Dad hasn't mentioned hiking with me since the first morning he and my mom picked me up, but I'm thinking today, when I enter Manitowoc County, might be a good time for him to get a little taste of the trail. It'll just be a connecting road route, I know, but I won't have to worry about him stumbling on technical singletrack. Plus the terrain here is flattening out as I near the shores of Lake Michigan, a glacial by-product of stupendous proportions, so he won't have to march up a steep incline. I just need to make sure the three of us stay close together this afternoon so he can quickly hop out of the car and join me when I find an appropriate spot.

I jog up to my parents' white sedan on South Cedar Lake Road near Millhome, shortly after crossing from Sheboygan to Manitowoc County. Studying the map, I decide a good spot to hike together will be along Moraine Road, which appears to be one that should be less traveled. I don't tell him, though, in case it doesn't look appropriate when we get there. I simply show him and my mom the spot on the map where they should pull over and wait for me next: the intersection of Moraine Road and County Highway XX. As the navigator, Dad carefully marks the spot on the map. Then they climb back into the car and motor off. I wave good-bye, watching as they approach West Washington, where they need to turn to reach Moraine. But the car chugs right past the road, continuing along South Cedar Lake. Two minutes later it comes puttering back toward me, this time taking the correct route.

As I near Moraine Road, I notice the street sign at this intersection is set at a cockeyed angle, making it difficult to read. I instinctively know my parents missed this turn. Sure enough, they're not waiting at our rendezvous point, which is a shame because Moraine Road is, indeed, a nice spot for walking. Fishing out my cell phone, I try calling them, but I don't have cell service. I'll just have to keep going, trusting that at some point they'll figure out the correct path.

I'm almost finished with the stretch along Moraine Road, nearing the spot where it hits XX at a T intersection, when my phone buzzes. At last!

"Hi, Melanie," Dad says. "We missed the turn on Moraine Road, so now we're parked at the intersection of Moraine and Highway XX."

I glance up at the intersection, which is straight ahead of me. There are no cars there.

"No, you're not."

"Yes, we are. We're at XX and Moraine," Dad insists.

"No, you're not, because I'm walking up to that intersection as we speak, and you're not there."

Silence.

"Then where the hell are we?" Dad shouts in frustration.

"I don't know where you are. I only know you're not at XX and Moraine. Can you get out and read me the names on the road signs?"

Luckily, they're quite close, and we soon reconnect. But Highway XX is not a good one for hiking. I'll have to find another spot for my dad to join me. I find it at the end of the day, on a stretch of Marken Road just north of Carstens Lake Road, where the road unrolls northbound in a gentle swell. A soft sunset to the left is bathing the dying cornfields in a warm, golden glow.

"Hey, Dad," I call out when I reach the car. "Want to hike this last mile with me?"

Dad lifts his head from the Ice Age Trail Atlas he is studying, a grin spreading across his face. "Oh, yes!" he says, immediately scrambling through their belongings to find his trekking poles. So as the sun continues its glide down the western sky, Dad clicks his way along the road next to me, chattering animatedly about how exciting my adventure is, how beautiful our state is, how great the Ice Age Trail is. Our pace is slow and relaxed, just a father and daughter enjoying a pleasant fall walk in eastern Wisconsin. There's something deeply satisfying about sharing the trail with my father like this, even if the trail here is a nondescript road in Manitowoc County.

When we reach my mom and the car, now pulled over on a field access road, my dad tosses his trekking poles inside and collapses into the front seat. "I'm exhausted!" he puffs. "I don't know how you do it all day." Smiling, I kiss the top of his head and climb into the backseat.

◦∽

Thursday, October 3. The Manitowoc County skies are painted a light pewter this morning, providing a welcome reprieve from the past month's near-constant sunshine and heat. I haven't been on the trail for more than an hour or two when I spot a small green-and-white sign: Pine River Dairy. I'm not actually on the IATA's prescribed connecting route; I'm on English Lake Road, taking a slight shortcut that saves me about 1.5 miles. The shortcut also runs past the Pine River Dairy, a favorite of hikers (and many others, I presume) because of its twenty-five-cent ice cream cones. They also sell more than 250 varieties of cheese here. Unfortunately for me, it's not quite 10 a.m., my stomach is still full of my morning breakfast, and for once I'm not hot and in search of cold food or drink. I contemplate stopping in anyway, since I missed out on the Mondeaux Esker pizza, Hillbilly Hilton, and Dot's, but I decide to continue on. I do have a record to set.

My parents are waiting up ahead as wisps of fog begin swirling above the ground. Their car is pulled into a farm driveway rather than along the roadside, as a safety precaution. A middle-aged couple, presumably the farmers, is standing in the driveway chatting with my folks. The couple begins cheering as I jog up; clearly, my parents have informed them about my adventure.

The man points out a large herd of elk in a field across the road, telling me the elk had just been bugling. If I've never heard elk bugle, he says, it's pretty cool. He motions me to follow, so I grab my camera from the car, and we both jog down the road, along the fence line. He shows me the herd's musclebound bull while I furiously snap photos, praying the elk will again bugle so I can capture the sound in a video. But a thick, velvety silence blankets the air, courtesy of the heavy clouds hanging low in the sky. I need to keep moving, so I ask the man if he will please take my camera back to my parents, plus the wrapper from the energy bar I've just eaten. He quickly agrees.

As he turns and jogs back toward his farm, my camera bouncing around his neck and an energy bar wrapper clasped in one hand, I call out to his wife, "I'm making your husband my temporary crew member!"

She starts jumping up and down in the driveway, fists pumping wildly in the air, then shouts, "We're part of this too, now! We're Dave and Margie by the elk! Don't forget!"

I wave good-bye to "Dave and Margie by the elk" and trot

down the road. Moments later a series of haunting, squeaking screams drift across the air, sharply cutting through the fog. The sounds are at once mechanical yet human, metallic yet vocal, unnerving and arresting. It's the elk. They're bugling. A shiver runs through me. The bugling sounds exceptionally prehistoric. And exactly like the sound I would expect a woolly mammoth to have made. Right here in this very spot, during the Ice Age.

∾

It's the first Friday in October, and the rain can't decide if it really wants to fall. So it falls to the earth in a smattering of increasingly thick drops, then abruptly stops. Then rains down in a thick sheet for a few minutes again, and stops. When I reach tiny Mishicot, everything is dripping, as if the town just stepped out of the shower. Water plops down from trees, rooftops, overhead wires, street signs. Walking along Washington Street past Mishicot High School, long strands of white, soggy toilet paper hang disconsolately from the trees dotting several lawns, too water-logged to wave in the breeze. That's right, it's homecoming season. The toilet-papered trees must mark the homes of some of the football players. Indeed, a sign at the high school announces homecoming is this weekend. Halloween is fast approaching as well; home after home is festively decorated with fat, orange pumpkins, grinning ghosts, and wart-nosed witches.

How quickly, how easily, landmark events slip from your consciousness when you're on the trail. What else is going on out in the real world that has slipped my mind, now that I'm preoccupied daily with following maps and markers, plotting rendezvous points with my crew, and picking my way across the trail as quickly as possible? The answer comes soon enough when I pass a giant, inflatable Packers player, grimacing sternly at some unseen foe as he sways gently from his tethered post on a front lawn. That's right. It's football season. And I have absolutely no idea how the Packers are doing this year. I contemplate these events—homecoming, Halloween, the Packers season—from some distant, detached perspective, not quite able to remember what it is, exactly, that makes these events so compelling. Right now, here on the trail, they all seem rather silly and inconsequential.

I wind through Mishicot then head out of town and up a wooded, thirty-foot-tall esker. Not too far from here, a little to the north, a much larger esker curls along land belonging to a dairy operation. The towering esker formed a barrier of sorts across the property, so at some point in time the landowner, seeking easier access to agriculture fields lying to the south, had a chunk of it cut away, the sand and gravel that had been sitting in its belly for the past ten thousand years likely ending up as anonymous fill. An understandable action, yet a tragedy. Wisconsin is considered to have some of the world's best glacial landforms, yet how many have been destroyed? And how many more will be ruined in the future?

Two hours later I jog up to my parents, waiting along Highway B at what should be the start of the Tisch Mills segment. Mom says they can't find it. I study the map. It should be right here all right, a little south of Highway BB and north of Freedom Court. But all we see are a series of homes set far back from the road on spacious lots. There does appear to be a path mowed into someone's lawn; it runs parallel to the road, then climbs a little hill before jogging toward the back of the property. It could be the trail, but it could also be a path marking the property boundary, or the family's own route to their backyard. I trot back and forth between Freedom Court and Highway BB, finally deciding to try the path. If someone yells at me for trespassing, I'll apologize profusely. Once I'm actually on the path, a Carsonite post materializes at the top of the hill. The trail. From my lofty perch I wave my parents on ahead.

The trail here is quite pretty, quickly moving you along the mowed path and into a small pocket of woods in back of the homes. Not too soon after you enter the woods, the trail jumps across Tisch Mills Creek; at the crossing, a wooden sign scolds, "Wading would be safer than walking on rocks." I believe the sign, especially as my feet are sheathed in plastic bags. (I'd pulled out the bags after the guidebook warned this segment has many wet areas.) But the sign is also a challenge, so I skip across the rocks in my plastic-bagged feet, with only a slight bobble as I hop back onto land. Emerging from the woods, I'm formally greeted by the Tisch Millsians via a large sign:

Welcome to
Tisch Mills
No Mayor—No City Council
Life Is Good!

I love the humor found along the trail. I don't want to leave, although I know I must. Later that night, I climb the steps of the Red Forest Inn, the Two Rivers B and B where I'll be spending the night. Owner Kay Rodewald has placed a framed whiteboard sign on a chair sitting next to the front door. The sign welcomes the night's guests and lists their names and hometowns. I find my entry, which has an asterisk next to it. At the bottom of the sign, the asterisk is attached to this message: "Congratulations on Living Your Dream!" A lump swells in my throat. I hadn't thought of my adventure in quite those terms, but that is exactly what I'm doing. I'm living a dream. How many people are lucky enough to get to do that in their lifetime? How many are brave enough?

∼

I direct my parents onto Clark Street in Algoma, reassuring them they'll like the food here. I hope I'm right, as they're not the most daring diners. But I've wanted to eat at Skaliwag's ever since I learned about the place, and what better time to do so than the night before I'm going to finish hiking the Ice Age Trail? Skaliwag's is a highly acclaimed restaurant, creatively billed as serving "Food that's five star in a crazy little dive bar." Indeed, as we pull up to the restaurant, it looks a bit, um, low-brow. And it definitely lacks curb appeal.

Skaliwag's is squished into the lower level of a small, two-story building; dirty, worn tan shingles cover the exterior. The front door is set off far to the right, while an octagonal window is set just to the left of center. But all you can really see in the window is a lighted sign saying Open. The innkeeper where we're staying tonight told us to get here right when the restaurant opens at 4:30, because it's Saturday night and the place will be packed. So here we are at 4:25 p.m. A small cluster of customers is already gathered outside the front door, smoking. My parents give me an uneasy glance, but I assure them we'll be having a splendid meal.

Chris Wiltfang is the owner and chef here at Skaliwag's. He was an accomplished chef in Georgia when he chucked it all in order to open Skaliwag's in Algoma, a place he had visited and fallen in love with. It's hard to imagine Algoma, population thirty-one hundred, supporting a fine-dining restaurant, but Skaliwag's has been a hit since it opened in 2011. Chef Chris serves plenty of seafood with a Southern twist, but he also serves steak, pasta, and more typical Wisconsin fare. He creates whatever food he feels like making that day, so there's no use studying a menu. He also greets all of his customers and discusses their tastes in food before recommending the dishes he feels they'll like best.

We enter the restaurant's dim interior and quickly nab one of the few tables. It's small in here—really small. Chef Chris is soon standing over us, a thick, animated, mop-topped man with a slight Southern drawl. After chatting with my parents he steers them to something safe. For me, someone who likes a little heat, he recommends the New Orleans pasta with andouille sausage and shrimp. We're all willing to sample the fried shrimp with aioli sauce appetizer.

Soon the three of us are digging into Chef Chris's delicious fare in a now-crowded, noisy room. Chef Chris is pinging back and forth between the kitchen and all his customers, a thick headband keeping the sweat and hair out of his eyes, yukking it up, cracking jokes, suggesting dishes, checking back for customer feedback. Suddenly he hollers for attention.

"Hey, everybody! Quiet a moment! Quiet down!" The restaurant patrons comply. They love Chef Chris. "Everybody look over here," he yells, and I see, to my surprise, that he's pointing at our table. At me. "This woman here just walked eleven hundred miles on the Ice Age Trail! Isn't that something? *Eleven hundred miles!* Let's give her a round of applause." The place erupts.

I don't know how he knew that. I suppose the innkeeper must have told him. It's a small town, after all. His proclamation is exciting, but it also brings a tear to my eye.

Tomorrow, my adventure ends.

~

It's Sunday, October 6. The start of day thirty-six. My final day. Normally I'm on the trail by 7:30 a.m. or so. But rain has been splattering from the skies all night and into the morning, so I wait until nearly 9 a.m., when the rain stops, to head to the trail. I only have about twenty-four miles to hike, which seems a ridiculously small number after all of these weeks. I jog easily and lightly along the Forestville segment, which tags along on a portion of the Ahnapee State Trail.

At one pit stop, my mother grabs my arm in alarm.

"Be prepared. There's a big tree that's fallen onto the trail. I hope you can get over it."

How big can this tree be? I've had to fight my way over, under, and around a lot of pretty big monsters in the trail's northern reaches, where such passage was often made much more difficult because thick scrub was crowding tightly around the trail and downed tree. So it's hard to imagine something as challenging here, on a wide, open rail trail. When I step back onto the path, I try to hide a smile. The downed tree my mother is worried about is so slender I can easily run right over it without breaking stride. But in case she's watching, I stop running when I reach the tree, carefully step over it, then resume my run.

Ed meets me later in the morning, then sends my parents ahead into Sturgeon Bay so they will have plenty of time to park and wait at the eastern terminus. Fittingly, the sun pops out and the gray sky dissolves into a beautiful blue hue just as I step into the city. It's not hot today, finally. Just a lovely fall day. The perfect kind of day to be hiking in the woods. We hit Potawatomi State Park, and I slow to a walk. I want to continue running, but the trail here is rocky and rooty in parts, and I don't want to trip and break an ankle now, with the end so near. Or maybe I'm trying not to finish too soon. I'm not sure. My emotions are racing around my insides like a mouse on a wheel. I'm so thrilled and excited, and proud of myself for enduring trips and spills and scratches and banged knees. Cellulitis and bloating. Two trips to urgent care. Lost toenails and blisters. Sunburns and mild dehydration. Weeks and weeks of subsisting largely on various energy bars—how many *have* I eaten?

Through all of this, Valderi prevailed, even though I met so few people I was never truly able to grow into my trail moniker.

We're nearly at the tower when Ed pulls a hat out of the small pack he's carrying. It's a furry Viking-style cap, brown with white horns. We each received one a few years ago after doing the War-rior Dash, an obstacle-course race. Until now, I never had a reason to don it. But now I do. I pull the cap onto my head and, as I pop out of the woods, raise both arms in triumph as I give a little roar. My parents are there to cheer me in, along with my two sisters and their families. I check my watch to note my finishing time: It's just after 2 p.m. That means I have hiked the entire Ice Age Trail in thirty-six days and five hours, just two days and some change slower than I'd planned. And nearly two weeks faster than Sharon Dziengel, the previous women's record-holder, whose thru-hike took fifty days. I'm ecstatic to have achieved my goal.

Walking up to the eastern terminus rock, I give it a gentle pat to make things official. The moment I feel the cool stone beneath my fingers, I know in my heart that I will be back in this spot once again, this time setting out to hike the trail from east to west.

CHAPTER TWENTY-ONE

Jenni Heisz, Warrior

Damn the wars but bless the soldier.
—T. L. MOFFITT, SINGER

Ping! My phone beeps just as I'm climbing into bed. It's Friday night at ten forty-five, nineteen months after I finished my thru-hike of the Ice Age Trail. Immediately, I know who it is, and I can't believe she's still awake. And showing no signs of hitting the sack.

"Who's that?" Ed asks in a voice thick with sleep. He'd gone to bed a half hour before me, but the phone's tone brings him to the brink of consciousness.

"It's Jenni. The Warrior Hike person. We've been chatting on Facebook tonight. I'm surprised she isn't passed out with exhaustion by now."

Jenni is a military veteran who spent time in Afghanistan. Now she is on the Ice Age Trail, hoping to hike her way back into civilian life.

I glance at my phone's screen, glowing brightly in our dark bedroom. "Just one more note to her, then I'll turn the phone on silent."

Ed is already snoring softly.

JENNI: I honestly can't tell you [where I am]. I've been letting
Natalie do most of the decision making since she is sore.
It's been a few days since I looked at my maps ☺ she is
going off trail for a week starting Monday so I'll have to
use my maps again ☹ I would guess I'm about 15 mile
or less away from the dam rec area. The French sounding
dam that starts with an M.

MELANIE: Mondeaux Esker. There's some great guy who does
pizzas. Sadly, when I passed through (on my birthday,
no less!) it was a Sunday morning and he was closed.
Let me know if you get a pizza and how it is!

JENNI: I'm passing thru on a Sunday as well so I guess that
means no pizza for me. ☹

MELANIE: Waaa! For pizza. ☹

I slide the phone's button to silent mode, set it down, and
climb into bed.

↩

Earl Shaffer was born in 1918 in York, Pennsylvania, in the
shadow of the Appalachian Mountains. A dreamy loner, poet,
and outdoorsman, he often escaped into the mountains' sheltered embrace. It was during his childhood, as he wandered in
and out of the mountains, that the Appalachian Trail was con-
ceived and built. Shaffer and a buddy, Walter Winemiller, were
captivated by this immense trail, and they formulated a grand
plan to hike the entire thing together. But then World War II
erupted, derailing their plans. Shaffer shipped to the Pacific,
serving in the US Army Signal Corps. Winemiller also went to
the Pacific, but he perished in the fighting at Iwo Jima. Shaffer
returned home alone.

Now his idea of an Appalachian Trail thru-hike took on new
meaning. It would still be a grand adventure, sure. But to Shaffer,

the quixotic quest was also a way to walk off the horrors and trauma of the war. He'd "walk the Army out of [his] system," he told friends. Experts declared him crazy. Yes, a two-thousand-plus-mile trail had been created, but that didn't mean its creators intended it to be hiked in its entirety. In fact, they said, it was impossible. Shaffer disagreed. Armed with a diary and camera to record his trek, he started walking at Mount Oglethorpe, Georgia, in April 1948 and didn't stop until he reached Maine's Mount Katahdin four months later. And just like that, Shaffer became the Appalachian Trail's first thru-hiker.

His hike was as transformative as he'd hoped, and perhaps even more so. Shaffer spent the rest of his years talking and writing about the trail, helping maintain and publicize it. He thru-hiked it twice more, once from north to south, the last time at age seventy-nine.

In March 2012, nearly ten years after Shaffer's death at age eighty-three, Sean Gobin formally separated from the US Marine Corps and headed straight to Georgia. Dark-haired and handsome, with a muscular build and ready smile, he was mentally, physically, and emotionally exhausted after three combat deployments to Iraq and Afghanistan. And he hoped to resurrect a dream.

Since his undergraduate days, Sean had wanted to thru-hike the Appalachian Trail. Sometime in 2011, during his deployment to Afghanistan, he decided it was time to get out of the military and finally achieve his dream. He was stressed and at the end of his rope, for one thing, from deployment after deployment after deployment. And according to Marine protocol, with ten years' service he was also looking at transitioning to a staff officer, which would mean grueling hours tucked away in a claustrophobic cubicle, hardly an appealing thought. No, the time was right to make a life change. He'd hike the Appalachian Trail and knock that off his bucket list, then start grad school in the fall. Once he had his

MBA, he'd start a business. He already had a few ideas in mind. One was to start a solar energy company; another had to do with online patient medical records. Maybe he'd dream up something else while in school, too. He just knew he liked the idea of being an entrepreneur.

As Sean planned his hike, more pieces fell into place. He'd hike with a military buddy from Afghanistan, Mark, who suggested turning their hike into a fund-raiser for wounded vets. Sean loved the idea and decided that for him, the venture would be a way to honor the lieutenant from his 2011 Afghanistan deployment whose legs were blown off by an IED (improvised explosive device). The two decided the money raised would go toward helping disabled veterans obtain adaptive minivans through Help Our Military Heroes, a nonprofit group already established for this purpose. Next, Sean created the duo's fund-raising model. They would stop in at the small towns along the trail and connect with the folks at the local VFW and American Legion posts to help get the word out about their fund-raiser. They would also chronicle their journey on a Facebook page Sean created, which he dubbed "Warrior Hike."

The same month Sean separated from the Marines, he hit the road, flying toward Springer Mountain, Georgia, and the Appalachian Trail. Mark was behind the wheel. Sean was riding shotgun.

~

The men began hiking, generally covering about twenty miles per day. But when a fund-raising stop was on the agenda, they'd usually only be able to knock out five to eight miles. The dollars rolled in as the weeks rolled by. And then a funny thing started to happen along the trail. Actually, it was probably happening all along, and Sean just hadn't noticed. But now, about two-thirds of the way along the trail, after he and Mark had put some fourteen hundred miles behind them, Sean realized hiking the Appalachian

Trail was a powerful experience. Not because it was making him realize how much he was capable of, or because he was accomplishing something huge, so huge most people would never be able to do it themselves. No, for him, hiking the Appalachian Trail was proving a powerful means of transitioning from military life to civilian life. Being out in nature all day, every day, away from the endless jumble of *stuff* that was part of American life, forced his brain to process all that he had been through and begin to deal with it. It was an amazingly transformative experience.

When Sean and Mark stepped off the trail four and a half months later, they'd raised fifty thousand dollars, enough to present three injured vets with adaptive minivans. Ten days later, Sean entered grad school at the University of Virginia, where he planned to obtain his MBA, for that business he hoped to start. But he couldn't shake the Appalachian Trail. He couldn't ignore the realization of how therapeutic it had been for him, for a vet who had seen combat. He knew the military was struggling with how to best transition its vets from combat to civilian life. It wasn't working to pull someone off the battlefield and plop them into their hometown Walmart three days later. Back into a world of screaming babies and unopened bills, crowded stores and highways filled with road-raging drivers, and, everywhere, people. People who wanted to talk about the war. People who didn't get it. People who never would. It was too abrupt, and too much too soon.

Sean began doing some research and quickly came across the story of Earl Shaffer and how Earl reported having a really hard time when he came home after World War II. How he realized, once he began plodding along the trail, all of the horrible stuff, the terrible junk, he had stored inside himself. Sean read that ancient armies used to march home from distant battlefields, a process that took weeks and even months. They marched home, having no other form of transportation in those days. It must have been difficult and tiring, to be sure. But maybe it was also a great gift, because marching home was what helped them transition from war to peace. From battlefield to home.

Sean thought back to his hike, when he began to process his own military career. He was so glad his friend, someone he knew and trusted, someone who had had similar experiences, had come with him. He could understand what Sean was going through better than a spouse could, or some random military counselor who had never been on a battlefield, the kind so many soldiers were being sent to see.

While Sean was obsessing about the Appalachian Trail and how hiking it might help other veterans, a funny thing happened. The Appalachian Trail Conservancy (ATC) contacted him. They had read about his trek along their storied trail on his Warrior Hike Facebook page, and it greatly intrigued the ATC's board members. They had been considering establishing some kind of veteran outreach program, but they weren't sure what it should look like. Did he have any ideas?

"Funny you should ask that," said Sean, "because I was just thinking of how I could get other veterans to hike the trail. To help them heal." He signed on to the project, assuming he'd be helping the ATC set up a veterans hiking program. But when nothing happened after a while, he thought, *Screw it. I'll do it myself.* And with that, Warrior Hike the Facebook page became the Warrior Hike Walk Off the War Program.

Sean's Warrior Hike program works like this. Any veteran who has served in a combat zone and was honorably discharged is eligible. If selected as a participant, the vet is given hiking supplies and equipment, plus a hiking schedule for a trip along one of the six participating trails: the Appalachian Trail, Arizona Trail, Continental Divide Trail, Florida Trail, Ice Age Trail, or Pacific Crest Trail. Although it's the hiker's choice, they're encouraged to select a trail in their home area, if there is one, and Sean reserves the right to match hikers to the trail he thinks best matches their abilities.

Each week during their hike, the veterans stop and are fêted by local veteran organizations, hiking clubs, and communities, generally by hosting them for dinner and putting them up at a local home or motel. Making connections with people is a crucial part of the transitioning process, because many veterans return home with a cynical view of society and/or seclude themselves from the public. Hiking and continually meeting friendly people who are very willing and excited to help someone out can reestablish a vet's basic faith in humanity.

In 2013, after a simple message posted on the ATC's Facebook page, Sean signed up fourteen people for the inaugural Warrior Hike along the Appalachian Trail. He hiked with them the first week to ensure they were off to a good start. That they didn't try to stuff too much in their backpacks or hike too far too fast. He met them again somewhere during the middle of their hike and then again at the end, at Katahdin. The program was a resounding success, with the seven veterans who completed the entire trail reporting a positive experience. Even the seven who had to drop out for various reasons said their hike was exceptionally rewarding.

After that, applications for a spot in the program began raining from the skies. In 2014, the year Sean received his MBA, sixty or seventy people applied. It was great news for the program, but it put Sean in a bit of a pickle. He was still noodling over those business plans for a solar energy company or an enterprise dealing with electronic medical records, and he was in the midst of the hiring process to become a special agent with the Drug Enforcement Administration. Warrior Hike was merely a side project. Wasn't it?

Sean realized he'd reached a crossroads. He had to make a life choice—a moral one. Once he thought of it that way, the decision wasn't difficult. Warrior Hike was the enterprise he was meant to start.

~

I learned about the Warrior Hike program in early 2015, when applications had soared to 120 and the Ice Age Trail had just signed on as a program participant. Its first two hikers, two young women, would be starting May 3. Eager to assist, to hear their stories, and to see their reaction to the trail, I reached out and connected with one vet, Jenni Heisz.

Jenni, thirty-one, is a compact five feet, four inches with a cap of dark hair and a broad smile. A tiny stud twinkles from her right nostril. Like Sean, Jenni began her military service in 2001, when she enlisted in the Army Reserves as a high school junior. Jenni planned to make a twenty-year career of the military. After graduating from high school in 2002, she enrolled at Viterbo University in La Crosse, where she studied criminal justice and trained with the Reserves one weekend each month. In 2005, she deployed to Kuwait. In 2009, she deployed to Afghanistan. In between, she attended classes, now at the University of Wisconsin–Madison, studying wildlife ecology. After returning from Afghanistan she obtained an associate of applied science degree in adventure recreation and tourism from a community college in Maine, while continuing to train monthly with the Reserves. Then, in November 2012, unhappy about aspects of her Afghanistan deployment, she decided to leave the military. She had had enough of that life.

Jenni returned to her parents' home in Boscobel for a while, soon deciding to hike the Appalachian Trail. Her family had done a lot of camping when she was growing up, and her favorite part of camping was hiking the trails. She longed to be outside and to hear the birds singing in the trees. In spring 2013, Jenni stepped onto the Appalachian Trail. She made it a month before stopping.

Turned out she just wasn't ready. She wanted to go home to Wisconsin, where her stay had been too brief.

So Jenni returned home, but she still felt unsettled. Yes, she wanted to be there, but she also had unfinished business with the Appalachian Trail. She wasn't a quitter. She wanted to go back and try it again. Hoping to keep Jenni closer to home, Jenni's sister-in-law researched other options. When she discovered another National Scenic Trail right here in Wisconsin, she excitedly told Jenni about the trail, urging her to hike this one instead. The Ice Age Trail did sound interesting to Jenni, but it was only half-completed. She would hike it some other time, when it was finished. In the meantime, she wanted to return to the Appalachian Trail.

A nagging doubt in the back of her mind was still holding her back, though. What if she ended up dropping out again? Then what would she do? She'd have no job to return to, plus she still hadn't finished her bachelor's degree, definitely a priority. As 2014 wound down, still struggling over what to do with her life, including whether to hike either the Ice Age or Appalachian Trail, she applied to Black Hills State University in South Dakota.

She also applied to hike the Appalachian Trail through Sean Gobin's Warrior Hike program.

Jenni heard about the Warrior Hike program in 2013, during her month on the Appalachian Trail. Several veterans on the trail ahead of her were Warrior Hikers. She thought the program was a cool idea, but not something for her. At the time, she wanted nothing to do with the military, nothing to do with vets. But now she reconsidered. Time had softened the harsh edges of Jenni's anger toward the military. In fact, she found herself missing certain aspects: the camaraderie, working as a team. Besides, hiking through the Warrior Hike program should make the adventure slightly easier than tackling it solo.

Jenni was accepted to Black Hills State University, where she'd be pursuing a bachelor's degree in outdoor education. She was also accepted to the Warrior Hike program, where Sean encouraged her to hike the Ice Age Trail instead. It was her home trail, and any contacts she made along the way were more likely to be beneficial down the road. Jenni readily agreed. The decision finally made, she became stoked. This was what she was meant to do. And the timing would be perfect. She'd hike May through early August in 2015, then get off the trail just in time to head to South Dakota to finish her undergraduate degree.

And so on a cool, sunny day in early May, Jenni Heisz strapped a twenty-eight-pound pack on her back, touched the western terminus marker in Interstate State Park, and headed into the woods. Natalie Koffarnus, another Warrior Hiker, was hiking with her. So was Sean Gobin.

～

I eagerly follow Jenni's progress on her Facebook page. They're on the Gandy Dancer segment, which runs along part of the Gandy Dancer rail trail, then pitching tents by a pretty lake. They filter water. Spot a deer stand and a few strange makeshift porta-potties, then bid Sean Gobin farewell. The weather is sunny and nice, then rainy and cold. Jenni posts photos of swans and squirrels. Frogs, frogs, and more frogs. A tall, peaked beaver dam. Other photos show feet that are blistered and bandaged, a package of Epsom salt held over a bathtub filling with water, and someone poking a lumpy pile of bear scat plopped on the trail. On May 11, Jenni posts a photo of pine cones carefully fashioned into the words "Happy Mother's Day." A lump forms in the back of my throat when I see it, but I'm not quite sure why.

The Chronotype, a Rice Lake newspaper, publishes a story about the two women and their hike. When they pass through the Mondeaux Esker segment about three weeks into their adventure,

Steve, the guy who runs the Mondeaux Dam Lodge via a contract with the US Forest Service, takes their photo; he's collecting photos of the military folks he meets. The next day, Natalie steps off the trail to attend to a military obligation, leaving Jenni to soldier on alone for the next week.

◟

On June 4 I drive up to Antigo to meet with Joe Jopek to ask him some questions for this book. As we're speaking in his living room, Joe's cell phone rings.

"The girls are ready to be picked up," he says. "Do you want to come with?"

"What girls?"

"Jenni and Natalie. They're staying at the campground in Veterans Memorial Park in the Old Railroad segment. They want a ride into town tonight to grab some dinner."

Jenni and Natalie are here in Antigo on the one day I decide to visit Joe? What are the odds? "I'd love to come with you!"

Soon the two of us are speeding out to the campground in Joe's van. As we're driving along, Joe gives me a little tour of the area's glacial history.

"These are the Antigo Flats," he says, gesturing toward a vast expanse of perfectly horizontal farmland stretching along both sides of the road and far into the horizon, where it's eventually stopped by a towering ridge. "You can see the Antigo Flats from satellite photography in pretty good detail at 150 miles above our planet. And its arrowhead shape is still visible at over 1,000 miles above the earth." A flat patch of land doesn't sound very impressive, but the area is so large, so level, that the view is actually quite spectacular.

The Antigo Flats are technically something called an outwash plain, formed when the glacier's Green Bay and Langlade Lobes—tongue-shaped fingers of ice extending from the forward-moving edge of the ice sheet—bumped together and, later, began melting.

"The Flats were scoured by the huge volumes of meltwater coming off of the two lobes," Joe explains.

According to Ray Zillmer's vision, the Ice Age Trail should run along the edge of the Antigo Flats, where it bumps into that distant ridge, which is actually the glacier's terminal moraine. But the trail is tucked just behind the terminal moraine, so you can't see the Flats while on the trail, a real tragedy.

I worked in our state legislature in the 1980s, and I tell Joe I recall the day something called "Antigo Silt Loam" was decreed the state soil. Did that have anything to do with the glacier? As a matter of fact, yes, Joe says. Antigo silt loam is a wonderful mixture of sand, clay, and silt. Fertile and easily drained, it contains some coarse cobbles and gravel, but none of the immense boulders, or erratics, the glacier can drag for thousands of miles. Those were encased within the ice sheet behind the terminal moraine. But here at the terminal moraine, the melting ice water snatched some of the gravelly debris from the edge of the moraine, and then, flowing rapidly and broadly in front of the stopped glacier, it neatly spread its cargo over the land it was scouring to pancake-flatness. First the larger pieces, then the medium-size ones, and eventually the fine particles. The resulting outwash plain, the Antigo Flats, is prime agricultural land and especially suited to the growing of potatoes.

We reach the campground and find the Gobblers Roost cabin where the women are staying. Two soggy tents are set up outside to dry, one on the cabin's concrete front porch, another off to the side in the grass. As we step out of the van, the door of the Gobblers Roost bursts open and the two women tumble out, laughing and giggling. I'm a little shocked. I first met both women back in April, coincidentally the day they had first met each other, and a mere three weeks before the start of this hike. They had greeted each other formally, reservedly, as most strangers would. Now they look like sisters or best friends. As they climb into the van, they chatter nonstop about the terrible swarms of mosquitoes they've been battling, Jenni's near-constant obsession with finding pizza, and how Natalie calls Jenni "one hundred percent" because Jenni keeps saying she is 100 percent sure they're going the right way on the trail, but she's often wrong. They tease each other, make inside jokes, and laugh, laugh, laugh. So much laughter wells up in the van, I think it's going to blow the doors open, but instead it bursts out through my mouth and Joe's as we join in their merriment.

Joe eases the van to a stop at the veterans' memorial that lent its name to the park. We hop out, and the girls snap photos of themselves near a large painting of a bald eagle flying over a lake with the phrase Freedom Is Not Free emblazoned above it. Then Jenni asks me to check out her foot and ankle for a minute. The top of her foot and ankle were hurting the other day, and now the area is kind of puffy. What do I think it could be? I look at the area, and it's just as she says, a bit puffy. It could be shoestring tendinitis, I say, which you can get from tying your shoes or boots too tightly. Maybe a stress fracture if there's one real hot spot that's painful to the touch, especially if the pain sort of radiates out from the hot spot. I advise her to ice it and keep off of it as much as she can until tomorrow. If things get worse, she can go to Antigo's urgent care center, the same one I used two years prior.

"I hope it's not from my little marathon," she says quietly. "I wanted to do my first marathon on the one-month anniversary of being on the trail, so yesterday I walked twenty-six miles."

~

Jenni ices her foot and ankle that night, but the next day her entire lower leg is so painful it takes her five hours to walk the three miles or so to finish the Old Railroad segment. Natalie was by her side the whole way, but Jenni tells her to go on ahead into Lumbercamp. She'll stay here at County Highway A, which divides the segments, and hitchhike back to Antigo. It should be easy. It's about 3:30 p.m. and a number of cars are zipping along the road. So Natalie hikes on and Jenni stands along the road, thumb out.

After fifteen minutes, not one vehicle has stopped. Which is so annoying and crazy, because all of these weeks, every time she stopped along the roadside to rest or eat her lunch, people would stop and ask if everything was all right, or if she needed a ride anywhere. Sighing, she flops to the ground, removes her shoe and sock, and puts her injured foot up on her pack. Then she tries to look as pitiful as she can. It works; almost immediately, someone stops to ask her if she needs a ride. "Yes, please," she says, "to the hospital in Antigo."

The medical personnel tell her she has tendinitis and that she needs to take a few days off. But the next day her leg is worse, with the swelling marching up her calf. Her leg is also warm, and it hurts like hell. A childhood friend picks her up in Antigo. That night, tucked into bed at her friend's house, the pain in her leg is so intense she can't fall asleep. Something serious is going on. It's after midnight, but Jenni grabs her friend's car keys and drives herself to the Madison VA Hospital's emergency room, where she's diagnosed with cellulitis. When I hear the news, I'm stunned. Her cellulitis looks nothing like mine.

Jenni hopes to be off the trail a few days, maybe a week. But after a few trial hikes, she knows it's going to be a while before she can get back on the trail. Every time she walks more than an hour or so, her leg instantly swells like a balloon and the pain flickers back to life. Frustrated and upset, sad that Natalie is marching through the woods alone without her, she decides to do something positive. She'll take a road trip to South Dakota and find an apartment for August, when she'll head there for school. Once that mission is accomplished, her leg should be healed and she can get back on the trail.

Finally, on June 27, Jenni is ready to resume her thru-hike. Natalie is somewhere around Lodi now, about three hundred miles ahead of the spot in Langlade County where Jenni stepped off the trail. There's no use joining her full-time quite yet. Jenni wants to ease back into it, for one thing. Plus back in April she'd purchased tickets to Lifest, a four-day concert in Oshkosh that starts July 9, and she doesn't want to miss that. No, she'll hike a little bit here, a little bit there, heading west to east or east to west, it doesn't matter. She'll fill in as many gaps as she can and meet up with Natalie whenever possible. After Lifest, they'll be together until the end.

So on June 27 Jenni hikes the three miles of the Portage Canal segment. On June 28, she knocks off Lodi, Lodi Marsh, and East Lodi Marsh, which enables her to join Natalie for one of the weekly VFW dinners sponsored through the Warrior Hike program, this one courtesy of the Prairie du Sac VFW Post 7694. This is the first time they've seen each other since June 6. The two dine on sloppy joes, the favorite meal of their host. Then the other members of Post 7694 join them for a bonfire in his backyard overlooking the Wisconsin River. *I'm back!* Jenni thinks. *Life is good!*

～

July 5 finds Jenni hiking east to west along a connecting route, then tackling the Verona segment and the Madison segment up until the University Ridge Golf Course. She sends me a Facebook message to see if I can join her. Yes, I say, and you can stay with us for the night.

I park at the golf course and start jogging back toward her. It's a sunny, humid day, and I wonder if she has enough food and water on her. I've gone a couple miles and am about to cross South High

Point Road at McKee when I hear someone call my name. It's Jenni, who is across the street, waving wildly at me.

"You're going the wrong way! The trail's over here!"

I feel stupid. This is my home turf, plus I've done the Ice Age Trail before. Yet here I am, about to go the wrong way. Jenni jogs across the street and joins me. She doesn't look like a thru-hiker today, clad in shorts, a black, sleeveless top, and running shoes—coincidentally the exact same pair I own. Her dark hair is pulled back in a short ponytail, and a lightweight, blue Sea to Summit bag is strapped on her back. We turn and head west, chatting easily about the trail (beautiful), the weather (a little too hot), her leg (doing great, thank you). When we reach the golf course, we duck into the clubhouse to get some cold water. It's Sunday and we expect it to be packed, but we're the only ones in the bar area.

The chef comes out to say hello and tells us no one realizes the Fourth of July weekend is always slow at the golf course. He asks what we're up to, and Jenni tells him about her hike, showing him her maps and other essentials. Then she hands him a little business card.

"You can follow my hike here," she says.

"What are these?" I say, taking one of the small cards. A close-up of a smiling Jenni, head topped in a Wisconsin cap, is on the card's left half. On the right half are the words:

Ice Age Trail
JD
Thru-Hike 2015
www.trailjournals.com/jd

At the bottom, her email address is listed.

"Hiker cards. I made them myself. I picked up the idea from other hikers on the Appalachian Trail. They're really handy

because people you meet always ask how they can follow your
adventure. When they ask you that, you can just hand them one
of these."

I turn the card over in my hand. This *is* a really good idea.
Here I thought I'd be giving Jenni some tips on her thru-hike. It
appears she'll be the one instructing me. For the remainder of the
summer, I follow Jenni's progress online.

~

JD's 2015 Ice Age Trail Journal
Friday, July 10, 2015
The temperature has been warm the past two weeks. I've
been taking a lot of breaks throughout the day to hide from
the sun and rehydrate. I have bug bites over my entire body
and a few rashes here and there. My Brooks are forming holes
along the side of my shoes and the sole is starting to detach
from one of them. So the question is, am I currently enjoying
my hike?
The answer is yes. Even when it's bad it's good. Sure I
had bad days and at times I hated the Ice Age Trail but those
moments were brief. I love it out here. Trail life is soo peaceful. I wish I could explain how I feel while I'm out here but I
cannot put it into words. I've tried many times. I love it. I love
nature. I love being outside. I love the sound of everything
around me (excluding manmade noise). I love the feeling of
freedom. I just love it.

~

It's mid-July when Jenni finally catches up with Natalie at Lapham
Peak. "*Awesome sauce!*" as Jenni is fond of saying. Everything has
changed and nothing has changed. Jenni easily falls back into the
all-day, every-day hiking routine. The two are still their own independent selves. They start their days together but sometimes

hike separately all day or even pitch their tents in different locales. When they're together they sing along to songs played on
their phones, tell stories, play 20 Questions or weird, made-up
games. But where once Jenni was focused on pushing herself as a
hiker—seeing how many days she could stay on the trail without
detouring into a town, for example, or designating certain days her
"marathon" days, where she'd see how many miles she could log—
now she focuses on having fun and enjoying every step of the
trail. Because for her, the finish in Potawatomi won't really be the
finish. Jenni will still have some three hundred miles to make up
someday. She also wants to enjoy her time with Natalie, because
she's so happy to be back with her. The two had started connecting before her cellulitis, sure, but now their bond has solidified.
They're a team. They're the Ice Age Trail's first two Warrior Hikers.

∼

JD's 2015 Ice Age Trail Journal
Tuesday, July 21, 2015

I'm kind of sad right now. My time with Natalie is about
to come to a bittersweet end. We plan to reach the Eastern
terminus on July 31st. Only 10 days left! Natalie and I had
a difficult time adjusting to each other's personality in the
beginning but now we are like two peas in a pod. She is peanut butter to my jelly. I am the frosting to her cake. When
we are together we can conquer the world. We are already
talking about her coming to visit me in South Dakota. I can't
wait! I'm really excited about going back to school to finish
my Bachelor's degree and to explore the Black Hills but I'm
not really ready to go back to the 9 to 5 lifestyle. I'm going to
miss sleeping outside. I'm going to miss having everything I
need for survival strapped to my back. I'm going to miss the
freedom. These are the things I'm trying not to think about.
These next 10 days will be emotional for me. I'm going to try

and embrace every single minute I have left. I haven't been writing lately and this is probably the most important time for me to be writing down my experiences. My thoughts have been all jumbled up in my head and I don't really know how to organize them. It's like rapid fire thinking is going on. I've been doing A LOT of reflecting this past week. Natalie and I have been replaying the funny moments. We've had many funny moments together.

~

July 31. It's a beautiful, sunny day when Jenni and Natalie march into Potawatomi State Park. Jenni's feelings are as scrambled as the eggs in a country breakfast. She's finishing her hike, but she really isn't. So there's elation—*I've hiked eight hundred miles!* (or whatever the exact tally is)—and a bit of sorrow over the unfinished business—*I still have to hike those last three hundred miles.* There's the excitement of soon heading off to South Dakota—*I'll finally get my bachelor's degree!*—and the sorrow of leaving her new bestie, Natalie. Still, she touches the eastern terminus rock, poses for photos with a giant Warrior Hike banner, and dreams of the day she'll officially be an Ice Age Trail Thousand-Miler.

~

On August 1, Jenni logs onto Facebook to post an update:

> Dear Friends, I'm done hiking for the summer. Time for me to rejoin you all in the world of bills and obligations. I'm not looking forward to showering every day and eating things other than candy for lunch. Ha, I can't even type that with a straight face. Showers are overrated and candy is delicious!

A few weeks later, after some more reflection, she turns to her online trail journal.

JD's 2015 Ice Age Trail Journal
Friday, August 21, 2015
After the Trail Update

My last day on the trail was July 31st. I was pretty bummed about ending my hiking season but thankfully Natalie and I had one more VFW stop. After pictures were taken by the plaque at the eastern terminus, Natalie and I headed into Sturgeon Bay to have lunch with VFW Post 3088. There were many questions to be answered during lunch. How was your hike? What was your favorite part? Did you see any wildlife? People are always talking about changing while hiking, how did you change? Would you do it again? I've heard many of these questions multiple times throughout the summer and my answers varied due to new experiences taking place on an everyday basis. Overall, it was good and without a doubt, I would hike the Ice Age Trail again.

I'm still not sure what kind of lasting impression the trail had on me or how it had changed me. It definitely tested my intrapersonal skills. This summer, I had to accept that I can't control every situation, for instance illness or injury. I had to learn how to be a team player with an individual who is even more independent than I. I had to learn how to ask for help from complete strangers. This was the most difficult for me. At first, I was afraid to call a stranger and ask for help, but, towards the end of the hike, I had no problem calling up the trail angels and asking for a ride or a place to stay. The more I did it, the more I looked forward to meeting the next trail angel.

～

Jenni's post-hike longing and confusion don't surprise me. I'm still grappling with how my thru-hike changed me, and it's been two years. I think about the trail all the time. I spread the trail gospel to all who will listen, and I hike its enticing paths whenever

I can. I confide in a few close friends that I'd love to thru-hike the trail again. It's my secret dream. And really, I should do it sooner rather than later, because as Agnes Breitzman pointed out two years ago, I'm no spring chicken. My friends smile at me indulgently, but they don't really understand. I don't think you can, unless you've hiked the trail.

~

Twenty-nine days after Jenni touches the eastern terminus boulder in Potawatomi State Park, on a gray morning wringing itself out in a gentle mist, I gently place my hand on its top and smile. Then I slip into the woods, my eyes immediately scanning the trail for yellow blazes.

Epilogue

*Twenty years from now you will be more disappointed by
the things that you didn't do than by the ones you did do. So
throw off the bowlines. Sail away from the safe harbor. Catch
the trade winds in your sails. Explore. Dream. Discover.*
       —H. Jackson Brown, Jr., American author

Melanie Radzicki McManus completed her second thru-hike of
the Ice Age Trail on October 2, 2015. This time she traveled east
to west and took the western bifurcation. While not trying to set
another thru-hike record, she completed the trail in thirty-four
days, four hours, and forty-four minutes, besting her previous
time by two days. She is the only person to thru-hike the Ice Age
Trail twice, in both directions, and taking both sides of the bifurcation. Melanie planned to return to the Ice Age Trail in 2017 to
do a flip-flop thru-hike. (Don't tell Ed.)

Pat Enright section-hiked the Ice Age Trail between April 1
and October 2, 2013. He used his hike to raise $13,585 for the
Waupaca County Senior Nutrition Program.

Jim Staudacher collaborated with Rep. Henry S. Reuss in 1981
when the congressman updated his book *On the Trail of the Ice
Age*. In 1982, he hiked the two hundred-plus-mile Cross-Michigan
Trail (now called the Shore-to-Shore Trail) with a friend after
graduating from Marquette University with a degree in law enforcement. Today a retired police detective who runs a small
organic vegetable farm with his wife in southwest Wisconsin,
he still has the backpack and leather boots he wore on his 1979

thru-hike, plus his original notes, journals, and topographic maps. And, yes, the .22 Magnum revolver his dad brought to him after he was attacked by a pack of feral dogs. Jim says today's Ice Age Trail route is substantially changed from the one he hiked in 1979.

Sarah Sykes died of cancer on September 30, 2011, at the age of sixty. Her obituary, published on the *Milwaukee Journal Sentinel's* Legacy website, read, in part:

> Sarah will be best remembered for her work on the Ice Age Trail. She fell in love with the project as a staffer for the late Congressman Henry Reuss and spearheaded efforts to bring it into being. Over a period of several years, she drafted the legislation creating it, successfully steered the project through a maze of federal, state and bureaucratic rules and regulations, secured the cooperation of private landowners and coordinated the efforts of early volunteers to transform the Trail from an imaginary line on a map to an actual, tangible, 1,000-mile hike across more than two dozen Wisconsin counties. . . . In lieu of flowers, please consider making memorial donations to the Ice Age Trail Alliance or Neighborhood House of Milwaukee.

Bob Fay finished hiking the Ice Age Trail on October 17, 2015. It took him seven years to hike all segments and connecting routes. Bob left Lions Park in St. Croix Falls that morning with his two daughters, Erin and Meghan. Erin traveled from Oklahoma City, and Meghan from Milwaukee, to accompany him over the final seven miles. Bob reports it was thirty-three degrees when they left Lions Park, but warmed up to the low fifties by the time they finished—a beautiful, sunny fall day. His wife, Georgia, shuttled the trio to the trailhead and met them afterward at the western terminus.

Bob meticulously kept track of his Ice Age Trail adventures over the years. A few of his more interesting calculations and notations:

- Hiked 1,106.3 total miles, averaging 8.4 miles per hiking day (longest hike 19.6 miles)

- Hiked 92.2 additional miles (natural trails, paths to designated camping areas, etc.)

- Biked 768 miles

- Received 25 shuttles

- Hitchhiked once

- Drove 24,454 miles

- Hottest hiking day 97 degrees (June 6, 2011, Hartman Creek State Park)

- Only months never hiked: December and February

- Picked up 178 aluminum cans while hiking 17-mile connecting route from John Muir Park segment through Packwaukee to Westfield (most were beer cans)

Adam Hinz finished thru-hiking the Ice Age Trail on October 18, 2013. The experience was a life-altering one, as he'd hoped. Adam returned to school, initially to obtain a bachelor's degree in environmental health and water quality control. He later became a certified phlebotomist and, as of 2016, was pursuing a career in the medical field. Adam finished the Ice Age Trail shod in the low-cut Keens he purchased in Green Bay. They still didn't feel quite right on his feet, he says, but "it was as good as it was going to get." Not surprisingly, Adam says one of the many bits of wisdom he's learned on the trail is that most boots or shoes won't last longer than five hundred to seven hundred miles, so if you find a pair that works for you, buy several pairs. He never did burn his Editors' Choice hiking boots, thinking they still might be wearable if he ever took the time to break them in. (Note to Adam: No, they won't be! Get rid of them!) In fact, he still has every pair of boots he wore on the trail piled up in his garage. When he sees them, he thinks of his journey along the Ice Age Trail. And that makes him smile.

Drew "Papa Bear" Hendel hoped to thru-hike the Pacific Northwest National Scenic Trail in 2017. This trail stretches twelve hundred miles from the Continental Divide in Montana, across Idaho's panhandle, and all the way to Washington's Olympic Peninsula.

Paul "Hiking Dude" Kautz took 2,248,576 steps during his Ice Age Trail adventure, according to the pedometer he wore. His trail journal also shows he generally ate two Pop Tarts or granola bars for breakfast and a mixture of peanut butter and honey on Ritz crackers for lunch. ("I didn't get tired of it, but came close.") He drank mostly water, sometimes diluted Gatorade, and he downed a daily vitamin. His favorite snacks were Snickers or peanut M&Ms. His total thru-hike expenses—travel, gear, maps, food, and lodging—came to $1,500, or about $1.33 per mile.

In the fall of 2015, Hiking Dude began section-hiking the Appalachian Trail. In 2016, he hiked the one-thousand-mile Florida National Scenic Trail.

Jason Dorgan raised more than $15,000 for the Ice Age Trail Alliance during his record-setting 2007 thru-run. He calculated the following statistics about his effort:

- Covered 1,079 miles in 22 days and six hours
- Spent 248 hours on the trail

- Averaged 4.35 miles per hour

- Averaged 48.5 miles per day

- Got up at 5:30 a.m. each day

- Started running between 6:30 a.m. and 7:30 a.m. each day

- Rotated five pairs of running shoes

As of January 2016, Jason's speed record still stood. He planned to section-hike the Ice Age Trail in 2017, the tenth anniversary of his 2007 thru-run.

Jenni Heisz returned to college to obtain her bachelor of behavioral science degree in outdoor education. She was on schedule to graduate in May 2017. Jenni says, "I'm thinking about what I plan to do once I graduate and the only thing I can think about doing is finishing the two hikes I started."

Sean Gobin says introducing Jenni and Natalie to the Ice Age Trail was the "funnest first week I had on the trail." He also praised the Ice Age Trail for offering hikers such great diversity, moving them from rail trail to wilderness, through small towns and past dairy farms.

In 2015, Sean added Warrior Paddle to his company, now renamed Warrior Expeditions. The 2,300-mile paddle, created for injured veterans who can't hike long distances, takes veterans down the entire Mississippi River. In 2016, the Warrior Hike program received 350 applications, up from 14 in its inaugural year (2013). In 2017, Warrior Bike will debut a 4,228-mile journey along the TransAmerica trail running from Oregon to Virginia. Like Warrior Paddle, Warrior Bike is designed for wounded veterans who can't hike long distances. Sean asks readers to recommend Warrior Expeditions to any combat veteran who is struggling to find peace. And, he adds, his program is always looking for volunteer assistance. Nudge, nudge.

The **Ice Age Trail** continually improves. Bear Lake and Kettle-bowl, the two segments that most confounded Melanie and other thru-hikers in 2013, are now well blazed, as is all of Langlade County.

Acknowledgments

We must find time to stop and thank the people who make a difference in our lives.

—JOHN F. KENNEDY

This book—and the thru-hikes that helped produce it—could not have occurred without the support and assistance of many people. I'll start by thanking Kent Williams, a friend and talented writer and editor who critiqued my book proposal and gave me the courage to submit it. Once it was accepted and I began writing, I relied heavily on the wonderful folks at the Ice Age Trail Alliance (IATA) to supply me with trail information from the past, present, and future: Dave Caliebe, Luke Kloberdanz, Tim Malzahn, Tiffany Stram, Kevin Thusius, Mike Wollmer, and, most especially, Eric Sherman and former IATA employee Drew Hanson, who answered the bulk of my questions. I also had much assistance from Ice Age Trail volunteers and chapter chairs: Ruby Jaecks, Randy Lennartz, Dolly McNulty, Buzz Meyer, and the incomparable Joe (and Peg) Jopek, who answered innumerable questions via phone, email, and in person.

As you know by reading this book, this Ice Age Trail story does not belong solely to me, but also to those whom I met along the way or who inspired me in some way. A huge thank-you to the other hikers mentioned, who were so kind to take the time to share their backstories with me, often digging up their old notes and photos to provide the most accurate information possible: Pat Enright, Bob Fay, Jenni Heisz, Drew Hendel, Adam Hinz, Paul Kautz, James Staudacher. And, of course, Jason Dorgan. Jason, your inspirational 2007 thru-run and subsequent chatter about the trail were major factors that propelled me to thru-run the trail in 2013. I appreciate your sharing all of your memories, blog entries, and tapes, and for crewing me on the trail.

Sean Gobin, bless you for starting Warrior Hike—now Warrior Expeditions—and for helping with this book. (P.S. If anyone wants to get involved, the group can always use assistance.)

Thanks, too, to everyone who assisted me with my two thru-hikes, whether crewing, housing, shuttling, or feeding me, or by performing any of the many other tasks that make a thru-hike easier: Peggy Afable, Bobbie Joy Amann and Patricia Gates, Chet Anderson (the Gray Ghost), Phil Brinkman, Terie Cebe, Bunny and Tim Collins, Jerome Converse, Dean Dversdall, Sharon Dziengel, Mary Jo Grabner, Ann Heaslett, Stuart Horwitz and Xavier Saint-Luc, Sue Matheson, Marge McManus, Molly McManus, Maura McManus, Tim McManus, Tim McRaith, Dan Mitchell, David Mix, Paula Moore, Tess Mulrooney, Marilyn Nash, Alison Radzicki and Michele Walker, John and Liz Senseman, Lauren Weaver, Gregg and Marie-Anne Westigard, and, again, Ruby Jaecks, Randy Lennartz, Dolly McNulty, Buzz Meyer, and Peg and Joe Jopek.

I certainly cannot forget to thank Dr. Lisa Tenold of Eau Claire and Dr. Curt Draeger of Antigo, chiropractors who both stayed at their clinics after-hours to treat my injured knee in 2013. Plus Dr. Andrew Schupp, my regular chiropractor who treated me on-site when I passed through Madison, and Tom Harding, massage therapist extraordinaire, who traveled to my Whitewater and Waunakee lodgings in 2013 and 2015 to give me a massage. Thanks as well to Dr. Derek Grenfell of Sturgeon Bay's Cherryland Chiropractic, who treated me on a Saturday morning at the start of my 2015 hike, even though it meant coming in with his toddler (thanks, Charlotte Rae, for letting your daddy help me out).

I was exceptionally fortunate to have my book published by the Wisconsin Historical Society Press and its talented staff, namely my editor, Erika Wittekind, who helped me figure out how best to say what I wanted to say, and Jere Foley, who oversaw the production process—thank you!

Finally, my most special shout-outs. An enormous thank-you to my parents, Richard and Roberta Radzicki, who crewed me for a combined ten days; my mother even postponed her knee-replacement surgery to crew me in 2015. Many, many thanks to one of my very best friends, Doug Erickson, who crewed me eight days between my two hikes, staying the course even when he turned an ankle (2013) and twice ran into a naked thru-hiker (2015). P.S. Thanks for doing my laundry on the trail! Last, my most special thank-you to my husband, Ed. Thanks for letting me disappear into the woods for weeks at a time, supporting and cheering me every step of the way. You are amazing, and I love you so very much.

About the Author

Trish Kaiser, Remember
Me Portrait Studio

Melanie Radzicki McManus has worked as a news reporter at a Green Bay radio station, as a press secretary at the Wisconsin State Capitol, and as editor of two local publications. Since 1994, McManus has worked as a freelance writer and editor, specializing in travel and fitness. She has won numerous awards for her writing, most notably prestigious Lowell Thomas Gold and Grand Awards for her travel journalism.